Cuban-American Literature of Exile

Cuban-American Literature of Exile

FROM PERSON TO PERSONA

Isabel Alvarez Borland

New World Studies

A. James Arnold, Editor

University Press of Virginia

Charlottesville & London

The University Press of Virginia
© 1998 by the Rector and Visitors of the University of Virginia
All rights reserved
Printed in the United States of America

First published 1998

∞ The paper used in this publication meets the minimum require-
ments of the American National Standard for Information Sciences—
Permanence of Paper for Printed Library Materials, ANSI Z39.48-
1984.

Library of Congress Cataloging-in-Publication Data
Alvarez-Borland, Isabel.
   Cuban-American literature of exile : from person to persona /
Isabel Alvarez Borland.
      p.   cm. — (New World studies)
   Includes bibliographical references and index.
   ISBN 0-8139-1812-X (cloth : alk. paper). — ISBN 0-8139-1813-8
(pbk. : alk. paper)
   1. American literature—Cuban American authors—History and
criticism.   2. Cuban Americans—Intellectual life.   3. Exiles in lit-
erature.   I. Title.   II. Series.
PS153.C83A58   1998
810.9 ' 8687291073—dc21   98-15446
                                                                              CIP

for Neil, my American and Cuban son

But when the text *is* the homeland, even when it is rooted only in the exact remembrance and seeking of a handful of wanderers, nomads of the world, it cannot be extinguished.

GEORGE STEINER, "Our Homeland, the Text"

Contents

PART 3

Encountering Others: Imagined U.S. Cuban Communities

Preface

THE IDEA for this study had its beginnings in the winter of 1990 when I first taught a seminar at Holy Cross entitled "Cuban Literature of Exile, Immigration, and Ethnicity." Students responded enthusiastically to reading a series of texts, not grouped in any chronological fashion or specific genre, but rather organized and juxtaposed in such a way that they told a story: the story of the aftermath of the revolution of 1959. What we were doing in class that winter, and in subsequent versions of that seminar, was actually bridging a gap between the textbook history of the events of 1959 and the authors' personal experiences and fictions about these events. Each reading seemed to illuminate the next, and at times quite dissimilar texts seemed to be in dialogue with one another. By reading one text against the other, students were able to construct their own inside view of the 1959 diaspora and to understand how history could become dramatized in this literature.

The seminar's success and the way the readings seemed to reach my students were quite important to me as a teacher-scholar, but they mattered even more from a personal standpoint. As a Cuban-American daughter of exiles who came from Cuba in 1962, I also shared vivid memories with the authors and the narratives that I was teaching, as well as the same sense of rupture between my languages and my cultures. Paying attention to the voices of my peers speaking to me from their writings, I found a world characterized by displacement and a search for self as well as by a need to re-create a community away from home. I also realized that by inventing themselves in their literature, these Cuban and Cuban-American writers were in the midst of producing a new American literature of Cuban heritage.

This book's subtitle, *From Person to Persona*, reflects the trajectory of a narrative. If *person* here refers to the individual writer in history, the term *persona* conveys the distance achieved in time through the artifice of literature. In between, we have the analysis of representative works that explore the tension between the historical person of the writer and his or her created persona. I was particularly interested in determining how contemporary Cuban writers utilize the historical events of the 1959 diaspora as an inspiration to write and create their narratives. Above all, I was interested in the literary strategies these writers used in order to explore and revisit their past. The fictions analyzed in this study are engaged in a dialogue with the history that produced them. The poetic transformation of the literature of the post-Castro exile into an American literature of Cuban heritage will be evident through the study of specific works.

Choosing representative texts has not been easy. The heterogeneous nature of extraterritorial Cuban writing forced me to make choices regarding the type of cultural production that I felt could best tell the story of the contemporary exodus from Cuba to Cuban America. The criteria for selection centered around the degree to which the narratives rendered an explicit retelling of the story of the 1959 diaspora and the degree to which certain recurrent themes were present in these literary renditions of exile. I was not interested in the factual veracity of these versions of exodus; instead, my aim has been to examine their narrative strategies in order to determine the writers' perspectives on the aftermath of 1959.

The narratives I have selected are the product of several immigrant waves writing outside Cuba today. Although each work varies greatly with regard to content and ideology, many of the same themes are emphasized. Also, while I am aware that the authors discussed have a variety of political views toward the Cuban revolution, I have not made those views a factor in my selection. Choosing a particular political stance over another would have forced me to exclude works crucial to the literary trajectory I seek to trace for the reader. The common element of these works is that they all foreground the events of 1959 in their fictions since the very conditions of the production of the literature force the dialogue between the writer and history into the open. Unlike traditional history, however, the fiction analyzed here is rooted in a desire to explore the historical events of the aftermath of 1959 in the narrative in order to find a coherence unavailable in the real lives of these authors. The analyses examine representative prose writings (by well-known and not so well known writers) that, if read collectively, describe how a people viewed a traumatic historical change through their literary expression. Most of the narratives chosen were written originally in English; others were written originally in Spanish and later translated into English. All are available to the English reader, with the exception of the stories of Lino Novás Calvo analyzed in part 1, which to date have not been translated into English. Not included in this study are exile narratives written exclusively in Spanish. A prolific tradition especially in the area of poetry and theater, the literature in Spanish produced outside Cuba falls beyond the scope of this study.

By writing this book I am committing my energies to the broadening of American literary discourse to include the voices of Cuban-American writers. Scholars and teachers interested in the tradition of Cuban letters outside Cuba, as well as students of ethnic studies, especially Latino studies, should find this book useful. I also anticipate an interest from the Cuban-American writers themselves, for the study forces their reflection again on the historical, sociological, and personal influences that have shaped their lives and their work.

Acknowledgments

WHILE THIS book was in progress, I was sustained by the advice and encouragement of friends and family. I am especially grateful to Gustavo Pérez Firmat and Roberto Fernández, whose friendship, conversation, and scholarship provided a rich field of thinking. They and fellow authors Pablo Medina, Eliana Rivero, and Lourdes Gil generously sent me their published and unpublished works. I am grateful, too, for the support I received at the earlier stages of this project from Roberto González Echevarría and Raymond Souza, whose knowledge and good sense have long been helpful. I must also thank John W. Kronik, who has been a constantly supportive adviser and friend. My brother Carlos and Vincent Lapomarda S.J. have been sending relevant newspaper clips for what seems a lifetime. I am also indebted to acquisitions editor Cathie Brettschneider and to editor Jane Curran for their interest in the project and for their helpful suggestions. I would also like to thank the anonymous reviewers at the University Press of Virginia, who offered valuable criticism that helped me revise the final manuscript.

Finally, and most importantly, I thank my husband, Kermit, and my mother, Dulce, for their confidence in this book, their generosity, and their love for me. And a special thanks to Neil, who patiently endured endless hours of his mother at the computer.

I am indebted to the Committee on Research and Publications of the College of the Holy Cross, which supported my research during its preliminary stages through a semester's Faculty Fellowship and most recently with with a Summer Faculty Fellowship in order to finalize the manuscript. Portions of the material presented in chapters 5 and 8 appeared under a different context in my article "Displacements and Autobiography in Cuban-American Fiction," *World Literature Today* 68, no. 1 (winter 1994): 43–49. This material is reprinted here by permission.

When I comment on texts that have not been translated into English, I use my own translation unless I indicate otherwise. Dates listed in the chapter titles or in the subheads indicate the original date of publication and, if applicable, the date of the English translation.

Cuban-American Literature of Exile

Introduction

> Someone who's been uprooted, exiled, has no country. Our country
> exists only in our memory, but we need something beyond memory
> if we're to achieve happiness. We have no homeland, so we have to
> invent it over and over again.
> Reinaldo Arenas, "Last Interview"

WHAT HAPPENS to a culture when two or three generations
of its artists and writers become displaced and dispersed in places like
Miami, New York, Union City, or Los Angeles? What happens when
this culture changes languages in the process? This book traces the story
of an extraterritorial body of literature that begins close to the nation
and by virtue of historical change eventually becomes something else. As
Clifford Geertz tells us, an artist's response to a social reality can allow a
better assessment of that reality.[1] Understanding the process and the
conditions under which some of these works were written heightens our
sense of culture and allows us to consider the story of the 1959 Cuban
diaspora beyond the issue of geographic displacement.

This study focuses primarily on the way that one type of narration,
the prose narratives of the 1959 diaspora, explores a particular period in
Cuban history and makes it understandable to the reader. My appraisal
of the Cuban and Cuban-American narrative dramatization of the post-
1959 exodus has a double objective: to trace the evolving perspectives of
these writers toward their history, as expressed in representative works,
and to tell the story of the reformulation of Cuban literature as it
crossed cultures and changed languages during the years that correspond to the Castro regime (1959–). Here I examine issues common to
emergent U.S. minority literatures: the need for the authors to reinvent
themselves through autobiographical and testimonial literature and their
need to confront issues affecting their minority communities within their
fictions. By studying the trajectory of displacement in the history of the
post-1959 Cuban literature of diaspora, I examine the relations of self to
history and culture.

But a dispersed culture is more than one tradition and has more than one expression. As Cuban literature is no longer being written and published exclusively in Spanish, the very classification of works by Cuban and Cuban-American writers has become problematic. Thus a study of the literature of the 1959 diaspora implies a concern with linguistic, ideological, and methodological issues of interpretation. Implicit in all approaches to this literature are a variety of issues: What is the relationship between these writers and their own history? From what perspective can we speak of the Cuban and Cuban-American literary output, given its varied stance before its diasporic history, as well as the diversity of languages and ideologies that inform it? What are the differences between an ethnic and an exilic perspective?

The prose narratives of the 1959 diaspora chosen for analysis evoke the experience of exodus and its aftermath through memories most often, although not always, narrated in the first person. The past that each narrative examines (the historical context) is the past of the first decades of the Castro revolution, the trials and tribulations of those who, because of their dissent, were forced to become exiles. These works, if read collectively, describe how a people viewed traumatic historical change through their literary expression. Thus this is a study of variants of one theme: the theme of displacement in the aftermath of the 1959 exodus.

The History within the Fiction

Understanding the relationship between fiction and the history that produces it can give us a new perspective on both the art of fiction and the portrayal of history in literature. In an article entitled "Is Fiction the Art of Lying?" Mario Vargas Llosa compares history and fiction and proposes the idea that in the creation of fiction, a lie is told. This lie, if told well, can uncover the startling truth about humanity's fears and foibles. Vargas Llosa asserts that history and fiction both recount life and happenings associated therein through language. Yet, while history tries to maintain a pretense of fact, it serves no truth from the perspective of the fiction writer. In fiction, the greatest truths are revealed through the artistic use of language, which, unlike history and other kinds of narratives, is not rooted in a form of inquiry that must respond to reality. The truth of fiction, according to Vargas Llosa, is contained not within its facts but within "its own persuasive powers, on the sheer communicative strength of its fantasy, on the skill of its magic . . . submerged in the human experience" (Vargas Llosa 40). Moreover, Vargas Llosa asserts that fiction also possesses a "subversive quality" since its readers are encouraged to form their own perceptions of reality and to formulate their passions and desires about what goes on in history. In fiction, the unattainable for history is completed, the state of humanity is addressed, and the institutions that govern the lives of all of society are called into question. Thus fiction acts as a vehicle to pass on basic human truths and desires that create the reality we record as history.

In a second article entitled "Latin America: Fiction and Reality," Vargas Llosa continues to meditate on the interrelationship of history and fiction, this time from the perspective of the historian. Praising Raúl Porras Barrenechea, a former history teacher whom he deeply admired, Vargas Llosa speaks of Barrenechea's unique manner of looking at the history of Peru: "Whenever Porras Barrenechea spoke, history became anecdote, gesture, adventure, color, psychology" (Vargas Llosa 65). For Porras Barrenechea, as well as for Vargas Llosa, the chronicles that narrated the discovery and conquest of Peru were important not only in their factual content but also for the way in which they were written. According to Vargas Llosa, by looking at these New World chronicles as both narratives and historical accounts, a reader could comprehend how the early historians thought and how they formulated explanations about things and events they did not understand: "Because they narrate these events under the passion of recently lived experience, they often relate things, which to us seem like naive or cynical fantasies" (67). The chronicles of Peru were indeed both fiction and history, and, according to Vargas Llosa, both aspects had to be taken into account in order to truly understand their significance. "History and literature—truth and falsehood, reality and fiction—mingle in these texts in a manner that is often inextricable" (67). Through his admired teacher, Vargas Llosa was able to understand a deeper truth contained in these New World accounts.

Vargas Llosa's keen observations on the differences between fictional and historical accounts offer a contrast in many ways to the work of the New Historicists of the last decade. For historiographers such as Hayden White, the process of fusing events into a comprehensible totality is a poetic process, for facts are not given but are "constructed by the kinds of questions which the investigator asks of the phenomena before him."[2] For White, the writing of history is essentially a creative process in which historians must use precisely the same strategies for representing relationships in words that are used by poets and novelists. The writing of history, White tells us, involves choosing and eliminating, coordinating, and subordinating the elements that make up historical events.

In this process the historian gathers fragments, imbues them with significance, and constructs with them an ordered world—thus the importance of rhetoric in what he calls the "emplotment" of history. These tropes, according to White, are inherent in language itself.

The view that history is textual and that literature and history are engaged in a relationship of exchange is a crucial one. Like Vargas Llosa, Hayden White reflects on the linkages between history and literature, providing us with important insights about the nature of both disciplines. But while Vargas Llosa diminishes the intricacies of history in order to privilege literature, White's conceptions of history emphasize the literary qualities inherent in the historical account.

Vargas Llosa's and Hayden White's questioning of the objective categories of historical discourse has found an echo in the concerns of postcolonial scholars who have taken an interest in how "received history" is tampered with, rewritten, and realigned from the point of view of the colonizer. For instance, in "Histories, Empires and the Post-Colonial Moment," Catherine Hall proposes that the metaphors of fiction be considered as an alternative way to rethink the distorted and manipulated histories of the colonized cultures. For Hall, the task of the fiction writer is crucial in the rebuilding and reconstruction of the history of a decolonized society, "a history which involves a recognition and a re-working of memory" (Hall 76). According to Hall, fiction can become a language in which a history can be retold and imagined communities reconstructed. Through fiction, Hall continues, the colonized can find their identities and can recognize their diasporised condition.

Seeing history from the perspective of fiction can be a valuable experience because it allows the reader a deeper knowledge and insight into that history. My inquiry into the Cuban narratives of the post-1959 exodus seeks to capture precisely the living quality of history that is essential for the understanding of the cultural and literary aftermath of the Cuban revolution.

The Narratives of the 1959 Diaspora

Contemporary Cuban exile and Cuban-American writing of the last forty years represents the latest stage in Cuba's long history of émigré literature.[3] Exile is not a new theme in Cuban letters, as the literature of exile dates back to the years of Cuban independence from the Spanish in the nineteenth century. José María Heredia, a well-known Cuban poet, fled the island in 1823 in order to avoid imprisonment for his anti-Spanish sentiments. After Heredia, the poet-essayist José Martí captured in both his life and work the spirit of independence in nineteenth-century Cuba, producing his main works during his many years as an exile. Also in the same century, women writers such as Gertrudis Gómez de Avellaneda and Mercedes Merlín produced a significant body of writing related to their own experiences of exodus. In the twentieth century, novelist Alejo Carpentier elected self-imposed exile in 1928 rather than face dictatorship on his native island.

The Cuban revolution of 1959 initiated many political and social changes in Cuba and also had a profound impact on Cuban culture. Cubans who could not agree with the new demands of the Castro regime left Cuba for the United States and other continents, although they often did not realize that they were leaving their homeland for permanent exile. Large numbers of Cubans began to arrive in the United States during the 1960s, a pattern of exodus that has been repeated several times across the four decades of the Castro dictatorship.

Since 1959, more than 700,000 Cubans have settled in the United States. The first migration, from January 1959 to October 1962, was composed of about 250,000 men and women as well as their children. Between December 1965 and April 1973, another 400,000 Cubans emigrated. In 1980, the Mariel boatlift produced a third wave—nearly 120,000 people. The Mariel migration was different from the previous waves in the way it was perceived by the larger society. Unlike the Cubans who immigrated between 1959 and 1973, the Cubans of Mariel were not considered legitimate refugees.[4] Historian María Cristina García indicates that the Mariel exodus is one of the most fascinating case studies of migration because of the controversy it engendered. According to García, public opinion turned against the so-called Marielitos when the press revealed that Castro had used the boatlift to rid the island of undesirables.[5] In Miami, the Marielitos faced many obstacles. Jobs were scarce because the country was in an economic recession. Also, since many of the Mariel immigrants were black, they faced racial discrimination in addition to political discrimination from their fellow Cubans.[6] Because of these factors, the Marielitos have had much more difficulty in adapting than the immigrants of the first two waves. The *balseros* or raft people comprised the latest and fourth wave of immigrants, a wave that reached its peak in August 1994: "In one five-week period alone, from August 5 to September 10, the U.S. Coast Guard picked up 30,305 Cubans at sea" (García ix). The literary and social impact of this last wave remains to be fully assessed.

The consecutive yet different waves of immigration have brought with them artists and writers producing a unique pattern of exchange and renewal among the various generations of intellectuals in exile. While these exchanges have been quite fertile in creating an artistic renaissance of sorts, especially in the realm of music and the plastic arts of painting and sculpture, the new voices coming from the island have also added complexity to the study of extraterritorial Cuban literature. Indeed, what we have is several generations of writers producing literature simultaneously in English and in Spanish and often from contrasting perspectives. The generational diversity of these Cuban writers is further complicated when we try to discern the issue of language choice since some of the writers, equally versed in both English and Spanish, can choose the language in which they will create their works.

Presently Cuban writing outside Cuba is being created by a variety of generational and linguistic groups reflecting the migratory waves that have occurred since 1959.[7] Even if the themes of exile and displacement seem to be a constant in the literature of the various generations, the perspective from which the story of diaspora is conceived and told varies considerably among the groups. For instance, the amount of time the authors lived in Cuba before coming to the United States becomes a barometer that determines the way the writers perceive their native country in their stories of exodus and the manner in which they engage the United States as their adopted country. These variations in perception and engagement toward the native and the adopted land become evident if we compare the narratives of diaspora written by the first generation of exiles with those of the second generation. Moreover, a different attitude toward the native and adopted countries is also evident *within* the second generation when we compare the literature of those writers who left Cuba as adolescents or preadolescents and those who left as infants or who were born to Cuban exile parents in the United States. If we take into consideration these variants, two main groups of writers seem to emerge: the first generation and the second generation.

The *first generation* of writers left Cuba as adults and were fully educated on the island. This group includes internationally known figures such as Cabrera Infante and deceased writers Reinaldo Arenas, Severo Sarduy, and Novás Calvo, as well as Hilda Perera, Heberto Padilla, and Antonio Benítez Rojo, many of whom had begun successful literary careers while in Cuba. Most of these writers continue to write for a Spanish readership while in exile.

The narratives of first-generation authors selected for this study record the experience of exile in its most naked stages. Because of the temporal proximity to the physical experience of exodus, this writing displays indignation and anger toward the traumatic events or individuals causing the exile. This is a literature with an overt political content that expresses angry feelings of betrayal reflecting the chronological proximity of the events to the writing. While the United States appears as the setting in some of these narratives, the presence of the adopted country is not central to these writers' narratives since most of them write from the sometimes bitter and nostalgic perspective of exile.

This first group is multilayered in terms of chronology, for it also includes those writers who arrived in the United States in migratory waves subsequent to the first exodus of the 1960s. For instance, writers such as Reinaldo Arenas and Carlos Victoria, who arrived from Cuba in the 1980s during the Mariel boatlift, were educated in Cuba and had begun to write their first works on the island. Their Spanish writing shares many of the concerns of the older exiles from the first wave, although their life experiences growing up under Castro are necessarily different from those of the first exile group. These writers are grouped together in this study because of the similarities in their conception and relationship toward their country of origin, Cuba.

The *second generation* of writers, the children of the first exile generation, can be divided into two subgroups: the *"one-and-a-half"* generation and what I have chosen to designate as *Cuban-American ethnic writers*. The chronological factor of age combined with the amount of time these writers lived in Cuba before coming to the United States produces a literature of a markedly different sensibility toward both Cuba and the United States.

The *"one-and-a-half"* generation is the subgroup of writers who left Cuba during their early adolescence and thus had Cuban childhoods and U.S. adulthoods. Gustavo Pérez Firmat, who was the first critic to popularize this rubric in his *Life on the Hyphen*, feels that Cuban artists and writers who came to America during their adolescence or preadolescence have had a crucial impact on twentieth-century U.S. popular culture. Citing the findings of Cuban sociologist Ruben Rumbaut, Pérez Firmat explains the unique conditions that characterize this group: "These refugee youth must cope with two crisis-producing and identity-defining transitions: (1) adolescence and the task of managing the transition from childhood to adulthood, and (2) acculturation and the task of managing the transition from one sociocultural environment to another" (Pérez Firmat 4). In *Life on the Hyphen*, Pérez Firmat studies this particular chronological placement across the lives of Cuban artists and musicians of the 1940s and 1950s in addition to writers belonging to his own generation. For the purposes of this study, however, the designation of *one-and-a-half* will refer exclusively to the writers of the post-Castro diaspora who immigrated as adolescents or preadolescents.

Many one-and-a-half-generation writers have opted to publish their narrative works in English even if their earlier poems, short stories, and novels were written in Spanish. They feel that the content and the spirit of their works make them Cuban writers. They are both Cuban and American, or perhaps they are neither. Their English works are configured in two predominant forms of prose narratives: autobiographical writings and fictions of community and geographical crossings. The production of Cuban letters in English by members of this one-and-a-half generation is currently undergoing a creative explosion, as can be witnessed by the dozen or so novels that are the subject of this book. Many others, not represented here due to reasons of scope, have also appeared in the last two years. These writers recognize the disruption of their exile and create for themselves a new persona in the adopted language. This hyphen generation, also dubbed *los atrevidos* by poet-scholar Carolina Hospital,[8] writes in two languages.

Interestingly, a significant number of these writers continue to write exclusively in Spanish. Poets such as Lourdes Gil and Maya Islas, who arrived in this country as children or preadolescents, continue to write in Spanish, as do first-generation writers such as Heberto Padilla and Hilda Perera. The publication of Cuban letters in Spanish in the United States is a significant dimension of extraterritorial Cuban culture. This prolific tradition falls outside the boundaries of this study, although its current status is reviewed in the conclusion.

Cuban-American ethnic writers are the group of younger writers who came from Cuba as infants or who were born in the United States to parents of the first exile generation. These Cuban Americans have moved further away from Spanish since some of them learned English and Spanish simultaneously as young children. Others, in fact, never really mastered the Spanish language, although they heard it in their homes from their parents and relatives. These authors write simultaneously for an American and a Cuban audience. Their literature places greater distance between the writers and the events of the diaspora. Their novels join an already existing corpus of U.S. literature of Cuban heritage, *not explicitly* about the 1959 revolution, which is central in the appraisal of the English literature of Cuban heritage in the United States. This body of writing would include authors such as the 1990 Pulitzer Prize winner

Oscar Hijuelos, who lived in the United States *prior* to the 1959 diaspora and whose perspective toward Cuba is quite distant. This pre-1959 English production of Cuban heritage written in America has been studied by Gustavo Pérez Firmat, who devotes a chapter to Hijuelos's works in his *Life on the Hyphen.*[9]

While the choice of Spanish seems natural for writers of the first exodus, whose intellectual formation took place on the island, and the choice of English also seems natural for the Cuban-American writers, who came as infants and were fully educated in the United States, choosing one language over the other becomes a complex matter for the Cuban Americans of the one-and-a-half generation. After all, for these writers, Spanish was the language of their childhoods, and English became the language of their mature lives. At times, neither choice produces entirely satisfactory results, since by choosing either Spanish or English these writers give up the idea of belonging to intellectual communities that are essential for their creative survival.

During the years encompassed by the narratives studied here, the historical perspective on the events of 1959 undergoes a dramatic evolution: from the pressing reality of the Cuban exile writer to the distance of the ethnic writer of Cuban heritage. The narratives of the Cuban exile writers of the first generation reflect nostalgia and anger toward their homeland as well as a feeling of alienation from the world of English. In the case of the Cuban Americans of the one-and-a-half generation, we trace the literary dramatization of the Cuban voice from Spanish to English and explore the solutions or substitutions that these authors have devised in order to compensate for linguistic loss. Finally, for the Cuban-American ethnic writers, their search will be oriented toward issues of recovery as they set about the task of constructing a U.S. identity that very much needs to take into account their Cuban heritage. By looking at the common features in the works of these authors, it is possible to assess these texts from a perspective that is based on their common diasporic center.

An Overview

As indicated in the preface, the texts that are analyzed in this study encompass representative writings from all of the above groups. The study follows a trajectory that is *not strictly chronological* since the readings are grouped according to the evolving relationship of these authors to both their native and adopted countries. In part 1, the readings selected dramatize a confrontation between the writers of the first generation and their history as the pain and the loss caused by exile become explicit. This first segment concentrates on the literature of recognized exile writers and studies how their fictions are intertwined with the depiction of the history of the 1959 diaspora. The texts examined in part 1 are living proof that the wounds of history heal slowly, if at all.

The narratives of Guillermo Cabrera Infante, Lino Novás Calvo, and Reinaldo Arenas, chosen as representative of this first stage, display openly the authors' relationship to their own history as they offer us literary representations of the early years of the revolution and its subsequent exodus. For these Cuban exile writers of the post-Castro era, exile meant loss and, above all, indignation and a sense of betrayal by the revolution. Belonging to three separate generations, these authors have produced narratives of diaspora reflecting how exilic writing can fluctuate from the immediacy of political diatribe, in the case of Novás Calvo, toward a dialogue with aesthetics and politics for Cabrera Infante. In the case of Arenas, an exile from a different migratory wave than Novás Calvo and Cabrera Infante, exile becomes an enabling metaphor that asks broader questions of the human condition. Arenas's literature bridges the first and second stages of the exile writing of diaspora because of its strong exilic ties to the previous writers, and also because it shares many of the concerns of the autobiographical writings of the second generation.

In part 2 the writers themselves begin to create their own history. Through the autobiographies and personal essays of these writers, the personal and historical dimensions of their lives come together. In order to write about Cuba, the Cuban-American writers of the second generation had to make present a history that had been past and marginal to them. Part 2 studies how these children of exile utilize the autobiographical stance in order to reinvent themselves in a new language. Most of the writers examined in this section spent childhoods in Cuba and adulthoods in the United States. Their works confirm Paul J. Eakin's dictum that "an autobiography dramatizes the experience of a writer's living in history."[10]

Pablo Medina's *Exiled Memories* and Gustavo Pérez Firmat's *Next Year in Cuba* recall the prerevolutionary Cuba in which they spent their first decade, whereas Virgil Suárez's memories in *Spared Angola* are grounded in a different historical time and provide a contrast to Medina's and Pérez Firmat's happier recollections. The memoirs of all three authors revisit experiences of a Cuban childhood while simultaneously exhibiting an emotional and ideological interaction between the writing self and the self recalled. On the other hand, the autobiographical essays of Eliana Rivero and Ruth Behar exhibit a different perspective than that of their male counterparts. In the case of the women writers, the deployment of identity takes into consideration issues regarding the traditional place of women and minorities in U.S. society, as well as the lack of freedoms accorded to their gender. Cuban and American cultural mores are juxtaposed as these writers try to make sense of cultural contrasts. Although these autobiographical accounts are radically different in their perspectives, all become a means to ensure the survival of a collective identity.

Cuban-American personal constructions of self are inextricably connected to the historical traumas that fueled the writings. They are both intimate and public since they reveal personal details of the lives of these authors and undertake the reconstruction of a culture and of a lost past. There is a documentary or testimonial character to these texts that stems from a desire to sound real, to achieve authority. These authors need to appear factual in order to gain credibility because their works are dispersed and are rejected by the culture and country of origin. Their thematics, although situated sometimes in opposing ideological perspectives toward the Cuban homeland, engage the issue of biculturality as a lived reality and as a social construct.

The readings selected in part 3 tell about encounters between the exile's own history and the history of others. This segment focuses on fictions that directly address the reality of Cuban Americans as a minority group living in the United States. In chapter 6, the writers address issues of their community as a collective entity. The novels of Roberto Fernández and J. Joaquín Fraxedas look at life in exile and beyond and ask how the Cuban community coexists within the dominant Anglo culture. The narrative perspective in these works changes from the autobiographical writings featured in part 2 to a more distanced and critical outlook that centers on issues that affect U.S. Cubans as a group. In chapter 7, autobiography becomes fictionalized so that gay and lesbian writers can engage community. The novels of Elías Miguel Muñoz and Achy Obejas dramatize the intersection of these authors' gay and lesbian fictional selves and, in Muñoz's case, tell stories of U.S. Cuban communities that do not always accept them.

Finally, chapter 8 examines novels that imitate the structure of autobiography via protagonists who seek the capacity to tell their own stories. The novels of Pablo Medina, Omar Torres, Margarita Engle, and Cristina García feature protagonists who become *writers within the text* in order to collect the memories of their Cuban communities in exile. These fictions utilize modernistic narrative strategies, such as embedded texts and fictional writers, in order to articulate issues of cultural displacement. Some of these narratives go back to the pre-1959 Cuban past, while others consider the Cuban present and the aftermath of the revolution. Communication is a central theme in these works, as the characters meditate on the problem of language and try to come to terms with the possibilities of English as well as Spanish. The way in which the fictional characters in these novels dramatize this issue demonstrates how linguistic choice is deeply tied to these characters' relationship to their adopted country.

The fictions studied in part 3 demonstrate geographical and historical crossings that make the various Cuban communities communicate and interact with one another. These narratives become central in the validation of Cuban-American ethnic culture and values as they exist in Miami and other parts of the country. By looking at fictionalized accounts of these writers' Cuban-American communities and their interactions with their dominant Anglo counterparts, we learn a significant amount about these writers' own conception of the history of their community as it evolves outside their native country.

In *Nations without Nationalism*, Julia Kristeva studies minority groups in France, examining the possible relationships of "outsiders" toward their homelands.[11] The author defines the relationship between ordinary citizens and their home nations according to two different models: an organic model and a contractual model. For Kristeva, the *organic* nation, founded on origins and tradition, relates to its citizens by integration since all must adhere to a uniform concept of nation. The *contractual* nation, on the other hand, places emphasis on the present more than the past. Kristeva's findings illuminate our discussion of the literature of the 1959 diaspora, for the older Cuban exiles dramatize the moment of rupture of the organic relationship of individual writer and nation, whereas the Cuban Americans of the second generation eventually develop a contractual relationship with their adopted country as they become Cuban and American, although not necessarily at the same time.[12]

The poetic rendition of displacement in the writings of Cuban exiles and Cuban Americans is central to this study. These narratives of exodus record a crucial and personal trauma for these writers and document the changing identity of a nation in exile. This book seeks to reflect the evolution of a narrative, a trajectory that is at once historical and literary.

The analyses of the various works encompass a movement from narratives that reflect the personal loss caused by the historical fact of exile (part 1), to autobiographical writings that reflect the need to search for a new identity in a new language (part 2), to fictions that dramatize an encounter between the diverse U.S. Cuban communities and the authors' fictional personae (part 3). Following the progression of this literature, from the texts produced by well-known Cuban exiled writers to the younger and lesser-known Cuban Americans, provides an understanding of the changes that can occur once a literature loses touch with its culture of origin.

PART 1

Exile as Loss

Bearing Witness

You will leave everything loved most dearly;
and this is the arrow
that the bow of exile shoots first.
You will learn how salty the bread tastes
in others' houses, and how hard
is the going up and down of others' stairs.
And what will weigh heaviest upon you
will be the evil and senseless company
into which you will fall in this valley,
A company which, ungrateful, mad, and impious,
will turn against you, but soon they,
not you, will blush for it.
Their ways will give proof of their brutishness
so that it will be well for you
to have made a party by yourself.

Dante, *The Divine Comedy*

1 Exile and Retribution

Lino Novás Calvo's *Maneras de contar*
(1970)

Who but an exile like Dante, banished from Florence, would use
eternity as a place for settling old scores?

Edward Said, "Reflections on Exile"

EXILE LITERATURE has always been intimately related to
history because the banishment of the writer is usually caused by some
historical event beyond his or her will. In a recent article on the subject of
exile, Vytautas Kavolis reminds us that the condition of exile places a
particular burden on three dimensions of human experience: history, language, and community.[1] However, Kavolis adds that if the original language and community have been lost, "history is precisely what the exile
writer most surely has" (Kavolis 43). If we apply this idea to the Cuban
narratives of the 1959 exodus, we can see a literature that encompasses
these issues in a dramatic way. The texts analyzed in this chapter claim a
place in retelling the history of the aftermath of 1959 as these writers
cope with the loss of their native country and original community.

In December 1987, a group of novelists, poets, and journalists met in
Vienna at the Wheatland Conference on Literature to present essays that
spoke of their common experience—that of being exiled. With origins in
lands as varied as the Middle East, Latin America, and East Africa, each
writer explored different facets of their common experience. William
Gass's keynote lecture at that conference defined the philosophical significance of exile in the following terms: "Birth is your first experience of
exile, the Greeks maintained. That's why a child bellows when it is born.
. . . The second exile is never really to belong. . . . And the third exile is
to forget the enormity of your loss."[2] In its first stages, exile writing relates mostly to the politics that originated the condition in the first place.
In its middle stages, this writing has to do with resistance against the
erosion of identity as related to the new space. In its last stages, exile

transforms itself into ethnicity as it confronts issues related to assimilation and heritage. Yet, regardless of its historical moment, it is clear that exile writing makes for a variety of losses as well as some gains.

Cuban exile writer Guillermo Cabrera Infante, himself a participant in the 1987 Wheatland Conference, presented an essay entitled "The Invisible Exile," which stressed issues of loss of identity and lack of recognition for Cuban exiles who, like himself, had left Cuba for Europe in the early 1960s.[3] According to Cabrera Infante, Cubans in exile had to face further alienation than other writers in exile due to the fact that the exiles from the other Latin American countries did not accept the Cubans on political grounds: "As for me (a nonpoet), invisible is not the word to define my status. Even the Latin word is different when it applies to a Cuban. . . . There are no exiles from Cuba. As we know, this is a model country when it comes to dissidents and malcontents, who are usually going, rather than coming" (35–37). Cabrera Infante's resentment for the lack of sympathy shown to Cuban exiles abroad, as well as his feelings of alienation from the community of Spanish-speaking exiles in Europe, confirms Gass's dictum that exile always has to do with invisibility and loss (of language and of place) as well as with change. Moreover, for the exiles from Cabrera Infante's generation, these feelings were intensified due to the hostile political climate during the 1970s and 1980s toward exiles from the island of Cuba.

Michael Ugarte's study of exiled writers of the Spanish Civil War provides a definition for exile that is suitable to the group of writers treated in this chapter.[4] Ugarte indicates that while the term *exile* is usually attributed to someone who suffers "punishment by expulsion," the Spanish word *desterrado* conveys a much stronger meaning (10). *Desterrado*, Ugarte tells us, means literally to be unearthed, to have lost the essential link between land and soul. For this author, *destierro* rightly signifies the loss of a necessary and integral human component.

In part 1 of this book, the selected narratives of Lino Novás Calvo, Cabrera Infante, and Reinaldo Arenas tell stories that are overtly political in nature and present the authors' ideological stance against the injustices of the revolution. Whether they left Cuba in the early 1960s, as did Cabrera Infante and Novás Calvo, or in the early 1980s, as in the case of Reinaldo Arenas, these works reflect themes of treason, betrayal, and existential solitude by means of a tragic discourse of lamentation and denunciation. By virtue of their exile, these writers feel unearthed and in a sense "amputated" from their place of birth.

Maneras de contar (1970; Modes of narrating) constitutes Lino Novás Calvo's first and only work published outside of Cuba and reflects the tragic events of the revolution as the author experienced them firsthand.[5] The name of the collection evokes a plurality of approaches to the writing of these tales, as *maneras* can be translated as modes, manners, or ways of telling. This title also demonstrates a clear ambivalence on the part of the author as to how to dramatize in his creative work the catastrophic events that had turned his life upside down. Woven around the theme of revenge and retribution, the stories look back to events related to the first months and years of the 1959 revolution. As an exile writing in Spanish in the United States during the early 1960s, Novás had no guarantee of a secure or receptive readership.

The narratives of this first Cuban exile writer of the 1959 revolution depict stories about marginal, isolated individuals whose only power lies in their ability to bear witness. Born to a poor family in 1905 in Galicia, Lino Novás Calvo was sent to live in Cuba by his mother when he was only seven. As an adult in Cuba, Novás Calvo established his reputation as a short story writer and published seven collections of stories, all of which received wide critical acclaim. The 1940s represented the most significant period in Novás's career. In 1942, he won the Hernandez Catá prize for the short story; in 1944, the National Prize for the Short Story for his collection *La luna nona y otros cuentos* (The ninth moon and other stories).[6] Shortly after the 1959 Castro takeover, Novás Calvo sought asylum in the Colombian embassy and later moved permanently to the United States, where he died in exile in 1983.

Novás Calvo's literary career was shattered by the advent of the revolution, and his personal sadness is reflected in the stories written in exile. The disillusion and hopelessness found in *Maneras de contar* describe an experience common to exile writing as the author suddenly found himself cut off from his language, environment, and sources of inspiration. The stories selected for analysis are united by the thematics of retaliation. Most of these pieces revisit the first days and months after the Castro takeover; they attempt to relive this time of crisis in order to document history and to find some sort of coherence to the upheaval. These narratives vividly dramatize Novás Calvo's anger and indignation toward the events that followed the 1959 revolution, as the challenge for this writer in exile is how to effectively dramatize the human passions of revenge and retribution within the context of the history of 1959. As such, these stories make clear Novás Calvo's political distance from the

Cuban revolution, as his exile engenders a moral discourse against the abuses of the early days.

For Novás Calvo, writing about exile meant testifying about what happened: "There have always been victims and executioners. It is the responsibility of the humanitarian writer to denounce them" (152). Through an exploration of the literary possibilities allowed to the writer by the short story as genre, Novás Calvo explores reprisal in its psychological and social dimensions. His objective in writing these tales is clearly political, as documentary history is too tangible and impossible to put aside. Revenge becomes a major theme in the development of stories populated by exiles who seem obsessed with their need to get back at those who wronged them while in Cuba. Novás's literary re-creation of these bloody exile encounters frequently involved the clash of Cubans who had arrived during the various immigration waves. Indeed, Novás was quite convinced that those who supported Castro at the beginning would eventually become exiles themselves. Old debts between the new and the older exiles would have to be repaid in exile.

The narratives collected in *Maneras de contar* probe the experiences of Cubans from all levels of society who were caught in the middle of an unprecedented historical upheaval. Loss, in its many variations and manifestations, is the most vivid image in Novás's prose, as he looks upon the condition of being an exile with indignation, powerlessness, and, eventually, sad resignation. The short prologues that accompany the stories indicate the author's reason for their inclusion in the anthology and often include the author's own criticism of the pieces. Readers are guided and told, not only Novás's assessment of his stories of diaspora, but also the way he wished his stories to be read by his audience. Fearful of being misunderstood by his new readers in exile, Novás wanted the readers to be clear about his objectives and to fathom the individual stories in a prescribed way.

With this goal in mind, Novás Calvo makes brilliant use of the ancient narrative strategy of the frame, a device that serves him well for many reasons. The framed story allows Novás a much needed temporal distance from his recent experience of exile, a distance that in real life did not exist, since these tales were written soon after he left Cuba in 1961. Most importantly, the use of the literary frame *creates tellers and listeners* within the text, fulfilling Novás's real need to conjure up an audience for himself. A great number of Novás's frames in this collection feature narrators who usually claim to have been witnesses to the injustices of the revolution and who allege to possess the true version of these events. In addition to providing a needed historical context to these tales of revolution and diaspora, these fictional narrators allow Novás to explore the psychology of the victims as well as the victimizers during the days following the 1959 upheaval. In the stories that follow, Novás's narrators usually act as mediators for history as the author experienced it himself.

The narrative frame is of extreme importance in the story "Nadie a quien matar" (No one to kill) for it introduces the reader to the treacherous character of Romilio, the narrator and the murderer of Aranguren, his half brother.[7] "Nadie a quien matar" is aptly titled, for this story accurately depicts a historical period of vengeance, treason, and eroded family loyalty. The fate of Lauro Aranguren, a medical doctor who initially survives the change from the Batista to the Castro regime but who soon falls from grace, is not an uncommon story during the early days of revolutionary unrest. Aranguren is sent to jail on a false accusation and experiences the changes of the new regime in a very personal way: his children are sent abroad to live, and his wife dies en route to the prison on one of her visits. Once Aranguren is released, he is consumed by a desire to get back at those who caused his misfortunes: "I needed to kill someone. . . . The thing is to do something, to kill someone. Because what one has to do is to start killing. Whoever it might be, we are all guilty" (87–88).

From the beginning of the story, the revolution looms large in this tale and is referred to with devastating nomenclature: *El huracán* (The hurricane), *La Candela Grande* (The great fire) (79–80). The radical changes to Cuban society instituted by the revolution are well depicted by Novás, with privileged professionals such as Aranguren the first to suffer from such changes. Aranguren clearly had no sympathies for the new regime and only wanted to survive the times. Reminiscent of Desnoes's protagonist in the film *Memorias del subdesarrollo* (*Memories of Underdevelopment*), Aranguren sees history changing before his eyes.[8] He does not agree with what is going on, but he stubbornly decides to stay in his country. The revolution in this story meant the destruction of family ties, with members ready to harm each other in the name of some material gain.

Unable to find his original accusers, Aranguren decides to punish the unknown individual who resided in his confiscated home while he was in jail. What Aranguren does not know is that the new owner of his former home is Romilio, his half brother and the only person he has ever trusted. At the end of the tale, Aranguren is shot by his half brother as he returns to reclaim his former home. The reader is further shocked when the unknown narrator of the story identifies himself: "That is the truth. Let no one say that Dr. Lauro Aranguren is still out there trying to avenge his fate. Let things be! What I have just told is the truth pure and simple. I have a reason to know. I am Romilio Candón" (90). Novás Calvo, the exile writer, presents this story from the point of view of the victimizer in order to make events even more sordid.

The idea that historical facts are actually versions created by those in power is evident from the start in the words of Romilio: "This is the true version and the true story of the last days in the life of Lauro Aranguren" (77). The tension regarding historical truth is doubly evident: once victims such as Aranguren are out of the way, the victimizer (Romilio) is free to lie to the reader and retell the events from his own perspective. Both at the beginning and at the end of the story, Romilio alludes to other versions, which he obviously claims to be false. Romilio sets himself up as the authority on the facts, although once the reader knows he was Aranguren's assassin, his version also becomes rather suspect and horrifying.

Romilio, as narrator, stands not as a witness of events—as he pretended initially—but as the originator of the abuses perpetrated on Aranguren. Novás's narrative strategy makes the reader experience, along with Aranguren, the uncertainty and the lack of trust felt by those who had endured the first years of the revolution. According to Romilio, the exiles, having nothing left to do in their adopted country, had taken up fabricating their own versions of the historical events of 1959: "That's up to them and their musings. It's about all they have left" (77). The exiles, Novás among them, were defenseless before what happened to them and opted to portray in literature their own versions of the aftermath of 1959.

As a first-person "historian," Romilio claims to tell the real truth about what happened. He is a witness of events, a *narrador testigo*, and later, as the reader will find out, he is also victimizer of and traitor to his half brother. Interestingly enough, the words of Romilio betray Novás Calvo's true feelings of futility and impotence before a fate imposed by history. With this narratorial option, Novás Calvo displays the anguish of a writer who feels that the events of the aftermath of 1959 were better told by those in charge of the fate of his country.

In "Fernández, al paredón" (Fernández to the firing squad), reprisal takes on an aleatory dimension.[9] Set during the days and weeks immediately following the downfall of Fulgencio Batista, this story continues to be critical of the revolutionary excesses of the early years by portraying the bloodthirsty revolutionary tribunals and the sentencing of *batistianos* to death by firing squads. In reality, Fernández never has a chance, although the narrator creates suspense by making the reader feel that the familial link between victim and executioner will prevail over the need to avenge Batista's people. This is one of Novás's more unified pieces, as the theme of injustice becomes the center of the actions perpetrated on Fernández, the protagonist and victim.

A policeman for the Batista regime, Fernández is a pathetic figure who is prey to forces much larger than himself. The story begins at the time of Fernández's execution and then works itself back to the Batista years and eventually to the actual moment of the murder. Fernández is imprisoned by the rebel government, tried without recourse, and sentenced to death; his fate is sealed before the story begins. Fernández's closest relations—his wife, his former mistress, and Ciro, his illegitimate son—are all presented as unfeeling characters who do not believe in family ties and who refuse to intercede on his behalf. When Fernández is ready to face the firing squad, the reader is astonished to find out that Ciro is the leader of the firing squad that eventually kills the father. The unnamed narrator keeps a cold distance from the events narrated, especially at the end, when the reader realizes that Ciro, the son, is responsible for the murder of his own father.

In the story's short prologue, Novás Calvo presents his reasons for writing about the injustices of the revolutionary tribunals: "For me the story is above all a testimony outside time, which is beyond its current historical context" (152). For Novás Calvo, Fernández becomes a prototype, since many like him were executed during the bloodthirsty days of early 1959. The need to set things straight led to the establishment of makeshift tribunals that needed very little evidence to condemn those who had to pay for the Batista injustices. These killings were an all too real happening during those days, as was the reluctance of friends and family to lend support to those who had former ties to Batista. Linked to the prevailing theme of injustice, the dissolution of family loyalty becomes central in the development of this piece. Novás clearly saw the impact of the revolution of 1959 as deleterious to nation and family.

In fact, it is the injustices perpetrated against the characters' families that often motivate the crimes related in these tales. "Un buchito de café" (A sip of coffee) seeks to give the reader an alternative historical perspective to the events that precipitated the revolution.[10] "Un buchito" is told by a narrator who declares himself the only survivor of a

1958 massacre of his entire family by an unknown group of thugs. A Cuban exile in New York City, he relates in detail how his mother and two younger brothers died at the hands of five individuals whose identity is never known. His listeners are a mysterious group of newsmen who never really identify themselves although they indicate that they too are Cuban exiles. The end suggests that the newsmen, who had come to speak to the narrator, are the possible perpetrators of the 1958 massacre. The sound of a rifle, conveyed by the onomatopoetic "tac tac tac," suggests that a second massacre has indeed taken place during the last lines of the tale. As the bloody battle of revenge is fought across time and in the adopted country of exile, the narrator becomes the murderer of his listeners, thinking them to be the assassins of his family.

In the story's prologue, Novás expresses a need to lend documentary veracity to his tale in order to give exact testimony of what happened: "If letters could have sound, this story would begin with the humming of a tape recorder. Precisely what the story pretends to be is a tape recording of events" (209). The theme of the unfair victimization of poor and innocent Cuban farmers is well wrought in a tale of misunderstandings and cold-blooded murder.

Written by Novás Calvo in 1961, the narration shifts in geography from Cuba to New York City as the narrator (within the story's frame) tells his tale from the space of exile. The title, "Un buchito de café," lends interest to the story; Novás uses the very Cuban gesture of offering coffee to visitors as a deadly motif that structures the events of the tale. Hospitality is never denied to either the Batista or the Castro side by the *guajiro* (peasant farmer) family members that are soon to be massacred: "For that reason, she never said anything to anyone or ever denied coffee to anyone who went by their house, whoever it might be. . . . Using the same pot and cups, mother would serve them coffee" (217, 18). Eventually, the *guajiros* in this story become more than innocent bystanders. They are exploited by both factions since even their food is taken from them: "On our little farm there was little left. Chickens, pigs, rabbits, they took everything" (219). Novás Calvo's need to tell the sad stories of those who stood to gain the most from the changes brought about by the revolution is crucial to his appraisal of the aftermath of 1959.

"Un buchito" is a story about the *guajiro,* the country folk who were to have been redeemed by the coming of the revolutionary era but who instead suffered abuse from both the Batista and the rebel armies. Novás portrays this humble segment of the population as fed up with events, only wishing for the conflict to be over so that they can be left alone: "God willing, they will be finished soon. Whoever might win, let this mess be over. Things are becoming impossible" (219). The author's intention here is political, for Novás wants to show the fate of those who were caught between warring sides of the conflict.

"Un bum," written in 1964, revisits the theme of revenge of individuals from rival factions trying to avenge each other in exile.[11] Novás Calvo was deeply worried about the subject of factions and groups that harmed each other in Cuba and that, in exile, would seek to avenge the wrongs of the past. This particular story relates how Pallares, a Cuban exile, spots Corbeta, an old enemy from Cuba, in the New York City subway. Corbeta, as it turns out, had been responsible for atrocities done to Pallares during the first months of the revolution and had even demanded his execution. Now it becomes Pallares's turn to avenge these atrocities. The action is reduced to the dialogue that takes place between the two men during a long walk through the streets of Manhattan, a walk the reader knows will end in the murder of Corbeta. At the end of the grizzly tale, Corbeta is thrown by Pallares into a construction pit, and his body is left there to be covered by the imminent snowfall of a New York winter.

The story's interest lies in Novás's efficient use of irony: the reader all along knows more than Corbeta, the character whose death avenges the previous atrocities, thus creating the intense pathos of the situation. The reader is allowed into the thoughts of Pallares and thus into the motivation that leads this character to seek revenge. The brevity of this tale, along with its eerie detachment from the sordid events narrated, gives ample evidence that for the author, the story of exile was indeed a tragic and a violent one.

For Novás Calvo, the past and the wrongs of the early days of the revolution are all too recent. As a writer, he is not willing to concede forgiveness to latecomers such as Corbeta. Moreover, Novás considers zealots such as Pallares and Corbeta responsible for what happened in his country: "and who but you and others like you created our exile?" (293). In the short prologue to this story, Novás indicates that, in fact, the events of the story were taken from his personal experience: "One of my friends actually wanted to do exactly as I told it (in this story). He admitted it to me himself. But he was glad, of course, for not having done such a thing. These were his words: 'the intention was mine, but yours is the crime'" (281). Through his narratives of retribution, Novás wants to help his exiled peers understand and experience the negative emotions of exile. Novás's readers thus become vicarious participants because of their own inevitable need for settling old scores in exile.

"La noche en que Juan tumbó a Pedro" (The night Juan victimized Pedro) combines Novás Calvo's thematics of revenge with his desire to explore the ways in which this theme could be dramatized in literature.[12] In terms of the thematics of exile, it presents the idea of revenge from a double perspective: as an aesthetic abstraction that the writer might explore in his work and as an exploration of the psychological effects of obsessive behavior in his characters. In terms of literary strategy, the story shows Novás Calvo's skills as a writer and his willingness to explore modernistic techniques such as metafiction and the introduction of fictional creators within the story.

The tale is about Portelas and Artigas, former neighbors in Cuba, who visit one another in New York City. It is Artigas's obsession with the idea of revenge that becomes the reason for a tale centered on retribution as an abstraction as well as a historical reality. With the tacit complicity of Portelas, the two friends fabricate a situation in order to confirm the validity of Portela's theoretical musings on the subject of vindictiveness: "History is written in order to confirm that if yesterday Pedro victimized Juan, today Juan should victimize Pedro" (266).

Just as writers would choose their characters, Artigas and Portela become surrogates for Novás Calvo as they arrange for a meeting of Morales and Pereira, two former enemies now in exile. By setting up this meeting, Artigas and Portela initiate an instance of revenge. Once the participants are introduced and recognize each other, both Artigas and Portela become cold-blooded spectators of the murderous drama they themselves have created. The results are predictable. Pereira kills Morales and later dies himself of a heart attack. At the story's end, Portela and Artigas remain quite unaffected by the violence they have caused.

Seldom commented on by critics, this story is significant in conveying Novás Calvo's perception of the aftermath of 1959. By dramatizing authors within his story, Novás Calvo seeks to understand for himself the sordidness of life in exile so that he is able to relate it to others. The story helps the reader comprehend the thinking of Novás Calvo regarding the immediate consequences of the 1959 revolution and the inevitability of a bloody battle of revenge among the exiles themselves: "When they return, many Pedros will have to die before the Juans and Pedros are able to live peacefully" (271).

Novás Calvo's stories of exile confront the official history of the events of 1959, as his narratives show a concern for exploring the human dimension of history. His narratives suggest that alternative perspectives on the events of the revolution should be examined because they can lead to a more complete understanding of what really happened. History, to Novás Calvo, is variable and uncertain, for it suffers from the effects of time and the modifications in the memories of those who recorded it. Concerning Cuba, history is seen as having played a negative role, for it has hidden injustices and abuses in the name of enfranchising a figure or an event. The last lines of "La noche" bring out the author's ideas about the writer's role in narrating the cruelties of history: "After all, at times things happen just as one would have imagined. Almost always . . ." (280). For Novás Calvo, no one is truly innocent in the historical drama created by the revolution. Furthermore, the idea of a collective responsibility for what happened is dramatized by characters who act in accordance to the dictates of a history that they did not create but that will rule their lives.

Maneras de contar contains many more stories than are analyzed here. In all these tales, Novás Calvo leaves the mark of a narrator who vigorously pursued objectivity in his art. A Spaniard who became a Cuban, and later a Cuban who became an exile, Novás always lived within two cultural contexts, thus providing his readers with a unique perspective on reality. Of the Cuban exile writers who settled in the United States during the early 1960s, Lino Novás Calvo has only recently begun to receive the critical attention he deserves.

2 Challenging History from Exile

Guillermo Cabrera Infante's *View of Dawn in the Tropics* (1974, 1978)

Facts are the worst enemy of truth.

Cervantes, *Don Quijote*

WHEN ASKED about what he thought of the relationship between literature and history, Guillermo Cabrera Infante had the following response: "History is no more than a book that has on its cover the title History. . . . The best proof that history is just a book that gets written has been given by those fanatics of history, the Marxists who, in China, Cuba, and the Soviet Union, have rewritten and altered the past in order to affect the future. . . . I have never thought of history as a muse or as a theme. To the contrary, for me, an ideal life is a life outside history, such as urban life."[1] In *View of Dawn in the Tropics* (1978; a translation of *Vista del amanecer en el trópico*, 1974), Cabrera Infante writes about history because he does not trust it.[2] The anonymous narrator in this text seeks to counter the history written in the annals of Cuban history by retelling it from the point of view of the defeated. As the title of the collection of vignettes indicates, the text is an *aperçu*, a view of the country's total history from colonial times to the revolution of 1959. In this fragmentary text, Cabrera Infante places the revolution and its indignities within a larger context of horror and unfairness.

Born in Cuba in 1929, Guillermo Cabrera Infante is probably the best-known exiled writer Cuba has ever produced. Cabrera Infante began his literary career in the 1950s as a movie critic. In the early Castro years, the author was editor of the influential literary supplement *Lunes de Revolución*. After *Lunes* ceased publication in 1961, Cabrera Infante was sent to Belgium as a cultural attaché. He returned to Cuba briefly in 1965 and has lived in London ever since. Cabrera Infante has published several collections of essays, short stories, and two fictional works since his exile (see the authors' bibliography). His most famous work to date is *Three Trapped Tigers* (1971; a translation of *Tres tristes tigres*, 1967), a work published in exile but written in Cuba.

View of Dawn in the Tropics has not received wide critical attention, perhaps due to its overtly political contents. Completed in 1972 and published in Spanish in 1974, *View of Dawn* can provide us with valuable information regarding the author's social and aesthetic responses toward language and writing at a crucial period in his career. Similar to Novás Calvo's collection of stories, *View of Dawn* is Cabrera Infante's first work written as a Cuban exile. Critic Terry Peavler provides some useful information on the author's life at the time of its genesis: "It apparently began as a sort of therapy: Cabrera Infante had sunk into a deep depression while working on a film script for *Under the Volcano*. During his recovery, which included shock therapy, he received the devastating news that his old friend, Alberto Mora, had committed suicide in Cuba. The book, dedicated to Mora and to Plinio Prieto (another friend, who had been executed in 1960) is a sort of catharsis, a hymn to Cuba and its violent history. . . . It is the author's most poetic work, and may someday be judged to be one of his best."[3]

For Cabrera Infante, the writing of a text that confronts historical narrative in its explicit thematics as well as in its aesthetic strategies was not just a way of seeking personal balance. This apparently fragmented narrative constitutes a search for Cabrera Infante's own identity as a writer without a country, a kind of reexamination of the past in order to rebuild a shattered present. The vignettes of *View of Dawn* carry within them an angry indictment against historical writing, since Cabrera Infante himself had experienced much of Cuba's painful past and had seen upheavals that made history in textbooks around the world. It is this feeling of disappointment toward history that is expressed in *View of Dawn*, for the writer's challenge is in fact to the language of history and to the way history has been recorded for posterity. To challenge history is not to deny it, and so, in his first work written as an exile, Cabrera Infante invites the reader to reflect on the process of how history is made. The presence of an anonymous historian and the juxtaposition of known historical events and fictional anecdotes in the telling of Cuba's history clearly point to Cabrera Infante's anguish in conceptualizing his own present as an exile as well as Cuba's own past.

The fragments that comprise the bulk of *View of Dawn* are mostly sketches of the lives of individuals who had to live under the various dictatorial regimes throughout the history of Cuba. In *View of Dawn*, Cabrera Infante's fictional narrator becomes a mediator of Cuban history, and the various versions he offers in the narrative become a way to make readers examine their own perceptions of that history. The text is a collage of 101 vignettes, a chronological account of Cuba's history from its physical emergence as a volcanic island to the early 1970s when the book was written. This is a book that portrays Unamuno's concept of *intrahistoria*, a book about the small, anonymous incidents and specific conflicts of unknown characters.

The chronological order of this text makes it resemble the structure of a history book, as the vignettes are based on a variety of epochs of Cuban history: colonial times, independence, and the bloody twentieth-century tyrannies of Machado, Batista, and Fidel Castro.[4] Ironically, Cabrera Infante uses these techniques and strategies not to maneuver an escape from history but rather to engage the central theme of the unfair recording of history. From both the selection of vignettes and their placement within the text, the reader gets a sense of disjunction that will also be reflected by the content of each piece. Time periods are not delimited; the markers are not there, although clues do exist. The book covers almost five hundred years of Cuban history, from colonial times to the first decade of the Castro regime. The reader, unable to judge by conventional methods of names, places, and dates, is forced to relinquish conventional ways of reading history.

Can history claim more truth than fiction? In *A Poetics of Postmodernism*, Linda Hutcheon coins the term *historiographic metafiction* in order to describe the nature of postmodern narratives that, according to Hutcheon, ask two central questions from history: "How can we know that past today? What can we know of it?"[5] My reading of *View of Dawn* proposes to show how the voice of the fictional historian in this text embodies a paradoxical stance that challenges the veracity of historical language because it offers no assurance of truth while at the same time it explores aesthetic and philosophical issues of perception and meaning.

The different styles and themes exhibited in *View of Dawn* are used to probe the historical truth of an event. Some vignettes are rooted in the historical, as they relate the occurrences the narrator presents. Others are stories within stories in which one character relates a tale to a listener within the piece, thus adding a dramatic, oral sense to the living history the author seeks to present. Still other stories are presented in the visual form of photographs, paintings, and engravings. In many of these pieces, the voice of the narrator explores the limits of language and its (in)ability to adequately represent reality. Throughout all of the vignettes, Cabrera Infante asks if fictional and historical writing are really that different and if a separation of categories is valid.

From its very first pages, including the book's dedication and its prefatory epigraphs, *View of Dawn* reveals Cabrera Infante's conscious challenging of the historical account:

> To the memory of Comandate Plinio Prieto,
> who was shot by firing squad in September 1960
> In memory of Comandante Alberto Mora,
> who shot himself in September 1972.

Cabrera Infante includes in this dedication the cause of death of these military figures who were his personal friends and the date of their demise. The fact that both deceased men were members of Castro's military force suggests a negative progression for the revolution, a fact that is confirmed by the reading of the text.

Likewise, the reference to one of Goya's etchings, *If It Dawns We Will Leave* (*Si amanece nos vamos*), also has a crucial significance in revealing the author's purpose in writing this fictional history of Cuba. This particular epigraph, taken from the title of one of Goya's *Caprichos*, offers clear parallels between Goya's story of repression under Fernando VII and the story of Cabrera Infante, the author in exile.

The influence of Goya's famous etchings on Cabrera Infante's *View of Dawn* is significant. First, the title of Cabrera Infante's novel, *Vista del amanecer*, links directly to the title of Goya's painting, *Si amanece nos vamos*. The use of the word *si* (if) in the title implies the same despair and pessimism that Cabrera Infante wants to convey in his narrative version of Cuba's history. For Cabrera Infante, as well as for Goya, the coming of dawn (*amanecer*) is filled with irony for it does not imply hope for resolution. Instead, the hope implied here is the prospect of escape, the possibility for exile in the case of both artists. Furthermore, although the etching title selected by Cabrera Infante for his epigraph pertains to Goya's *Caprichos*, a collection from the 1790s, the painter's later collection of war etchings, *Los desastres de la guerra* (*The Disasters of War*), completed in the early 1800s, has an even closer link to Cabrera Infante's narrative.

View of Dawn closely resembles *Los desastres de la guerra* in theme and in structure, as Cabrera Infante's vignettes become his own version of Goya's artwork in their didactic indictment of history. Both Cabrera

Infante's vignettes and Goyas's paintings are in a sense artistic records of war.[6] Furthermore, Goya's *Los desastres* were important to Cabrera Infante for a crucial reason: these etchings were not reproductions of official historical events; rather, they were paintings rooted in the everyday life of the common people, paintings that prepare the reader for a subject matter that reflects the suffering and humanity of the anonymous individuals living in history. In their rendition of violence, both Goya and Cabrera Infante present seemingly unrelated vistas of despair that could only be understood by their collective impact and carefully ordered display. Each image or vista in Cabrera Infante's text, and in Goya's visual texts, expresses an idea that in turn adds new dimensions to the general theme of violence and repression in Cuban and Spanish histories—and, for both artists, their sympathies are always with the victims.

Last but not least, Cabrera Infante's allusion to Goya's paintings also emphasizes his careful utilization of visuals in *View of Dawn*: engravings, photographs, and etchings dramatize how perception affects the process of writing. In the following example, Cabrera Infante uses the device of a photograph with multiple objectives that converge in stressing the idea of subjectivity:

> The ambitious general appears, surrounded by army officers, but he's dressed in civilian clothes. . . . The general is in the middle of the photograph, with a caption that says: "He is The Man!" That *ecce homo* is meant to be flattering. The general, in civilian clothes, is smiling, perhaps thinking of the historical forces he has just unleashed, but it doesn't show. Around him are colonels and captains who will soon be, in barely a few hours, generals and brigadiers. This strong-armed promotion will divide the island in two. But that doesn't seem to matter to the men in the picture. (66)

By capturing in his picture only that part of reality that he deemed important, the photographer becomes the ultimate interpreter of the reality described. While on the surface it looks like the use of photographs and other visuals would enhance the authenticity of the historian's perspective, in reality what matters here is how the photographer describes the photograph and his own role in the recording of history. The eye of the camera becomes an analogue of the written historical account, for it makes evident how every view on reality is really interpretive and thus vulnerable to the perceiver's subjectivity.

Another vignette, which tells about the rebel triumph in 1959, substantiates this point:

In the photograph you can see the head comandante entering the capital in a jeep. Next to him is another comandante and you can see the driver and another member of the escort. . . . But the photographer had a touch of foresight. As he didn't know the third comandante, he cut him out of the picture when cropping it. A few months later the third comandante was in jail, accused of treason and sentenced to thirty years in prison. All who had anything to do with him were immediately branded as suspects, and the historians proceeded to erase his name from the books. Ahead of his time, the photographer did not have to look for his photograph to cut it accordingly. That's what you call historical guesswork. (116)

The photographer, who records events with a camera, cannot claim any more authority to his visual account than the historian who tries to represent reality with words. In fact, one of the most illuminating features of *View of Dawn* is Cabrera Infante's dialogue with the very nature of perception and the problems that arise when a writer attempts to capture reality in writing.

It is through concrete examples such as these, which can be easily imagined by the reader, that Cabrera Infante develops his reflections regarding the relationship between fact and fiction. In the vignette entitled "The Photograph Is an Image," Cabrera Infante again creates a connection between objective and subjective realities. The irony in this vignette rests on the difference between what can actually be seen in the picture and the truth that cannot be seen. The objective photograph soon becomes a description of the moral character of the patriot being described. The anonymous historian concludes with an explanation for the reader: "Because of all that, this is not a photograph, rather that *rara avis*: the image of the dead hero when alive" (119).

A group of vignettes that seem to describe photographs or "freeze frames" are some of the most poetic in the collection, as many assume a lyrical style in their description of the violence inflicted. In one vignette, the description seems to center on a dead body, although the reader is allowed to "see" only parts of it: "The Only Thing Alive Is The Hand. In any case, the hand seems alive leaning on the wall. One can't see the arm and perhaps the hand is dead too. Perhaps it's the hand of an eyewitness and the spot on the wall is its shadow and other shadows as well. . . . A nearby object—a grenade, the shell of a high-caliber cannon, a movie camera?—looks black, like a hole in the photograph" (73). Vignettes like this one are still-frames in which the language vividly evokes the moment itself. Words are repeated, tones of gray and black accented.

The hand, "the only thing alive," is reflective of all the other hands of those who will also fall to their deaths in obscurity. The ambiguity about what is being described, the questions from the narrator, the blurriness of the objects described, as well as the possibility that a movie camera is in the photograph, present strong evidence that Cabrera's explicit task was that of evaluating visual perception and its relation to the recording of historical facts. It is also in vignettes like these that the naked brutality of Cuba's history comes alive to the reader as it becomes frozen and immortalized in time.

Another crucial dimension of this text's aesthetics is the interplay between the written and the oral versions surrounding history. If we pay close attention to the vignettes that relate specific events, we notice that the narrator's labor of interpretation exhibits peculiar features. The first, as some critics have pointed out,[7] is an intentional ambiguity regarding the historical veracity of the events narrated:

> History says: "The colored people began to nurture among themselves the goal of imitating the Haitians. The insurrections of the blacks in the sugar mills were more and more frequent, but they lacked unity and leadership." Legend has it that the largest uprising was crushed in time because the governor himself found out about it when, during his rounds, he heard some blacks talking in a hut outside the town walls. In reality, as often happens, the conspirators were betrayed by a neighbor who lived in the house on whose roof the conspirators would meet. All conspirators were hanged. (14)

In the above narrative, history and legend are both presented as different from "reality." The historian's voice mentions with irony and detachment that facts were omitted from the official record. While fiction (in this text represented by either "legend" or "in reality") is not always reliable, history is not entirely objective, because it is a story told from only one of many possible perspectives. History, for Cabrera Infante, is subjective and moldable, and can be used to serve one's own purposes.

The vignettes that present various versions of reality overtly challenge the reporting of historical accounts, since language becomes the medium through which public perception is altered and manipulated. The voice of the anonymous historian, however, has no more authority over the facts than other versions and becomes instead a critique of the historical process by telling the perceptive reader that this version, like the others, is only one of the many possible ones that can be offered as true to the reader. A subsequent example demonstrates that the ultimate role of this voice is *not* to claim it presents a true version, in spite of the voice's deep convictions that it does tell the truth:

> No one knows how the incident occurred. Some say that the president himself was surrounded by enemy forces and tried to evade capture. Others say that the president started running in the direction of the enemy. Still others speak of a runaway horse. The truth is that he received a bullet through his head, falling from his horse very close to the enemy troops, and it was impossible to recover his body. Recognized by the enemy, he was thrown over the back of a mule and the enemy took him with them as the spoils of war. (36)

In this vignette, Cabrera Infante confronts the reader with ambiguities and conjectures as the narrator once again tries to separate history from fiction. Just before the quoted passage, the narrator tells the reader that "pious hands tore out the pages of the journal that spoke of the meeting, and thus helped turn the meeting into historic gossip" (36). What we have here are multiple interpretations, all of them prefaced by subjective disclaimers that satirize the manner in which history can quickly become fictionalized. As readers, we are tested to select the narrator's point of view as truthful and to regard him as the voice of truth, although we have no way of knowing if his story is any more correct that the others cited. The task of Cabrera Infante's historian in *View of Dawn* takes various dimensions in the narratives. By presenting the reader with multiple versions of one event, Cabrera Infante is in fact exploiting the very methodology he seeks to criticize. The hesitation and mix of versions suggest that historians and their readers must be self-conscious about their narratives.

History, as Walter Ong has written, is a series of stories created by the people, stories that also needed to be heard or written about.[8] Although few in number, several vignettes in the text relate anecdotes or dialogues spoken by anonymous protagonists and represent the suffering of the common people. These narratives give preference to oral language as a way to challenge the official historical record. Throughout these narratives, a tension arises in that the official accounts and the narrated anecdotes appear to be at odds with one another. A rhythm is established within the narrative in which the oral anecdotes seem to undermine those vignettes that are rooted in the official record. It is precisely this tension between sources that cautions readers against the trap of fully believing one version or the other and confronts them with the intrinsic difficulty of the task as the historian tries to capture facts with words.

Some vignettes point to the lives of unknown heroes and indicate the importance of the day-to-day verbal interactions of living peoples. For instance, in "The Nephew Talked about His Dead Uncle," the characters are able to personalize their tales through their use of spoken expressions and familiar jokes (33). Others, such as "Someone Once Said" (98–99), describe the death of an anonymous hero from an unexpected gun that shot him after hearing a joke. The joke is reproduced for the reader, and the dramatic and experiential dimension of the youngster's story is captured. It is precisely the participatory quality and contextuality of oral speech that the anonymous historian values in reconstructing Cuba's history.

Other vignettes simply tell stories that remain in the realm of literature and seem to offer perhaps an alternative way to speak of and comprehend the world around us. This is illustrated by the vignette about the revolutionary poet who is immortalized by his own words: "'Over the poet's grave / there is no cypress tree, no weeping willow!' They finally shot him at Foso de los Laureles, which was actually a dry moat" (28). With such vignettes, Cabrera Infante is in fact recording history as the poet's own words give life and spontaneity to written history.

Just as visuals and oral accounts are central in the understanding of the subjectivity of the historical record, Cuba's geography appears as the only objective and unchanging reality for this author. Thus the first and the last of the vignettes in *View of Dawn* are of the island itself, of its geological origins and its enduring physical qualities. In the opening vignette, Cuba is presented as a "long green wound," while in the last, Cuba becomes "a sad," "unfortunate" island. Between these initial and final vignettes, a tale of violence and death is told. Strategically placed as metaphorical bookends to the entire history of Cuba, these vignettes give the reader the impression that geography will endure above all histories. For Cabrera Infante, Cuba's hope for the future will be in its physicality, Cuba's own link to nature rather than to humanity.

The experience of reading *View of Dawn* is unsettling, as the reader is bounced about in space and time in a manner that at times seems unnerving. The link between the segments is experiential, not one that connects between characters or personalities. By not being attached to a single plot line, the narrator is able to carry the reader through the history of the island in a most effective manner. Thus the narrative is able to brush against multiple lives through the isolated quality of these vignettes and convey Cabrera Infante's view that history is not simply made up of one single vision. The reader does not know the individuals in question and thus is truly kept at a fair distance from the information that is revealed, for his or her concentration is turned toward the recurring violence of each situation. The detached tone of the narrator is an integral part of Cabrera Infante's narrative strategy since reporting atrocious circumstances without comment or judgment gives the reader a clear responsibility in the position of observer.

Yet, this laconic reporting will change in the final episodes of the text. Here the narrator abandons the historical imitation, and a first-person voice narrates several of the vignettes (129, 133, 136). For example, in the penultimate vignette, the first-person voice of the mother who has lost a son conveys one of the most emotionally intense passages in the entire text. Leaving aside any care for objectivity, the character of the mother laments the outrage and the lack of freedom of the Cuba of the 1970s. She is anguished and impotent before what is occurring: "When they told me: Pedro Luis Boitel is buried, he's already buried . . . To say that to a mother . . . And they took me prisoner and beat me and everything. . . . Did you know that I was in prison . . . eight hours, when they finally told me: Your son is dead, we've already buried him, and I was in prison, they had me there . . . they did horrible things to me, those bastards" (136–40). Because the reader identifies with the feelings of the mother, this passage stirs up emotion and thus has a greater impact than the preceding pieces. Cabrera Infante demonstrates that the ways of fiction could inspire others to action in a manner that a historical account could not. The contrast in point of view is a lesson for those who attempt to record history, since the effect on the reader proves the efficacy of the perspective chosen.

In one of the final episodes, history becomes dramatized in a first-person narrative as life is pitted against death. As in the mother's narrative, the use of a *balsero's* perspective creates a new empathy in the reader, who is immediately drawn to the lives of those who speak and to their suffering. "Then I saw that the days and the nights were passing and I was still alive, drinking sea water and putting my head in the water, as long as I could, to refresh my burning face. . . . But I was sure I wasn't going to perish. . . . It was like the end of a novel, horrible. Someone had to remain to tell the story" (130). Such vignettes show that behind the anonymity of the suffering that was experienced in the previous historical periods, there was also a human face. Moreover, these last pieces, which correspond to the author's present as an exile, are indicative of the personal autobiographical dimension of the tale. Cabrera Infante simply could not pretend objectivity in narrating the events that led to his own exile.

Cabrera Infante's intent in *View of Dawn* is to deflate versions of official history and to recognize that all histories —Cabrera Infante's included—are interpretive constructions that refer to themselves and other fictions. The book addresses the lies and the violence in Cuban history as constructed, not just through the explicit themes and ideas of the author, but also through his style and his aesthetics. The play with versions, the use of oral language and popular scenes and topics, and the effective interplay of visuals and points of view present an effective portrayal of the links between writing and repression. Because of the lies of history, Cabrera Infante's book sets out to explore the different ways in which a better job could have been made of recalling and recording: listening to rumors and legend, telling stories, interpreting visuals such as engravings and photographs. These activities rebut both the classical ways of creating history and the classical accounts of that history.

According to Mario Vargas Llosa, "Novels aren't written to recount life, but to transform it by adding something to it."[9] Cabrera Infante's desire to come to terms with the fractured history of his country became the impulse for writing this crucial text. The author's indictment of history in *View of Dawn* goes further than Novás Calvo's *Maneras de contar*, as the task of Infante's anonymous narrator-historian is both literary and political. It is ironic that the text appears to follow a chronological progression because there was almost no progression for Cuban history. By rearranging and distorting history in a purposeful way, Cabrera Infante passes on his protest in hopes that his indignation would become part of the reader's experience as well. The author's hope is for a greater understanding of just what is at stake in the creating of histories of countries. Still, for Cabrera Infante, the person and the writer, the only escape from this suffering and this history was his own exile.

3 Existential Exile

Reinaldo Arenas's *The Doorman*

(1989, 1991)

*Hace mucho tiempo me declaré a mí mismo desgajado
de un tronco y de unas raíces. Yo no vivo, floto.*

(A long time ago I declared myself a severed branch
from a tree and its roots. I no longer live, I float.)

Gaston Baquero, "Letter to Eliseo Diego"

THE NARRATIVES of Novás Calvo and Cabrera Infante viewed exile as a confrontation with history that deterministically seemed to impose itself on their lives. In contrast, Reinaldo Arenas's *The Doorman* (1991) uses the history of the 1959 revolution as a metaphor for a broader exile encompassing questions that go beyond the historical reality of exile and explore the metaphysical and existential aspects of the exilic condition.[1] While the narratives of both Cabrera Infante and Novás Calvo integrate reader and text, Reinaldo Arenas's *The Doorman* proposes to do the opposite. In fact, Arenas wants his readers to experience otherness in the act of reading itself.

If for Novás Calvo and Cabrera Infante life and history were testimonial and experiential, for Arenas, on the other hand, history and life become metaphors that seek to express what we have not yet found or should seek to find. In an interview with critic Francisco Soto, Arenas spoke of the links between history and literature and explained how the two came together for him: "I'm interested fundamentally in two things about the world of narrative. First, the exploration of my personal life, of my suffering, of my own tragedies. Second, I'm interested in the historical aspect of the world. And in taking that history to a wholly fictional plane. To interpret that history as it was seen by those people who experienced it."[2] In his struggle to find meaning in his life as an exile, Arenas finds the existential dilemma of the human condition, and because of his own personal despair, he leaves us with very few answers.

Published eight years after Arenas had gone into exile, *The Doorman* denotes the evolving trajectory of exile writing as it changes perspective from the native to the adopted country. *The Doorman* appeared first in French in Paris in 1988, where it was selected as one of the three best foreign novels of that year. The next year the Spanish version appeared in Barcelona (*El portero*, 1989), and finally it was translated into English and published in New York in 1991.[3]

What does it mean to be human? Can we hope to attain some level of humanity through awareness of our role as human beings and our responsibility to others? Arenas views political exile as part of humanity's larger exile, although he does not accept this realization without a fight. His rebellion is the creation of a grotesque story destined to make his readers think about their own existence. The novel conveys the dimension of exile as alienation through both its aesthetic strategies and its surrealistic content. The reader is challenged to examine this novel's themes and narrative technique and, in so doing, to reflect upon the role of the individual and his or her condition.

Born in Cuba in 1943, fourteen years after Cabrera Infante and almost thirty-five years after Novás Calvo, Arenas is one of the first Cuban dissident writers who was fully educated under the Castro regime. Arenas's only published work inside Cuba was *Celestino antes del alba* (1967), a short novel later translated and published as *Singing from the Well* (1987). His second work, a novel entitled *El mundo alucinante* (1969; *Hallucinations*, 1971), was banned in Cuba, although it was published in Mexico and honored in France. Arrested for smuggling his work out of Cuba, Arenas served two years in prison and finally arrived in the United States during the Mariel boatlift in 1980. Two years after his arrival, Arenas published *Otra vez el mar* (1982; *Farewell to the Sea*, 1986), his first novel written in exile. Suffering from AIDS and too sick to keep writing, Arenas committed suicide on 7 December 1990. Before he died, Arenas had completed eleven novels, half of which have appeared posthumously. During the last years before his death, Arenas actively collaborated with a group of writers who had also come from Cuba during the 1980s Mariel crisis and who are known today as the Mariel generation.[4]

The Doorman begins within the context of exile but soon transforms itself into a grotesque tale. Juan is a Cuban who, like Arenas, had arrived in the United States during the Mariel boatlift. His job is that of a doorman in a luxurious apartment building. As a doorman, Juan also assumes the duty of a quasi-evangelical figure for a metaphorical door to happiness. The text's surrealistic story is presented to the reader in two parts, which are quite different in both content and style. In the first part, the book relates the story of Juan and his relationships to the tenants in his building. In the second, it is the animals who become the true protagonists of the story.

When the reader meets Juan, he is already obsessed with one idea: to get the tenants of his building to follow him in a search for a deeper happiness, symbolized by his references to a mythical door that would allow humanity a fuller experience of life. The rest of the tale is dedicated to his search for the door and to converting the tenants to his cause. This attempt is a foretold failure since the tenants themselves are caricatures, cardboard characters who look out only for themselves and for their obsessions—sex, science, politics, or even suicide. During the second half of the book, the narration takes on the deeper subjects of freedom, existential angst, and despair. The doorman is adopted by the tenant's animals, who definitely see in this tragic figure a way out of the oppression and claustrophobia of their owners' apartments. Here the text unravels, as the voices of the pets of these obsessed tenants are heard.

Nothing is left sacred in the world of Arenas, for the distance he creates between the reader and the literary world of this text allows the reader to examine closely the life of the doorman and the elusive door. The author's stark prose and lifeless characters are created not in the deepest of affection for his creations but in the most literal sense of duty. Arenas indirectly mocks all that is human in the figures he creates. They are simply what they practice: religion, sexuality, money, materialism, vanity, and even death. In fact, Arenas's somber prose and lifeless characters convey the impression that the author is separated from them as well. The tenants are stick figures without any depth, a parody of humanity and its obsessions.

The thematic content of *The Doorman* deals precisely with both the ontological and physical experiences of exile, for it addresses issues of self at a most fundamental level. With Juan as his created exile-immigrant protagonist, Arenas gives us his utmost rendition of the exile condition: the context is Cuban, although the meaning transcends any nationality and goes to the roots of humanity and existential philosophy (after all, the doorman's reading was none other than Sartre's *Being and Nothingness*).[5] In fact, it is the novel's Sartrean desire to create distance in order to promote reflection that causes the reader's separation from the characters and from the action.

At the start of the novel, the first-person-plural narrator (*nosotros*), which is supposed to represent the entire Cuban community in exile, brings about a distinct break between the action and the reader. This collective narrative voice is not friendly and at times even sounds defensive as it seeks to justify the reason and purpose for telling us about Juan's story. Yet it is through this plural narrator that Arenas articulates the anguish suffered by the protagonist: "It all came out of the need, unavoidable for us immigrants, to go back to our own world. . . . But all of this we see again and again as if through a dense fog, and when we come back to our senses and return once more to this place we have been living so many years, we cannot be sure if all these memories, even of hell itself, are fictions we cannot forget, or true events we cannot clearly remember" (167–68). Arenas did not want a comfortable reader; instead, he wanted to place his readers in a position to face the nothingness experienced by his protagonist, Juan, and the bleak reality of an impossible and distant door. The challenge for Arenas's readers is to read as this author hopes they would do to become the Other in order to feel the alienation in the reading that is the life source of Juan, the protagonist.

In *Strangers to Ourselves,* Julia Kristeva considers the figure of the outsider from a psychological perspective, analyzing the process of otherness and the response of the foreigner (the exile).[6] For Kristeva, exile is a manner of perception that involves seeing one entity through the eyes of another entity: "How could one tolerate a foreigner if one did not know one was a stranger to oneself?" (183). The exile or stranger's role is then to show others who they are. Arenas's protagonist has precisely the role Kristeva describes, for this character seeks (albeit unsuccessfully) to make others aware of the limitations in their lives. Through Juan, the animals in the story struggle with their own shadows. In fact, both the tenants and the animals teach us the otherness that, in the words of Kristeva, is also "within" them. It is only the freedom attained through writing that provides Arenas a way and an avenue to explore what it means to be the Other and to confront the shallowness of society at large. For Arenas, exile becomes a separation of self from others, as well as the loss of close ties with the group.

In exile, Juan is able to define himself more sharply from the others, from whom he is culturally different. This separation leads him to a deeper understanding of himself and to a desire to have others understand themselves better. In his task of helping others, Juan assumes upon his shoulders the weight of the failure of the lives of all the tenants and animals and is left to confront them himself. In other words, for Arenas, being an outsider is the only way to salvation from the ills of the times.

Being outside means a possibility of redemption exists, whereas being inside only assures the superficial and materialistic life of the tenants and some of the animals. Thus Arenas's doorman, in the manner of a tragic antihero, struggles daily to make meaning of life, to make the door open for himself as well as for the others. He is constantly torn by doubt, fear, and despair; his character is impotent and unable to transcend this despair even if, as a doorman, he will be able to save the animals. It is precisely in these passages of despair and existential pain that the lyrical voice of this text finally appears, and the distancing and coldness of the previous style cease, even if only for a short while:

> Juan sees himself in a rage, walking along the carefully patrolled beaches of his country, trying to find out, fearfully trying to find out how to get to the other side of the sea. . . . Forever trying to escape from that place, where his whole childhood and early youth, his life, had been a frustrated attempt to be accepted somewhere besides the work camp, the compulsory military service . . . the obligatory assemblies and meetings, the mass rallies, the official, irrevocable decree that he surrender the only thing he had, and which anyway he could not enjoy: his ephemeral, and therefore wonderful, youth. (167)

The happiness for which Juan searches is not to be found in Cuba or in the United States, for it is illusory and impossible. Perhaps in Cuba the happiness was more authentic because it entailed suffering, and grief affirmed his existence. In America, he has escaped the adversity of an oppressive regime and must learn to survive a life that is different from the one he previously knew but that is also equally strange. It takes coming to the United States to truly feel the repercussions of existential alienation, of a solitude that transcends the mimesis of existence: "And here we are again, amid the unending mechanized din of this life, in which— even though we may publicly deny it, and we do—we can't help but feel alien" (168).

In his *Literature and Inner Exile*, Paul Illie views the experience of exile as a mental condition, as a set of feelings and beliefs that isolates the expelled group from the majority.[7] According to Illie, the deepest level of exile manifests a converging semantics that conveys a common dislocation from the homeland but also from the self. In the case of *The Doorman*, political exile helps Arenas crystallize his ideas about human despair and suffering. In exile Juan can distance himself from the physicality of anguish and can better see the issues of a self alienated from itself as well as culturally separated from community. If the escape from the tenants' apartments means freedom to the animals, Juan realizes that this freedom is also false.

During the second part of the text, as we listen to the speeches of each animal, the message of the doorman becomes clearer, although it remains somewhat elusive. The animals and their positions help us understand what we might call human attitudes toward our own role and existence as human beings. In many ways these animals are the true human component of this text, for it is they who listen and learn from the message of the doorman. As Francisco Soto has shown, the genre of the fable is turned upside down by the author since the animals in this text are placed in a position superior to the humans who share the world of the doorman.[8] For the animals, Juan's message to seek a higher way of living becomes real. In fact, for these animals, the doorman becomes liberator and leader in promoting their escape from their tyrannical owners. With the animal's pronouncements, Arenas presents his existential view of the exile condition.

Chapter 39 describes Juan's escape from the mental asylum to which he has been sent and presents one of the most important monologues: that of Cleopatra, the genial, humanlike dog. The chapter underlines the important need felt by the animals to find themselves, to know themselves better, and to encounter happiness. The animals speak as exiles (after all, they have escaped their own domestic prisons) and are all striving to find their own happiness. Cleopatra's criticism of the weaknesses and failures of humankind is worth noting: "they don't know anything and are incessantly tangled in sorry contradictions" (179).

Human beings, according to this unlikely narrator, truly do not know what they want and are therefore always submerged in a dire unhappiness. This, of course, is in direct contrast with the animals, who know what they want and who only have to decide if they want to pursue their search. The dog's critical comments are bitter and constitute Arenas's own indictment on the human condition: "we simply are not able to pursue happiness because we truly cannot know what happiness is. . . . Our true identity is an incessant disguise, an infinite joke" (161).

As Jacques Derrida observes, the activity of the writer is not unlike that of the exile, for the exile and his writing are twice removed from meaning.[9] Thus the Derridian notion of "differance" becomes an allegory for exile since, for Derrida, meaning can never be present in language. In his essay about Edmond Jabès, the exiled Jewish poet, Derrida further links the reality of dislocation to language by relating the marginality of the writer to the experience of exile.[10] Arenas, like Jabès, orchestrates his fight through writing, his only weapon being the creation of a surreal world destined to promote reflection in its readers. Writing about his isolation and sadness becomes the only protest possible to the ills of both his native land and his adopted society.

There is in *The Doorman* a conscious election of the marginal as the preferred space for the writer. Through Juan's narrative, Arenas invites his readers to find their own door, their own alternative to a life that by its essence invites displacement rather than a sense of belonging. For Juan the doors are never found, although he must continue to search for them. Juan's suffering arises because he feels a part of him is missing. The animals in the novel can return to their homelands—the country, the lake, the river—but for humans, above all for exiles, there is no return:

> the now familiar sensation of despair and suffocation, of unbearable frustration, once again took hold of our doorman. Another year had gone by, and he had not yet found the door; worse yet, he had not even been able to convince anyone of the importance of finding it. . . . And looking at himself . . . in the tall mirror in the lobby, in his splendid uniform with golden buttons and braid, his high cap and white gloves, Juan experienced the horrible but clear vision of himself as a clown—rather than a savior—just another lackey in the ridiculous scheme of things. . . . What sense did it make for me to stay here or there or anywhere? (104–5)

Juan's solitude is so intense that he cannot hide it within himself any longer. His outburst is interpreted as proof of his madness, rather than as a cry for acceptance. Eventually, the doorman is put in a mental asylum because his need for reflection remains outside human and animal concerns. Toward the conclusion of the text, Juan seeks and shouts for help. Is there life after exile? To Arenas, the answer is clearly no. In the author's own words: "*The Doorman* is a quest for a world we did not leave behind in Cuba but which we haven't found in exile either."[11]

Arenas's own life has to be taken into account in any reading of *The Doorman* since this author was also a man who was "dying of grief." The novel conveys intense feelings of solitude and pain that reflect situations from Arenas's experience as an exile, his failure to feel accepted in either Cuba or the United States. Moreover, the pain Juan derives from being an outsider, not only culturally but also spiritually, could easily parallel the experience of author Reinaldo Arenas—especially if *The Doorman* is read in conjunction with Arenas's autobiographical memoir, *Antes que anochezca* (1992; *Before the Night Falls*, 1993). Arenas had no illusions about exile or life in America and claimed that "In exile one is nothing but a ghost, the shadow of someone who never achieves full reality."[12]

Arenas's rendition of exile is broader than that of Novás Calvo and Cabrera Infante for it involves a critique of the values of modern U.S. society. By using strategies of distance and alienation, Arenas initiates an exiled Cuban literature of otherness, margins, and displacement. The feelings of invisibility and anguish evident in his writings help us understand the Cuban-American writers of the second generation who, in spite of their chronological proximity to Arenas, had a much different experience of exile. Arenas's literary works, *The Doorman* in particular, are pivotal in the emergence of a new American literature of Cuban heritage, for this author combines in his writing the loss of exile and the need to find a new life after exile. Indeed, the Cuban Americans' search and fight against the erosion of the writer's identity begins with Reinaldo Arenas, a writer who bridges the concerns of the first exiles and those of the second generation.

PART 2

Self-Writing as Search

The Second Generation

¿cómo no seguir viviendo con dos
lenguas casas nostalgias tentaciones melancolías?
Porque no puedo amputarme una lengua
ni tumbar una casa
ni enterrar una melancolía.

(how can I not keep on living with two
languages homes nostalgias temptations sorrows?
because I cannot lose a language
nor tear down a home
nor bury a sorrow.)

Gustavo Pérez Firmat, "Provocaciones"

4 Issues and Patterns in Cuban-American Literature

> The exile knows that in a secular and contingent world, homes are always provisional. Borders and barriers, which enclose us within the safety of familiar territory, can also become prisons, and are often defended beyond reason or necessity. Exiles cross borders, break barriers of thought and experience.
>
> Edward Said, "Reflections on Exile"

IF ANGER, despair, and sadness were the traits expressed by the first exiles, vacillation and ambivalence will be the prevailing emotions for the Cuban Americans who came from Cuba as adolescents. The history challenged by the exiles has to be confronted by the second generation in order to put it aside and to go on, even if this process is painful and at times fruitless. Whereas works such as *View of Dawn in the Tropics* tried to address and redress the injustices of official Cuban history, the questions asked by Cuban-American writers focus on the relationship between past and present and on the importance of creating an identity in the adopted country.

In his commentary "Unique but Not Marginal: Cubans in Exile," sociologist Lisandro Pérez indicates that Cuban Americans as a minority culture existing within U.S. borders present a special case when compared to other ethnic groups in the country. Pérez uses the term *second generation* to refer to those individuals who arrived in the United States from Cuba as children or who were born in America of Cuban parents. He looks at the future of this second generation, stressing the lack of knowledge we have of this emerging group: "Thus far, this has been a community of exiles in which the immigrant who came as adult (during whatever period) has predominated. But in the years ahead, those who had the opportunity to shape their lives in this country will be emerging to the forefront. And we know very little about them."[1] Part 2 of this book takes up Pérez's challenge as we undertake the analysis of the various autobiographical writings of this displaced generation in the context of the exile literature that preceded them as well as the fictions and novels that are currently being written today by younger Americans of Cuban heritage.

From the outset, the term *Cuban American* evokes displacement and dislocation since this term implies a kind of Cuban cultural expression as perceived through an American perspective. In fact, while the tradition of origin (Cuban culture and literature) can be easily located, the Cuban-American literary tradition seems elusive because of its diverse makeup and ideological complexity. As indicated in the introduction, two groups of writers can be distinguished *within* the second generation: those who came from Cuba as adolescents or preadolescents, designated by Pérez Firmat as the "one-and-a-half" generation, and those who came from Cuba as infants or who were born in the United States, referred to in this study as Cuban-American ethnic writers. This subgrouping, as previously stated, is based on the manner in which these Cuban-American writers engage their native country and their adopted land in their narratives.

Writers of the one-and-a-half generation turn toward the past, not to confront history or lament their loss as the first exiles had done, but rather to search for a way to balance the disparate elements of their existence, such as their Cuban childhood and their American present. The issue of English as a linguistic choice for the literature of this in-between generation is a question intimately linked to the individual writer's conception of his or her artistic identity. Related to the optional use of English are issues connected with their utilization of a narrative persona in order to create a voice in a language that is adopted rather than native. On the other hand, for the Cuban-American ethnic writers, who had American childhoods and were brought up biculturally from infancy, linguistic issues are of a different nature. For these writers, a need to transcend contradictions and a need to cope with a loss of Spanish as a creative language are personal issues of concern. These writers take up issues in their narratives that have mainly to do with their bicultural selves and how their dual culture affects their present-day life in the United States. Both groups, however, are living the history that serves as context to their autobiographical memoirs and narratives.

Cuban-American writing is a body of writing that seeks authentication and therefore offers abundant testimonial instances of recounting that stem from a desire to gain credibility. Although situated sometimes in opposing ideological perspectives toward the Cuban homeland, Cuban-American writing often deals with historical issues: the horrors of immigration, the lack of historical truth, and a dislocation that at times is more spiritual than physical. Similar to many other literatures originating in exile, the literature of Cuban Americans of the second generation is centered on the experience of self-fragmentation, an experience that was first expressed in the poetry of these writers.[2] Perhaps the best way to approach the current state of Cuban-American literature is by reviewing what has been written about it by author-scholars who have contributed their own creative work to the body of writing that constitutes Cuban-American literature and who also have compiled anthologies and have written theoretical essays about their group as an emerging U.S. minority literature.

The Cuban-American Literary Boom of the 1990s

The last few years have been critical for the literature of the Cuban-American children of the first exile generation. The intellectual and political atmosphere in the United States made Cuban Americans more introspective, leading them to examine their own history and culture. Minority presses (such as Arte Público and Universal) and major publishing houses (Doubleday, Farrar and Straus, and Knopf, among others) are competing to publish the newly minted work of Cuban-American authors. This current publishing "boom" of Cuban letters in English shows no signs of decline. During the calendar year of 1996–97 alone, six novels have appeared in print. Achy Obejas's *Memory Mambo*, Himilce Novás's *Mangos, Bananas and Coconuts*, Cristina García's *The Agüero Sisters*, Virgil Suárez's *Going Under* as well as his memoir, *Spared Angola: Memories from a Cuban-American Childhood*, and Ana Veciana Suárez's *The Chin Kiss King* confirm that the 1990s have become a time when the second-generation writers have begun to establish themselves as a significant writing force in the United States.[3]

Beyond the tide of critical interest in and prominence of works by individual authors, five significant anthologies containing the work of over seventy Cuban Americans have appeared in print between 1994 and 1996: Behar and León's *Bridges to Cuba* (1994), Ballester, Escalona, and de la Nuez's *Cuba la isla posible* (1995), Barquet's *Puentelibre: Más allá de la isla* (1995), Suárez and Poey's *Little Havana Blues: A Cuban-American Literature Anthology* (1996), and, most recently, Hospital and Cantera's *A Century of Cuban Writers in Florida* (1996). All five mark a moment of emergence of artistic voices that have reached intellectual maturity. Not since the publication of *Contra viento y marea* (Against wind and tide) in 1978—an anthology of anonymous prose

writings by the children of exile promoting a Cuban-American dialogue—had a similar effort toward the expression of a collective identity
outside Cuba emerged in the literature.[4]

Bridges to Cuba, an anthology of essays and creative works by Cuban
Americans dispersed across the United States, was published in two vol-
umes of the *Michigan Quarterly Review* during the summer and fall of
1994. The collection, compiled by second-generation scholars Ruth Behar and Juan León, expresses a desire to establish links between those
artists inside Cuba and those writing outside. As its title indicates, this
two-volume compilation was born out of a desire for conversation, communication, and dialogue with Cuban artists on the island who are the
counterparts of those who grew up outside Cuba. In *Bridges*, we can
perceive some of the same goals of its predecessor, *Contra viento y marea*: an openness toward an intellectual dialogue with Cuba and its artists, a desire to share artistic ideas with them, and a desire to make extraterritorial artistic production of Cuban heritage part of the patrimony
of Cuban art.[5]

Cuba la isla posible (Cuba, the possible island) proposes an exploration of coexistence rather than a specific desire for dialogue. Edited by
Juan Pablo Ballester, Maria Elena Escalona, and Iván de la Nuez, intellectuals who abandoned the island in the early 1990s and whose formative years occurred under Castro's regime, the collection has broader objectives than *Bridges to Cuba* since it does not direct its attention to any
one geographical space. In the introduction, the editors stress the idea of
tolerance for the different exile ideologies and emphasize the lack of a
common political philosophy for the pieces included: "A scope in which
each fragment makes use of its discourse and no other has the function
to speak for it" (21). The anthology, which provides an English translation of the entire contents in an appendix, expresses a desire for understanding between the languages and ideologies that comprise the Cuban artistic experience outside the country. It views extraterritorial
Cuban culture as a multicultural and cosmopolitan body of writing that
claims recognition outside Cuba. While the contents of both *La isla posible* and *Bridges* are interdisciplinary and transnational, *La isla posible*
proposes a different angle to the Cuban-American predicament by seeking an extraterritorial dialogue rather than a dialogue with Cuba. Published in Barcelona in 1995, this anthology looks for a cultural exchange
among Cuban writers and plastic artists dispersed around the world. It
should be noted that many of the same authors who contributed to
Bridges to Cuba also appear in *La isla posible*.

Más allá de la isla (Beyond the island), the third anthology, turns its attention toward the Cuban homeland as it declares in its prologue the importance of promoting cultural continuity with the tradition of Cuban culture and Cuban letters. The collection was published in Mexico in 1995 and edited by Jesús Barquet, a Cuban poet who arrived in the United States during the Mariel exodus. *Más allá de la isla* contains the work of sixty-six artists writing outside Cuba, including many from the second generation, the work of older exiles from a variety of migratory waves, such as Benítez Rojo and José Triana, and a posthumous essay by Reinaldo Arenas.

Barquet's editorial objectives are different from and yet similar to those of the above-mentioned editors. *Más allá de la isla* resembles *La isla posible* because it promotes the idea of a metaphoric space outside any kind of political perspectives that might unite Cuban artists dispersed around the world. As in *Bridges to Cuba*, the Cuban homeland figures prominently as a glue that joins the contributors together. Indeed, a unique feature of *Más allá de la isla* is its desire to look at the extraterritorial production as part of the cultural patrimony of Cuba, even if its expression involves the English language. This anthology also includes translations into Spanish of texts created in English originally: "a plural and representative example of the thematic and aesthetic concerns of Cuban culture beyond the island of Cuba" (6).

Little Havana Blues appeared in print during the fall of 1996. Edited by Cuban-American novelist Virgil Suárez and Delia Poey, this anthology includes selections from thirty-two Cuban-American authors of several migratory waves, many of whom were born after 1960. Like the previous collections, it includes writing from all genres (poetry, essay, drama, narrative). Unlike the others, it concentrates exclusively on those writers who live on the U.S. mainland and who are writing their creative works originally in English. In the short introduction to the collection, Virgil Suárez, himself a child of the first exile generation who left Cuba as a young child, indicates that the central aim of his compilation is to carve out a place for the literature of Cuban heritage within the mosaic of North American letters: "a literature undergoing a transformation from infancy to maturity . . . it will continue to redraw and reshape its own limits as it establishes its own dynamic, though amorphous, place on the American literary map" (15). The inclusion of new names in this anthology, in addition to the better-known writers of the Cuban-American tradition as it exists in English today, also indicates that many of the younger writers are just emerging to the forefront.

The last anthology, *A Century of Cuban Writers in Florida*, compiled by Carolina Hospital and Jorge Cantera, includes first-time translations of literary works written during the nineteenth century by Cuban exiles living on U.S. soil, as well as works by many of the contemporary writers we examine in this book. The efforts of Hospital and Cantera to translate nineteenth-century Cuban texts and to present them with the work of today's writers are evidence that the activity of recovering a literary heritage and of preserving the community away from home is an essential one for today's Cuban-American scholars. As the diversity of breadth and scope of all five anthologies indicates, the study and criticism of today's Cuban-American letters is in the midst of being redefined because it encompasses broad concerns that are generational, ideological, and methodological.

The Individual Theorists: A Context for a Generation

Recent attempts by individual authors to explain the writings of Cubans in the United States might help us see the configuration of this emergent American literature. The essays produced by known scholars and creative writers such as Gustavo Pérez Firmat, Lourdes Gil, Eliana Rivero, and Carolina Hospital are foundational in nature, for these writings attempt to explain the origins of a generation as well as the individual writers' need to create away from their Cuban homeland. A useful and crucial point of departure is the writings of Carolina Hospital.

Hospital's ground-breaking 1987 essay titled "Los atrevidos" (The daring ones) delineates the features that characterize her displaced one-and-a-half generation. Herself a poet and a child of first-generation Cuban exiles, Hospital speaks of the uniqueness of the Cuban-American experience and provides a description of her own group:

> a different breed from the writer that had a strong early foundation in Cuba. . . . His very essence is a manifestation of departure, loss, and struggle. He must overcome this sense of loss and displacement before he can come to grips with his new freedom. . . . The Cuban-American writer resists perpetuating the *status quo* at the same time that he refuses to be categorized as an ethnic writer whose culture and tradition have become more mythical than real. . . . As such the Cuban-American writer has to deal with the ideological conflict that arises as an inherent part of his condition as a child of exile. (22–23)

Cuban-American writers, Hospital asserts, are different from the older exiled writers educated in Cuba who were much more defined in their native culture and language. However, according to Hospital, these writers also maintain a link with their Cuban tradition since their writing impulse is motivated by the experience of displacement. In their poetic expression, Hospital perceives the presence of an "exile consciousness," a dimension that unites the writings of these poets. Hospital asserts that Cuban-American writers feel part of a strong exile community and refuse to give up this consciousness in order to become ethnic writers. It is precisely the tension generated between wanting to be both Cuban and American that provides the energy for this new literature. For Hospital, even if the writers she includes in her anthology write both in English and Spanish, their writing remains connected to their experience as Cuban exiles.

Hospital's essay was followed in 1988 by the publication of her anthology *Cuban-American Writers: Los Atrevidos*, in which she compiles the poetry and short narratives of writers who were born around 1950 and who came from Cuba as preadolescents in the early 1960s. Hospital's collection was the first to identify the children of exile as a cohesive group and to point out the common features these writers exhibited in their works. Her selection of representative writers proved to be an excellent one. Roberto Fernández, Lourdes Gil, Pablo Medina, and Gustavo Pérez Firmat, writers who figure in "Los atrevidos," went on to become central figures within the Cuban-American intellectual community. Moreover, the anthology is significant because it collects the early poetry and prose of these writers and as such represents the first stage in the emergence of Cuban-American literature.[6]

Eliana Rivero's essays on Cuban Americans take a contrasting approach from those of Carolina Hospital and signal an emerging consciousness of ethnicity on the part of these writers. Rivero, a professor of Spanish at the University of Arizona, has published several collections of poetry and is a well-known literary critic in the area of Chicano studies. Born in Cuba, Rivero arrived in the United States in her teens and has lived in Tucson since 1967. Her first writings (several poetry collections) were published in Spanish. In the last few years, her decision to use English in her personal writings is intimately related to her own definition of self. In her essays "(Re)Writing Sugar Cane Memories," and "From Immigrants to Ethnics," Rivero asserts that the exile consciousness of the older Cuban Americans appears to be giving way to a different kind of writing that centers less on Cuba and more on the United States. According to Rivero, "a writer's transition from exilic to ethnic concerns entails coming into a personal awareness of biculturalism and takes for granted the reality of permanence in a society other than the one existing in the country of birth" ("From Immigrants," 193). Rivero's autobiographical essays (examined in chapter 5) also reflect on the inevitability of being "hybrid" and her desire to create a positive and personal relationship between her adopted and her native cultures.

It is worthwhile mentioning that Hospital and Rivero wrote about their generation during the 1980s, a time when these writers were beginning to be recognized as a group. Their work is thus crucial in signaling the presence of an emergent tradition that, as indicated earlier, is currently in the midst of a literary boom. More extensive theorizing by members of this same generation came in the 1990s with the recent book by poet-scholar Gustavo Pérez Firmat, *Life on the Hyphen* (1994), as well as with Lourdes Gil's essays on Cuban literature in the United States.[7]

Pérez Firmat and Lourdes Gil are author-scholars who have themselves produced a sizable body of poetry and creative writing to date (see the authors' bibliography for a listing of their publications). Their writings illuminate and expand Rivero's and Hospital's earlier findings about their group and bear directly on the definition and nature of the Cuban-American literary production in the United States. As theorists of their own generation, they provide contrasting perspectives that together bring out significant issues regarding the dilemmas of language choice, assimilation, and dissimilation.

Born in Havana, Gustavo Pérez Firmat arrived in the United States as a young boy of eleven and was raised in Miami. Today, he is a professor of Spanish at Duke University. The most prolific member of his generation and a key figure in the delineation of an emergent field of study, Pérez Firmat is the author of several books of literary criticism and essays. *Life on the Hyphen* (1994) is the first extensive attempt to organize or theorize about a sizable body of literature published by Cuban Americans in the United States. It claims a place for the cultural production of an ethnic group and nurtures the roots that account for this cultural production in America. As already indicated in the introduction, the scope of Pérez Firmat's book is significant because it antedates the 1959 diaspora and covers instead the last half-century of Cuban-American cultural achievement in the United States, from Desi Arnaz to Gloria Estefan, from television to mambo, as well as poetry and prose.

Pérez Firmat's theorizing is centered around those who belong to the one-and-a-half generation. These are artists who precariously live "on the hyphen," that is, those who share in one way or another the experience of living simultaneously in two cultures. By considering Cuban-American culture in its pre-1959 stages, Firmat solidifies the presence of a tradition that has been largely ignored by scholars interested in minority cultures in the United States. The book explores the richness of a hyphenated cultural zone as it undertakes to establish the identity and character of Cuban culture in the United States during the last half-century.

In spite of this text's wide historical and artistic scope, it is clear that the artistic production of the sons and daughters of the 1959 exile is also quite important to Pérez Firmat's theorizing, as evidenced by his detailed and careful analysis of the poetry of José Kozer, the son of Cuban exiles and a bona fide member of the one-and-a-half generation. In his study of Kozer's exilic poetry—as well as in his chapter on Oscar Hijuelos's 1992 Pulitzer Prize novel *Mambo Kings*, a story about Americans of Cuban heritage living in the Bronx—Pérez Firmat makes crucial differentiations regarding Kozer's and Hijuelos's relationship to Cuba: "If Hijuelos writes 'from Cuba' but 'toward' the United States, Kozer writes 'from' the United States but 'toward' Cuba" (156). According to Pérez Firmat, the one-and-a-half generation—to which he himself belongs—will reach its potential only when it assumes the unique double perspective on reality available to the bicultural writer: "only by becoming double, can he ever be whole, only by being two, will he ever be someone."[8]

According to Pérez Firmat, the two forces that shape Cuban-American culture are tradition (continuity) and translation (distance). Coining the term *biculturation*, Pérez Firmat defines it as "a situation where the two cultures achieve a balance that makes it difficult to determine which is the dominant and which is the subordinate culture" ("Transcending Exile," 6). Biculturation implies an equilibrium, however tense or precarious, between the two contributing cultures. Pérez Firmat sees this coincidence as beneficial rather than negative. Rather than seeing marginality, the author stresses the privileged position that allows Cuban-American writers to make the best of their unchosen situations: "the Cuban Americans are capable of availing themselves of the resources—linguistic, artistic, commercial—that both cultures have to offer. . . . Cuban-American culture has been to a considerable extent an achievement of the 1.5 generation. . . . Their intercultural placement makes them more likely to undertake the negotiations and compromises that produce ethnic culture" (*Life on the Hyphen*, 4–5).

In *Life on the Hyphen*, Pérez Firmat celebrates the dualities and juxtapositions of being bicultural and how these are used by the writers to their advantage. Cuban Americans, states Pérez Firmat, achieve a double vision by fitting their Cuban self into their American setting. They possess both an ethnic and an exilic vision of their heritage. His autobiographical memoirs, *Next Year in Cuba* (1995), studied in chapter 5, provide the reader with an account of Pérez Firmat's own personal attempt to achieve the precarious balance he proposes.

If Pérez Firmat's emphasis is on the historical dialogue that has taken place this century between Cuban artists and their American adopted homeland, for Lourdes Gil the hyphen goes in the opposite direction. Unlike Pérez Firmat, who concentrates his attention on America as the new setting for the production of Cuban culture, Lourdes Gil's position is to demand a place in her native tradition. Like Hospital, Pérez Firmat, and Rivero, Gil is both a poet and a scholar who deeply cares about her heritage and the role of Cuban writers in the United States.

Gil's participation in the 1994 conference held under the auspices of the Olof Palme International Center in Stockholm indicates her desire to bring together the literary strands of what she considers to be the extraterritorial Cuban tradition. Her writings on the subject also confirm her belief that a possible recognition of the writers of the Cuban intellectual diaspora by the Cuban literary establishment can and should occur.

In her Olof Palme presentation, entitled "Conjugar los espacios: hacia una liberación por el lenguaje" (Conjugating spaces: Toward a liberation through language),[9] the author poses a central question for writers such as herself: "Where does the Cuban writer place himself or herself in the United States? How do they conceive their work?" (87). Gil does not look to bridge American culture with Cuban-American culture. Instead, she looks at Cuba and demands a place for writers like herself in the tradition of Cuban letters. Herself a child of the one-and-a-half generation, Gil explores the dislocation suffered by her peer group. Her hope is that, in the near future, the different literatures of Cuban heritage produced outside of Cuba will be recognized as part of Cuban letters: "There will only be a true literary encounter when the books published abroad are available in Cuba and when the exiled Cubans have access to the literary works from the island" (94).

In spite of their philosophical differences, Pérez Firmat's and Gil's analyses are significant assessments of the Cuban literary production outside Cuba. Although in their perspective and content they seem at first to be diametrically opposed, both author-scholars share the same purpose—they seek a place in literature for writers of Cuban heritage writing outside the nation. Their contrasting appraisals exemplify the complexities involved in theorizing about a literature of a generation that, due to its historical placement, exhibits an equal distance from the world of English as from the world of Spanish and that is further divided by ideological positions vis-à-vis Castro's Cuba.[10]

For the second-generation writers of Cuban heritage, especially for the writers of the one-and-a-half generation, the experience of exile is filled with tension and anxiety as these writers find themselves both inside and outside the experience they describe. To write about their exodus in the context of Castro's Cuba, the Cuban Americans had to define their relationship to their homeland and simultaneously forge a new relationship between the self and the adopted country. Like many other exiles around the world, these writers endured a rupture between their present and their past selves, and thus at first they had to learn to see and perceive their history and their reality from an outsider's perspective. Exile thus provides the Cuban-American writers with a variety of perspectives of reality that these individual writers can opt to examine.

It is therefore not surprising that autobiographical writings and fictions of autobiography prevail among the narratives of this generation. The choice of autobiographical selves is an appropriate one for Cuban-American authors since the narrative act is linked to the achievement of identity and thus is frequently used by writers who belong to ethnic and minority groups. If an autobiography indicates a desire to examine origins in order to start anew, the use of English rather than Spanish also indicates the need to construct a new identity. Writing in a language other than the language of birth becomes the means of regaining an identity or refashioning a new one, and in the case of the one-and-a-half-generation writers, it also becomes a way to cope with change and feelings of inadequacy. For these writers, movement from one language to another is experienced as a shift in identity as well, and in many cases, the protagonist's growth is a growth in the control of a certain language, be it either English or Spanish.[11]

In his recent study on the fiction of West Indian writer V. S. Naipaul, Timothy Weiss looks at the advantages of marginality in the creation of Naipaul's fictional world.[12] "Exile is more than living life away from home, it is a break with the center and a manner of perception from the margins of other worlds" (5). According to Weiss, the exile leaves home and, in spite of the experience of loss, also goes outward and experiences an opening up of self and of this world. "Exile is a process of becoming, in between origins and destinations, and because the exile is in-between, his journey can be a two directional movement"(5). Recalling Bakhtin's writings on "exotopy" as a "vision from the outside through which a writer can see what those in the inside cannot" and also Todorov's writings on "outsideness," Weiss makes a convincing case for the deeper insight into reality possessed by an exile writer.

As the narratives analyzed in chapter 5 demonstrate, autobiographical conveyance provides the one-and-a-half- generation writers with a unique perspective on reality. For these Cuban-American writers, autobiography becomes a forum for ordering their history by allowing them to be reborn symbolically in their narratives. Because these personal accounts are created in English rather than in Spanish, autobiography becomes "a second acquisition of language" and "a second coming into being of self" for these writers.[13]

5 Autobiographical Writing

Negotiating an Identity

> For the nonfiction writer, as I can testify, personal history is directly
> an effort to find salvation, to make one's own experience come out
> right.
>
> Alfred Kazin, "The Self as History"

HOW DO Cuban-American writers define the terms of autobiographical writing? Cuban-American autobiographical accounts demonstrate how the historical events of 1959 became intrinsic to their attempts toward self-definition. As Cuban Americans of the second
generation, the writers analyzed here strive to assert their native Cuban
culture as well as the centrality of Cuba to their experience. These narratives conform to Phillipe Lejeune's definition of the autobiographical
project, which requires a signature or correspondence of name between
the author and the narrator of the story.[1] The "I" of these narrators is
dialogical as well as confessional. In all instances the narrators share a
burden with the listener and seek in almost every case a reconciliation
with the past. There is also in all of them a sense of emotional urgency in
the telling of their narratives. For some of these writers, autobiography
becomes an exercise in self-evaluation.

According to James Olney, autobiographical writings provide a variety of perspectives for the study of a culture: "a personal vision; a per-
meating cultural reality; a culture bearer's point of view; and, a record
from within of what the experience of the given culture might be."[2] Olney's work asserts that autobiography is based on a notion of life experience as the expression of an individual's capacity for growth and self-
realization. For Olney, autobiographical writing is at once intimate and
public, psychological and cultural, individual and collective. As a kind
of writing, autobiography is always based on tacit or implicit assump-
tions about the relationship between language and identity.

Cuban-American personal accounts provide a valuable perspective of a particular historical period for Cubans living in America. Because autobiography mirrors the culture that produces and consumes it, it is an important document reflecting the history of the Cuban-American community within the United States.[3] Second-generation Cuban-American authors turn to history in their desire to interpret and somehow control historical events that radically affected their individual lives. Sylvia Molloy asserts that the idea of crisis is tied to the autobiographical moment in Latin American letters.[4] For the Cuban-American writers who are members of the one-and-a-half generation, this crisis originates in two basic issues that they share with other cultures in exile: how to reconcile past experiences in their country of birth with present experiences in their adopted country and how to negotiate between bicultural and monocultural readers. In presenting the history of the 1959 diaspora, many of these narratives have the same story to tell, namely, the decline and fall of a world of unity and order (before and after 1959). The fact that many Cuban children were uprooted from their families in the early 1960s and that many were sent alone to live in the United States makes these writers' relation to history intrinsic to their self-definition.[5] Here we often find an intersection between the personal and the historical in which the need for healing and the search for coherence are provided by the exercise of writing down a life.

This chapter examines the book-length memoirs of Pablo Medina, Gustavo Pérez Firmat, Virgil Suárez, and the autobiographical essays of Eliana Rivero and Ruth Behar. Medina and Suárez focus on their Cuban childhood as told from their adult American present. Pérez Firmat, on the other hand, places more emphasis on his American present and tries to make sense of it by looking at his early years in Cuba and his adolescence in Miami. All three authors write in English about a past that took place in Spanish.

Whereas the rhetorical task of the memoirs of Suárez, Medina, and Pérez Firmat seeks to give homogeneity to a social group's awareness of itself socially and culturally, Eliana Rivero's and Ruth Behar's essays emphasize issues of definition and affirmation of identity. For the male writers this experience leads toward an unsettled view of the self and its relation to language; for the women authors the very separation from one's language and culture of origin becomes a step toward redefinition. Together, the autobiographical accounts of these male and female writers illustrate simultaneous but different stages in the evolution of contemporary Cuban-American narrative. Issues of representation will be concerned with the autobiographical strategies used by the writers and the manner in which each text inscribes the reader in its process of self-revelation.

Pablo Medina's *Exiled Memories* (1990)

Pablo Medina was born in Havana and has lived in the United States since 1960. He has published several scholarly articles, a novel, and various poetry collections, in addition to *Exiled Memories*.[6] More than any of the memoirs treated here, *Exiled Memories* traces the self's understanding of its relation to history. In the act of remembering, according to Medina, the personal goes beyond itself and into historical events that became tragic in his life.

Exiled Memories is aptly titled, for it denotes the author's anxiety in publishing an account of his Cuban childhood. Medina's memories are "exiled" because until their publication in 1990, the Cuban-American voice (unlike other Hispanic voices in the United States) had not become important enough to deserve a public record. This first-person autobiographical account of Medina's childhood in Cuba was to become the first in a series of memoirs that have been published in the 1990s by a number of Cuban-American writers of Medina's generation.

The language of Medina's childhood memories is filled with poetry but also tension. Because the stories and the events Medina relates took place in Spanish, whereas his narration takes place in English, this linguistic severance produces a noticeable anxiety in the narrator. In his preface, the author defiantly asserts that he wrote these remembrances because he "felt like it," leaving the reader disconcerted and curious as to the author's confrontational tone. Soon Medina corrects this impression by declaring his wish and his need to leave a legacy of a Cuba that was very much his but that will never exist again as he had experienced it: "On visiting my great-aunt and my grandmother . . . I was awakened to the fact that they and the other old folks of the family would not live forever. . . . When they went, they would take with them the myths and folklore I had grown up with. That, I thought, should never be allowed to happen. And who better than I . . . to chronicle our past for those generations who had never lived it?" (x).

Dislocation for writers such as Medina is, in a sense, more tragic than the experience of adult exiles who were secure in their identities as Cubans at the time they had to leave their country. Medina felt that the kind of childhood he lived in Cuba would never be lived again by either the Cuban-American children in the United States or by the children in

Cuba today. Historical changes on the island would not allow the children there to live as he had, and Cuban children living in the United States would be destined to grow up as Americans. Thus Medina's text assumes the task of preserving a way of life and a tradition that the author feels could be a source of strength and knowledge for other Cuban Americans. His memories become a means to ensure the survival of a collective identity.

In *Exiled Memories*, Pablo Medina's life in Cuba is chronicled via incidents that occurred in the places where he grew up: the grandparents' farm, the house in coastal Havana, and the child's wanderings and explorations of city streets. The book begins with a vignette that illustrates the narrator's arrival in the United States in 1960 and works back in time to return to this same moment in the text's final pages. Specific events of the narrator's own childhood—his traumas, triumphs, and discoveries—are interspersed with vignettes about the life stories of his ancestors and how they came to settle on the island of Cuba. The incidents Medina narrates are chosen by the intensity in which they stand in his memory, such as the frightening experience of a night crabbing in the Zapata swamp (14) and the finding of human bones belonging to a victim of the repression of the Batista dictatorship (100). Medina recalls these events vividly, and his prose at times possesses an eerie intensity.

According to Roy Pascal, autobiography is a mode of writing concerned not with the past existing in any concrete form but with a contemporary memory of that past.[7] The writer looks at important events in his or her life in order to evaluate the totality of what he or she sees. The present self of the writer then seeks to attribute meaning to these experiences. In Medina's text, the process of autobiography is self-reflexive, for the writer is involved in the activity of creating and communicating his own life. Indeed, the author's main motivation for writing down his life has to do with the need to leave a legacy of a period in his life that will have no continuity in the adopted English space.

For Medina, the 1959 revolution with its redemptive promise becomes a casualty of history just as his own life between two cultures becomes a personal tragedy that he seeks to heal by leaving his memoirs as a legacy. At times, critical of life in both societies, the author invites us to rethink the way in which life evolves in both cultures: "As I grow older and sink ever deeper into the loneliness of American society, this sense of family, of openness to others that she [the grandmother] and others of the family have deeded to me, becomes increasingly dear" (36).

Pursuing an understanding of the intimate relation between his own life and that of his time, Medina could better understand the collapse of the country in the years that followed 1959. From his present as an exile in the United States, the writer is now able to reflect that all in Cuba was not well. Even if it means his own displacement, Medina is not oblivious to the social disparities of the system under which he was raised: "It took the experience of emigration and exile, threatening as it did our sense of security, to come to terms with that difference. To accept it in the mind, in the heart, and in the body" (29). It is in fact the tension between the young and innocent Medina and the middle-aged autobiographer's feelings about that past that provides much of the interest in *Exiled Memories*.

Time after time during the reading of these memoirs, the reader is witness to descriptions of episodes of poverty and repression that become meaningful only in light of comments Medina interjects from the present of the writing. Witness the description of the grandfather as a "benevolent but firm caudillo": "To further emphasize his authority, he carried a .38-caliber revolver with an ivory handle. At the time, I did not understand why he always wore it in the field. . . . When I grew older, well after he was dead, I tried to reject men like my grandfather because they represented the exploitation of the poor and downtrodden" (10). The fact that Medina's own family was part of the class that in some way could be held responsible for the events that later divided Cuba is significant only when the narrator speaks from his present as an adult in the United States.

Equally moving are the writer's ruminations about the poor farmers who worked for his grandfather. These individuals, whom he knew well despite living in the city because he visited the farm every summer, are now evaluated in a different manner and from a historical perspective: "It dawned on me that the lives of these people had not changed much. They wore no leg irons, they weren't shipped or bought or sold, but the *freedom* accorded them by emancipation had been a dim promise, always just beyond the horizon. . . . I was a twelve year-old member of a middle class family and, as such, took for granted the most basic of freedoms—freedom from hunger, from disease, from ignorance that were still beyond the grasp of many of the people of La Luisa" (28–29). Medina's evaluation of his past experiences has to confront Cuba and its history of poverty and repression.

Against his idealized childhood memories, Medina also projects a darker vision of history recorded by the Batista police as well as by incidents of sabotage by Castro's rebels. Terrorism was indeed part of the child's early years in Cuba, as it was the experience for a generation of Cuban children who grew up during the turbulent years of the Batista regime. The vignette entitled "What Happened?" encapsulates how violence was part of the everyday life of middle-class boys such as the author: "I was in the movies by myself and had left my seat to get a drink of water. Just as I was bending over the fountain, I heard a loud explosion. For an instant my vision blurred. . . . A policeman ran by, gun in hand, looking in every direction, not knowing what to do or where to go. I looked at him hoping his face might offer reassurance, but he trotted down the street, dazed, his eyes mirrors to my uncertainty. . . . *¿Qué pasó?* I asked. Sabotage, they answered. . . . That night I had a nightmare where the world was in my stomach and it blew up" (97–98). Instead of the much-needed democracy and fairness promised by Castro and very much lacking in the Cuba of Batista, the revolution and its aftermath had robbed young Medina of the possibility of growing up in his own country. Episodes such as this, in which political repression appears in the life of young Medina, now become part of events that the adult autobiographer can assess and evaluate.

Memoirs such as Medina's can offer a significant historical form of self-expression. As Elizabeth Bruss reminds us, in all autobiographical accounts the narrator is at once eyewitness of the events narrated, participant in the same events, and, many times, historian of these events as he or she stands outside the story of a life (his or her own) and editorializes about it.[8] As narrator, Medina has selected from his past those moments of experience that appear to be pivotal to his present self. For instance, when the author describes the slaughtering of a pig in the Cuban countryside, the event witnessed by the narrator as a child is brought to the present by Medina's ruminations about his own imagined slaughtering: "He discarded the tools carelessly on the ground, grabbed each side of the crevice . . . and pulled until the ribs let go of the spine and the chest cavity opened like a pulpy fruit exposing a chaos of purple organs and blue and yellow intestines. And then I wondered if I were split so unceremoniously like that whether my organs too would shine amorphously in the sun like multicolored gelatin" (25). The pig's dismemberment brings to the writer associations of the fragmentation and dislocation of his own exiled condition. Such comments betray the apprehension of the narrator as he views his uncertain present in the United States.

Throughout the narrative, Medina injects the fears of his present self into the story of his past self: "I am terrified of growing old alone . . . because my children will be too busy to care for me or because my presence makes them feel uncomfortable, put-upon, and limited from pursuing that vacuous activity called self-realization" (36). Cuban and American cultural mores are juxtaposed as the writer tries to make sense of their differences. Medina's commentaries from his present as a writer in America reveal a desire to engage the reader in some value questioning: "Life in the United States for me has not been a search for roots (that presumes their loss), but rather a quixotic attempt to become a creature I never was nor can ever be: an American" (x).

By asserting his own marginal condition, Medina separates himself from the English-speaking majority. Yet, the author acknowledges that having spent so many years of his adult life in his adopted country has affected him in ways that separate him from the Cubans of his native island: "Nor do I wish to delude myself that I am immaculately Cuban" (x). For Medina, the genealogical self-exploration that at first seems to be the central issue of his memoirs leads to the narrator's conclusion that his self will forever and irremediably be split: "My childhood lies inside the bowl of distance and politics, unapproachable and thus disconnected from my adulthood. The two revolve around each other like twin stars, pulling and tugging, without hope of reconciliation" (113).

While *Exiled Memories* is primarily a revisiting of experiences of a Cuban childhood, Medina's story exhibits an emotional and ideological interaction between the writing self and the self recalled. The result of these contradictions produces in the author an unsettled view of self, a view he will confront once again as he creates for himself a fictional persona in the character of Anton, the protagonist of his novel *The Marks of Birth* (1994), analyzed in chapter 8 of this book.

Gustavo Pérez Firmat's *Next Year in Cuba* (1995)

In his essay "Reflections on Exile," Edward Said defines the exile condition as inherently "contrapuntal." Said, himself an exile, poses questions associated with not only the physical but also the psychological condition of expatriation. According to Said, most people are principally aware of one culture, while exiles are aware of at least two: "This plurality of vision gives rise to an awareness of simultaneous dimensions. . . . Thus both the new and the old environments are vivid, actual, occurring together contrapuntally" (172). The exile's dual condition, according to Said, can provide unexpected creativity for the writer since the exile is able to feel at home in many different places.[9]

Pérez Firmat's theoretical work and his creative texts reflect Said's description of the "contrapuntal" condition of exile, for his works have consistently explored issues of crossings and thresholds. Examining how the adopted country can be a source of new ways of perceiving reality and addressing the issue of marginality, Pérez Firmat's works consider precisely the advantages and disadvantages of being both Cuban and American, although not necessarily at the same time. In his *Literature and Liminality* (1986), the author explores *liminality* not as a transitional period or stage but rather as a state that could sometimes become permanent for certain groups of individuals. In *The Cuban Condition* (1989), he pursues the idea of crossings as he defines the essence of Cuban culture as the product of transculturation, of assimilation, and adaptation of the foreign. In *Life on the Hyphen* (1994), as indicated in the introduction, Pérez Firmat returns to the concept of liminality, applying it to his own times and his own exile. Indeed, the liminal dimension of exile is significant for him because it carries within it the possibility of a new understanding of the self through the lens of another culture.

Whereas Medina's narrative in *Exiled Memories* centers on the past due to his desire to leave a legacy for posterity, Pérez Firmat's objectives in writing his memoirs are very much oriented toward his own present, as he attempts to reconcile his Cuban childhood with his adult experiences in the United States. Although Medina's past was conceptualized in terms of his specific memories as a child growing up in Cuba, for Pérez Firmat the Cuban childhood of the 1950s competes with his adolescence in Miami during the early 1960s. In fact, Pérez Firmat's memories present a complex set of allegiances, first to Cuba as his native land, but also to Miami as the community of his adolescence and early adulthood.

According to Louis Renza, the predominant reason for writing an autobiography is the writer's present: "autobiography is the writer's de facto attempt to elucidate his present rather than his past."[10] This is true for Pérez Firmat since for him the autobiographical act is centrally motivated by his desire to transcend his exilic condition and move forward into his present: "I write to grasp and hold that unchanging core. I write to become who I am, even if I'm more than one, even if I'm *yo* and you and *tú* and two."[11] Not surprisingly, the reconciling of the author's past with his present in *Next Year in Cuba: A Cubano's Coming of Age in America* is a process that is not assimilationist but that seeks a balance between the host culture and the native culture. Similar to the theories he expounded in *Life on the Hyphen*, Pérez Firmat makes his own life narrative an example of the precarious search for balance he prescribes for his one-and-a-half generation.

In his memoir, Pérez Firmat's narration alternates between becoming psychoanalytic, when it examines the author's relationship with his father, sociohistorical, when it narrates Miami's evolution, and literary, when the act of writing becomes an instrument that might help the writer beyond the threshold of exile. If the psychological inquiry takes the form of the son's search for the fatherly model lost through the uncertainties of exile, the historical inquiry will follow the changes undergone by the city of Miami and how Pérez Firmat reacts to these changes as he undergoes his own personal transformation beyond exile. The text's aesthetic dimension becomes evident when the writer relates critical episodes in his life that become in themselves metaphors of the autobiographical act. In these autobiographical episodes of loss and frustration, the activity of rebuilding becomes a metaphor for the writing of an autobiography, thus replicating the narrator's task of reordering and reshaping the events of his life.

As the memoir's subtitle suggests (*A Cubano's Coming of Age in America*), the modes of self-knowledge that the author utilizes are contained within the autobiographical act and are closely related to public and private spaces. The private dimension reconstructs Pérez Firmat's past in two locations: Cuba and Miami. The childhood in Cuba and the upper-class identity to which the author was destined by birth and family training offer a stark contrast to the narrator's adolescence in Miami, as the family absorbs the diminishment and shock of expatriation during the early 1960s. The public dimension of the memoirs, on the other hand, describes the narrator's relationship to the places in which he grew to adulthood; by doing so it chronicles the history of Miami in the 1960s and 1970s. Finally, the literary dimension of the memoir is both public and private, for the reader is acutely aware of the autobiographer in the process of giving shape to events in his life.

The author's remembrances in *Next Year in Cuba* often move forward into the writer's present and back in time to the narrator's adolescence in Miami and his childhood in Cuba, as well as his adulthood in Chapel Hill, North Carolina. Havana and Coral Gables merge in the mind of the narrator as he seeks to transcend the influence and nostalgia of place in order to live fully in the present. For the children of exile belonging to the one-and-a-half generation, as Pérez Firmat designates them in his *Life on the Hyphen*, Cuba is barely a reality and almost a dream. This author is acutely aware that he, like most Cubans of his generation, will probably never return to live in his homeland. Viewed from this perspective, the text's title becomes ironic since returning to Cuba is a promise this narrator does not intend to keep.

Pérez Firmat's Private Self

In his study on autobiographical fields of reference, Paul J. Eakin has demonstrated that there is a clear engagement between the use of autobiographical forms, history, and culture. According to Eakin, "the self is an autobiographical text, a construct of a construct, and culture has exerted a decisive part, through the instrumentality of models of identity and in the process of identity formation" (Eakin 102). Eakin coins the term *models of identity* in order to show a construct that articulates the psychological structure of the self but at the same time is an example of selfhood that a given culture offers for imitation.[12] Pérez Firmat's autobiographical account illustrates fully Eakin's definition of the term *models of identity*. Throughout the text, the writer mourns the loss of a culture and of a way of life that would have been his had the diaspora not happened, but that have no relevance to his present in his adopted country.

The experience of loss of Cuban role models looms central behind the autobiographical impulse in Pérez Firmat's memories. Indeed, culture for this author is explained according to the models offered to him during his Cuban childhood and lost through the trauma of exile. How historical events beyond his control change his life expectations and his models of identity is indeed disturbing for Pérez Firmat and produces extreme tension and apprehension in the telling of his story of exodus. For him, autobiography becomes inseparable from the problem of self-conception, for he brings together the experiences of the writer and the shared values of his culture.

The central experience of private loss is centered around the narrator and his difficult relationship with his father, also named Gustavo. The father-and-son relationship is important, not only because the narrator devotes many pages of the memoir to the exchanges and conversations between the two, but also because the father represents a role model that loses relevance for the son in the new culture. The process for Pérez Firmat is deeply personal as it becomes at times, in the words of Lejeune, "an analogue to the psychoanalytic encounter," as the writer grapples with his unresolved feelings toward his own father.

The elder Gustavo Pérez represents the old values in many ways. Not only is his son unable to follow him in the direction and management of the confiscated family business, but the son is also unable to assume codes of behavior that in Cuba his father held in high esteem. As the son of a Cuban exile of the first generation, Pérez Firmat looks at his father with love but also with resentment for not having fought to preserve his future and thus for not caring enough about his own losses. Not being able to follow in the father's footsteps causes the narrator a profound sense of inadequacy in several dimensions of his life.

Moreover, Pérez Firmat's own career choice, professor and critic of Spanish literature, becomes a source of trouble for him. Throughout the text, the author articulates fears that his literary profession is not a valid one and that it would not be understood by his own father: "The only thing I criticize myself is for ending up in a profession that I can't explain to my father. . . . I wish I did something that I could explain to him. Say to him, I sell shoes, or I make loaves of bread, or I run an *almacén*" (209). A career in business was the way of life for all the men in his family while in Cuba, but this career path was severely interrupted by exile. Time and time again in this text, Pérez Firmat meditates on what might have been had he continued to manage the prosperous business his father owned rather than to become "a literary type," a university professor.

Yet following or not following in his father's footsteps went much deeper than just shifting careers in his adopted country. The author's father also represents the loss of a code of conduct that was common-place in Cuban society. *Machismo,* which equates and celebrates male power and superiority over women, was tantamount to a way of life for many middle- and upper-class men in Cuba in the 1950s.[13] In an episode that narrates Pérez Firmat's adult experience as a professor of Hispanic culture at Duke University, the author explains his own position on male gender roles to his students. By complementing *machismo* with *hombría* (its more humane counterpart), Firmat explains a code of conduct that, for him, does not undermine women but that entails the male's duty and sacrifice for his family. This explanation, although not accepted by all his students, allows the author to articulate ideas that might enable him to balance his Cuban models with his American reality. The narrator's anxiety and sense of disjunction are evident as he strives to search for explanations that might somehow "restore" the readers' reception to cultural codes of conduct that were held in high esteem by his native culture.

As an antidote to the loss of irrelevant and obsolete cultural mores, the narrator seeks healing and reconstruction by creating other role models for himself. Pérez Firmat's intellectual and emotional interest in the television character of Ricky Ricardo from the series *I Love Lucy* makes Ricky become a substitute role model about which he enjoys writing and teaching. Ricky allows the author to explain himself through Desi Arnaz's creation: "When he falls into Lucy's arms, he loses and he finds himself. What he loses is his primitive identity as his mother's son; but what he gains is a renewed self compacted from his Cuban past and his American present. . . . Ricky becomes for us a symbol of what it means to be Cuban in America" (236–37). If *hombría* replaces the more negative *machismo*, Ricky Ricardo and the author's admired uncles—Mike, Manolo, and Pepe—in many ways replace the father as role model. In fact, these esteemed figures constitute the writer's efforts in finding avenues for replacing and reconstructing role models lost by the disjunction of exile. For Pérez Firmat, the models of identity given by his Cuban culture have to be somehow integrated into his present. He cannot reject them, but he can attempt to understand and integrate them in an acceptable manner into his current sense of self.

Yet, even if the disruption of a Cuban way of life is related to family, it is to family that the narrator turns in his efforts toward reconstructing and healing his present. This author's middle-aged realization is that he has spent more time in this country than in the Cuba of his childhood and, most significantly, that his American-born children will never feel as Cuban as he does. He does not despair, for he feels a middle ground is possible. His children "raise him" into his own Americanization as he simultaneously "raises them" into their understanding of his Cubanness. Both his children and his American wife, Mary Anne, become viable bridges that might enable him to effect solutions and adjustments to life in North America.

Miami as Public Space

Cuban Miami, as it has been documented by a variety of recent sociological treatises, has effected a transplantation and a fabrication of Cuba and Cuban culture.[14] However, as these studies indicate, the Cuba recreated in Miami by Cuban exiles has little to do with Cuba as it now exists; it therefore becomes a model of a city that can be said to be frozen in time. Through the narrator's own recollections of his adolescence there, the "Cuban" identity of Miami comes to life as it imposes on the members of the enclave codes of living and conduct that might prove irrelevant in other U.S. locations as well as in today's Cuba. In fact, one of the text's unique features in representing the Cuban-American experience is the author's own analysis of the exile mentality in Miami and in its transplanted Cuban citizens. Miami, the city in which the narrator grew into a teenager, becomes the locus for narrating social history as well as the setting of many personal reminiscences. Nevertheless, the narrator is aware of both the dangers and the benefits of the ethnic enclave and especially the particular kind of exile that Miami represented for Cubans like him: "I know Cuban-American men and women of my generation who have never strayed from home, who lead happy and healthy lives in the warm shadows of Little Havana. As someone who lived that way for years, and as someone who at times would still long to live that way, I'm envious of those people, though I sense that their choice might not have worked for me. Even though I love Miami more that any other place I know . . . I can't conceive of not having left. If I still lived in Little Havana, I'm afraid I would be trapped by memory the way my father is" (270).

In Miami, the narrator finds a cultural solidarity, *"an ambiente,"* which he cannot experience elsewhere. This feeling of familiarity is evident every time he returns to the city of his dreams: "In Miami lady bus drivers talk about their kidneys. . . . renting a car can be a life-affirming experience" (92). The role of Miami in Pérez Firmat's upbringing is central, for it allows him to meditate on the condition of exile and on the nature of this experience: "Even if places brand people, one cannot reduce a person to his place" (269). The narrator feels at home in this city, although he also realizes that his attachment to the ethnic enclave is partly the source of his present dilemma.

The author's growing up in Miami is an important phenomenon in many ways. First, it allows him to describe the community from the inside. Second, it presents an idea of exile and displacement of a different sort, for here the displacement is not from the country of origin, as was the case with Pablo Medina, but from Miami as the ethnic enclave in which the narrator grew to adulthood. From a very personal perspective, the author documents what being Cuban in Miami meant for him and other children whose parents decided to make Miami their home after their exodus in 1959.

Autobiography as Process within the Text

Throughout the memoirs, the author utilizes narrative figures that at times both parallel and counterpoint each other as the events described reproduce and amplify the trauma of remembering and of starting anew. Two events, the theft of his credentials by his brother Carlos and the theft of his dissertation materials while he was a doctoral student at the University of Michigan, become metaphors for how an autobiography is created. Both episodes bring the reader to the beginning of the book, when the narrator expresses immense frustration for not being able to visualize his house in Cuba. In these episodes, the narrator is forced to undergo the pain associated with trying to reproduce events from memory and with the fear of not being totally successful in achieving the task.

Faced with his brother Carlos's theft of his credit and his name, Pérez Firmat turns him in to the police. The family reacts very negatively to this action, and their response deeply affects the narrator. His parents place family loyalty above everything else, and they expected him to protect Carlos from being prosecuted. The family's lack of support and their criticism dramatizes for Pérez Firmat how his life is split by the very different demands of two cultures: "On this July morning in Chapel Hill, I realize that there's an immense frozen sea between my brother and me, between my parents and me. According to my mother, family loyalty comes before everything. . . . I'm beginning to feel as if I'm the criminal, and my conscience is killing me" (181). Once again, the author feels he has somehow fallen short of the family's expectations, although he cannot justify their demands. With the brother's theft of his personal documents, Pérez Firmat experiences a metaphorical (and real) loss of identity, which sets in motion his efforts at literally recovering an identity stolen in exile.

Similarly, the episode that relates the theft of his dissertation materials at the Michigan library echoes the pattern of loss and reconstruction inherent in the autobiographical act. After an anguishing search for notes stolen from a library carrel, a detectivesque chase that lasted a few weeks, the narrator considers having to reconstruct his entire manuscript notes from memory or face the prospect of having to write a dissertation without notes: "I had read about other scholars who had worse catastrophes befall them. During World War II the great philologist Erich Auerbach had to flee his native Germany, leaving many years of research behind. . . . although I too had left my homeland, I was certainly no Auerbach" (194–95). Even though the documents reappear after several weeks, the idea of remembering and reconstructing in order to survive is echoed in this short episode and serves as a metaphor for the task of the writer. Recording these life recollections in *Next Year in Cuba* allows the author to confront his own losses while it simultaneously provides an opportunity for him to ponder the aesthetics of writing down a life.

Pérez Firmat's exploration of history and culture proves to be therapeutic by producing a kind of spiritual deliverance in his attempt to understand his family relationships and his Cuban heritage. A recent article by Esther Shapiro Rok, a Cuban-American psychologist of the same generation as Pérez Firmat, explains in clinical terms what might be considered part of the psychological motivation behind Firmat's memoirs.[15] According to Shapiro Rok, many adult exiles have somehow suppressed their trauma of displacement "because to weave back together the once fragmented connections is to feel fully the pain of loss. . . . As immigrants or exiles we push back the moment of rupture although it isn't until we weave together past and present that we can live a fuller life" (586). Shapiro Rok recommends that she and others review what she terms "unexamined grief"—that is, the lost past and the need to introduce Cuba into her current present: "Only when we can face the anguish of uprootedness can we regain access to a past that enriches our present and future, restores the forward movement in developmental time, permits the creative integration of a multicultural identity" (580–81).

Next Year in Cuba constitutes Pérez Firmat's own "examined grief" as it presents both the history of the Cubans in Miami and the story of this author's reading of that history. Both are narratives of losses as well as gains, of destruction of old models and construction of new ones. By inhabiting the space between two cultures, Pérez Firmat manages to refuse conscription into either. His purposive self-contradictions serve to render a self that is impossible to fix: "Rather than merging Cuba and America, I oscillate ceaselessly, sometimes wildly, between the two" (274). Displacement and instability work for this author, for his express goal is not to stabilize his identity but to understand it. In Pérez Firmat's narration we have ample proof of how history and culture can be expressed in the life of an individual.

Virgil Suárez's *Spared Angola* (1997)

Spared Angola: Memories from a Cuban-American Childhood revisits the traumatic memories of a child who lived in Cuba during the first decade of the revolution (1960-70). Suárez's memoirs thus depict a different historical time than the past evoked by Pablo Medina and Gustavo Pérez Firmat. Born in Havana in 1962, Suárez is the author of four novels and a collection of short stories. His family left Cuba for Spain in 1970 when he was eight years old. Four years later, the family moved permanently to the United States.[16]

The memoir's title, *Spared Angola,* is significant in the context of Cuba's history, for it connects Suárez's recollections directly with Cuba's foreign interventions during the 1970s. It was, in fact, during this time that over forty thousand Cuban troops supported by Soviet equipment were transferred to Africa in order to bring to power communist regimes in Angola and Ethiopia.[17] The poems and vignettes that make up this memoir constitute a vivid personal recollection of a time in Cuba that has seldom been recorded in English.

The past recalled by Suárez is not there to be preserved as a collective legacy but rather to be put aside as if exorcized through the act of writing. In a style reminiscent of Reinaldo Arenas's *Before Night Falls*, the autobiographical model used by Suárez does not depict an ideal, utopian childhood. Events recalled serve to evoke moments of maturation for the child, while some pieces stand as a collective testimony of a way of life that contrasts sharply with the happier Cuban past described by Medina and Pérez Firmat. The presence of poetry as a form of autobiographical conveyance is quite effective here, for it gives the work an intimate quality absent from the other two memoirs.

Suárez's childhood remembrances reflect the material poverty and political repression prevalent in Cuba during those years. By the late 1960s, the dream of the revolution was rapidly fading into a nightmare. Because these years brought severe shortages to all Cubans, the 1960s were known as "the hard years." Obviously the radical changes in the life of the country were felt in the author's household as well. The Cuban economy was collapsing, and the hardships of daily life caused many Cubans to become disenchanted. Though a strict rationing system was set up to ensure that everyone had enough to eat, food was scarce, and Cubans had to obtain basic foodstuffs illegally from clandestine markets. This was a time when those who remained in Cuba had to adapt to the harsh reality of a failed economy and to the radical changes in lifestyle that were about to take place.

There is no idealized nostalgia in Suárez's remembrances; rather, the adult looks back at his early years in Cuba and often narrates sordid or traumatic instances that marked his childhood: his father's depressive behavior caused by the events of the revolution, violence inflicted upon animals, and the poverty and scarcities all had to endure. Suárez describes the incidents and the people he remembers in a straightforward tone that at times contrasts vividly with the horror of what is being related. While there is clearly a healing impulse in the writing down of these memories, for Suárez the healing occurs not in leaving a legacy for others to read but in writing about these difficult episodes so that they can be erased from his mind.

The vignette that opens the collection, also titled "Spared Angola," relates the visit of Suárez's grandmother, Domitila, and his feelings upon seeing her in Miami after a twenty-year absence. Domitila stirs memories in the author about which he must write. She reminds the adult grandson of his fortune in having left before the political situation in Cuba grew worse: "You are a lucky young man. Your parents did the right thing. When they took you out of Cuba, your parents spared you. Yes, you were spared. Spared Angola."[18] Seeing the grandmother uncovers twenty years of buried memories for the author, memories of clapboard houses, of both physical and spiritual poverty, of childhood fears, and of emotional scars. This initial piece becomes a metaphor for the entire text since it serves as a trigger that literally brings back Suárez's Cuban childhood.

The episodes narrated in *Spared Angola* show clearly the effects of history on the individual and how children such as Suárez remember their impoverished childhood. Clearly these were not the children of privilege, and Suárez's memories do not seek to idealize the past—merely to record it. For instance, the poem entitled "Luz and Balmaseda" centers on the lack of material objects as it expresses what it was like to grow up in a country that had no toys for its children. Having little to do, Suárez and his friends had to look for more dangerous sources of amusement:

Our parents made
papalotes, kites, out of bamboo and rice paper,

with long strips of old bedsheets for tails. We put razor
blades on them or tied broken pieces of bottles and fought

air wars

. . . .

When the games came to an end because by 1969

none of us got toys, or relatives stopped sending
these small gifts, and our imaginations ebbed on dry

we resorted to flinging rocks at the street lights. (42–43)

Happier vignettes center on the description of objects or possessions the child remembers with affection. In "Pin Pan Pun" (55), Suárez recalls the foldaway cot used by his relatives when they visited Havana from the countryside. Here, the presence of relatives who came in from the interior and slept in Suárez's Havana living room provided a source of joy and company for an only child growing up in a household of unhappy adults. In the poem "1965 Dodge Dart," the author remembers the family's first years in exile and the used car that became a shared prize between himself and his father: "it was the biggest & / grandest thing we'd ever owned" (117).

Yet the prevalent mood of these memories is one of sadness. In "Ji-cotea/Turtle," Suárez relates how his father brought home thirty small turtles and how he was taught to kill them so that the family could have something to eat that night: "As reluctant as I was, I did as I was told. I grabbed every one of those thirty turtles' necks, pulled without looking into their eyes, and closed mine each of the thirty times the machete came down. Turtle, after turtle, after turtle. All thirty" (48). Clearly the incident caused the child a great deal of distress that he was unable to understand or share with anyone. Several episodes cluster around fear of animals or physical violence done to animals ("Animalia"; "The Trouble with Frogs"), always told from the perspective of a child too young to understand what he sees or experiences.

A gruesome vignette entitled "The Goat Incident" stands out in its description of raw violence. Here the child is made to witness the crude ways in which the Cuban farmers tried to settle a dispute among themselves. As in many other incidents related in the text, the child's feelings of anger and frustration are evident: "Again the men in the circle. Another glimpse revealed the men, sweating, bestial, fighting each other with goats. With goats over their shoulders. Both goats had not made it. They were limp in death. . . . A part of me didn't want to see, but the other did. . . . The men continued now with their death dance. The man with the knife kept stabbing at the goat. More blood, more entrails. . . . The other man, the one with the machete, swung and cut the man on the arm. The sharp blade cut through the flesh down to the bone" (68–69).

A pattern emerges as several other episodes in the book relate similar incidents. In all of them, the child seems unready to process the tremendous physical violence inflicted upon the various animals, but at the same time he is unable to prevent these incidents from taking place. These frustrating memories remain deep in the writer's unconscious and become obsessions he later attempts to exorcise through his writing: "But the goat incident I remember well from all the years that I've had to carry it blazoned in my memory, though I once tried to purge myself of it in one of my books" (66–67).

If the poverty and traumatic violence witnessed by the child seem to be the thematic core of the incidents recalled in *Spared Angola*, the vignettes and poems created around the figure of the author's father best encapsulate these themes, providing some of the best writing in the collection. It is precisely the sadness of an individual betrayed by his country that Suárez wishes to portray in his memories of his father, the portrait of someone so deeply hurt by historical circumstance that he refuses to have any interaction with those around him, including his son. For Suárez, the father becomes someone whom the narrator watches silently from his infancy, an unhappy figure who pays little attention to the child and who is never seen as a role model.

In "Bitterness," the reader learns how the author's father became physically and psychologically alienated from everyone as a result of having to remain in Cuba during the first decade of the revolution. During those years, all that the father could find for a job was to slaughter old horses that were later fed to other animals in the Havana zoo. The vignette is in reality two memories that the author condenses and links metaphorically in order to convey the trauma and the frustration of life in Cuba and in exile.

The first memory is a graphic description of the father's job at the slaughter house. The father is described as a man who, at thirty years of age, has become depressed and has stopped speaking to those around him. His brutal job has a further alienating effect on his moods: "Dark blood, this blood of the horses my father slaughters daily to feed zoo lions. . . . and when he comes home his hands are numb from all the chopping and cutting" (49). The second memory takes place in Spain and recalls the first months of exile, when the entire family slept together in one room. Here the child describes how he overhears his parents arguing during the late hours of the night. The father wants to make love to the mother, but she refuses. The child records his impressions of what he hears: "This, I think, is the way death must sound. Then my father begins all over again. The room fills with the small sounds. . . . the cleaver falls and cuts through the skin. . . . All that blood. It emerges and collects on the slaughter tables, the blood of countless horses" (50–51).

Suárez's father is depicted by the narrator as both victim and victimizer as a result of his own harsh fate. The mixing of temporal categories and geographical spaces is quite effective since the reader is forced to associate the element of force inflicted by the father on the horses to the author's mother as well. Yet the vignette also speaks of the bitterness of the child who cannot escape from witnessing many sad and sordid episodes. One of the best written pieces in the collection, "Bitterness" stands out as a testimony of the deleterious effects of the revolution on the individual lives of Cubans such as the narrator's father.

Suárez's writing displays very little nostalgia for Cuba. In fact, it is the past that seems to have chosen Suárez by embedding in his memory the sad remembrances of his early life in his native country. The split self of the one-and-a-half generation and the need to balance past and present seem much less evident in the stories and poems narrated in *Spared Angola*. If Medina's and Pérez Firmat's memoirs sought to leave a record for posterity for the Cuban-American children who left a country in transition during the 1960s, the memoirs of Suárez speak to a different generation and are written instead to erase the scars of an unhappy past. Clearly for Virgil Suárez, the Cuba of the late 1960s was indeed a "luckless country," a birthplace ravaged by history.

Personal Essays by Eliana Rivero and Ruth Behar

Although assimilation and its counterpart, dissimilation, are important dimensions of narrators such as Gustavo Pérez Firmat, Pablo Medina, and Virgil Suárez, personal writing has other meanings for the women writers. Following a tradition well established by other Latina writers, especially Chicanas, Cuban-American women seem to prefer the personal essay as a vehicle of expression as they attempt to reaffirm the survival of their female self in their narratives.[19] Cuban-American women writers such as Eliana Rivero and Ruth Behar look mainly to the future in order to assert issues pertaining to identity and minority politics. Interestingly, with the exception of Ruth Behar's anthropological, but also biographical, essays collected in *The Vulnerable Observer* (1996), no book-length memoir has yet been published by a Cuban-American woman. This situation, however, might soon change due to the current creative boom by the children of the first exile.

Essays by Eliana Rivero and Ruth Behar about displacement embody a distinctive feminine sensibility. As opposed to the autobiographical accounts by male Cuban-American writers, who took pains in narrating and articulating the Cuban past and the icons of their culture, in these accounts by female writers issues concerning their U.S. present as women belonging to an ethnic minority take precedence over cultural matters. These women writers exhibit what Adrienne Rich would term "a politics of location."[20] They claim a place and declare their rights to exist in and speak from such a place. Making full use of the authority of the first-person narrative, they speak about their main concerns regarding identity and how they have become who they are today.

Eliana Rivero, who arrived from Cuba in her teens, describes her marginal experience as a Cuban American living in the Southwest, af-

firming her own hybrid condition as a positive step toward self-realization. Ruth Behar, the younger of the two, relates her experiences as a minority scholar very much concerned with her Jewish-Cuban past. As
daughters of first-generation Cuban exiles, these women faced unique
challenges. Painfully aware of belonging to a minority group but also
aware of being women, Rivero and Behar often find themselves strug-
gling with conflicting cultural messages. In fact, both women writers
strike out in search of their own identity in a confrontation with a society that seeks to dictate to them how they should act or who they
should be. The responses vary from a reflection on identity (Rivero) to
issues of ethnicity and heritage (Behar).

Eliana Rivero's Border Writings

As indicated in the previous chapter, Eliana Rivero is both a literary
critic and a poet. Born in Cuba more than a decade before Ruth Behar,
she has lived in Tucson since 1967. Like most of her peers, Rivero's first
writings (poetry collections) were published in Spanish. Her decision to
use English in her most recent essays is intimately related to her own definition of self. The autobiographical essays analyzed here, "'Fronteraisleña,' Border Islander" and "Of Borders and Self: A Latina on the Margins," present a perspective of identity based on the author's acceptance
that her inner core can no longer be defined as Cuban or even American.[21] Instead of lamenting this fact, however, Rivero celebrates her condition of "hybridism" because it provides her with a variety of perspectives from which to view and accept her life.

In "'Fronteraisleña,' Border Islander" Rivero defines her concept of
self and concludes by accepting and acknowledging that, after living in
the United States for almost four decades, she is no longer as Cuban as
she thought she was or as American as she should be: "Yes I am Cuban
by origin and by culture . . . but I have lived elsewhere most of my life"
(673). Rivero stresses that this realization is not tragic; rather, it produces a kind of inner contentment. "The anguish is gone; a sense of
wholeness now presides over the process" (673). Curiously, this author's
experience of marginality is first lived through the experiences of other
U.S. Latinos, Chicanos in particular. According to Rivero, she was in
fact more Latina than American even if her own definition of being
Latina excluded her Cubanness: "My choice was not accidental: I had
recognized in them [Chicanos] the same quest for identity and similar af-
firmations of "being other" that had become an integral part of my
American *vivencia* or lived experience" (671). By living in Arizona and

by witnessing and being a part of the Chicano literary renaissance in the early 1970s, Rivero felt herself part of a minority that became a surrogate ethnic group for her.

Rivero's life until the late 1970s was a process of de-Cubanization but not necessarily of Americanization. Being Cuban was not a choice since her own group's politics isolated and prevented her from feeling ethnic solidarity. In Miami, she was not welcomed because of her radical politics. Yet, if Rivero was isolated from her Cuban ethnic community due to differences in ideology, she also felt isolated from her fellow Latinos due to the fact that Cuban exiles such as herself had little in common with the political issues of Chicanos or U.S. Puerto Ricans. Moreover, Rivero's association with Latina and feminist groups allowed her to find kinship with other minority groups but never to find her own.

In "Of Borders and Self," the author continues to write about "the crucial task of constructing identity" (1). This second essay is lyrical and deftly crafted around the frontier-border metaphor. The figure of the border is ideally suited to Rivero since by living in Sierra Vista, Arizona, she has an external physical space that corresponds intimately with her fragmented identity. Rivero was in Mexico and in the United States; she was Cuban and American, both at the same time. Hybridism, a concept defined by Homi Bhabha and adopted by Rivero in her essays about Cuban Americans in America,[22] is now applied to her own life but in a joyous, anxiety-free manner: "I envision my space and my inner being as a center with no partitions, no limits, unproblematized by this hybridity that is, proudly, my core" ("Borders," 19). For Rivero herself, the metaphor of borders and frontiers is a real and intellectual one and thus gives force to the ideas expounded in the essay: "I was ideologically anomalous, indeed rebellious within a reactionary exile culture which was assumed to inform my views and my world vision" (7). Eliana Rivero's scholarly interests in feminist theory coalesce in her own condition and provide for this author a unique perspective from which to assess her experience of diaspora.

Ruth Behar's Shadow Biography

Of the two women essayists analyzed here, Ruth Behar, born in 1956, is the younger. Leaving Cuba in 1962 at the age of five, Behar simultaneously mastered English and Spanish as a young child growing up in the United States. Consequently, Behar's writings about her bicultural condition evolve from a perspective unlike that of the previous writers analyzed in this section because her essays reflect concerns of heritage and ethnicity rather than the traumatic experience of rupture of cultures and languages evident in the writers of the one-and-a-half generation. In fact, Behar's perspective more closely resembles the recent writings of other ethnic Cuban Americans and Hispanic Americans who analyze their bicultural status, not from having lived part of their lives in another culture, but rather because their parents preserved their Spanish language and Cuban culture in their American homes.

Ruth Behar's recent publications combine her autobiography and academic research in her need to understand the strands of her identity and heritage. Her role as editor of the anthology *Bridges to Cuba* (1994), her ethnographic work in *The Translated Woman* (1993), and her latest collection of anthropological but also very personal essays in *The Vulnerable Observer* (1996) all demonstrate Behar's need to blend the personal and the academic dimensions of her life. Presently Behar teaches anthropology, women's studies, and Latino studies at the University of Michigan.

The essays reviewed here reflect Behar's double-edged concern: to validate her own Jewish-Cuban heritage and to make sense of her experiences in academia as a minority scholar. "The Biography in the Shadow," a chapter in *The Translated Woman*, stresses issues of authorship and self; "Juban," an essay that appeared in *Poetics Today*, addresses Behar's search for the strands of her own ethnicity, taking the author back to her Russian-Jewish ancestry; finally, the essays gathered in *The Vulnerable Observer* reflect Behar's personal advocacy in creating a methodological practice in the field of anthropology that would take into account the subjectivity of both the observed and the observer. By relating experiences taken from her own personal life, Behar becomes at once subject and object of her anthropological writings.

"The Biography in the Shadow" is Behar's capsule history of her identity as a writer and how she came to feel confident and justified enough to exert the right to tell her own story and to consider it relevant. The essay tells about Behar's academic success, from her humble childhood days in Brooklyn, where the only quiet place for study was the bottom of the stairs of her apartment building, to being the recipient of a prestigious MacArthur Fellowship in 1988. Behar relates to us how she gained admittance into an exclusive Ivy League college and the unhappiness she experienced throughout her college years, feeling perhaps that she was there only as part of her school's minority quota: "The world of the academy, where people seemed invested not in loving books but in being able to talk about them impressively, was a world for which my immigrant milieu had not prepared me" (325).

Behar's "Biography in the Shadow" reveals a sense of the costs of acculturation as it responds to the experience of assimilation not as a source of self-esteem but rather as a source of discomfort that requires endless explanations and apologies. Behar's humble family beginnings (her grandfather was a peddler in Cuba) get in the way of her education, for she feels unable to claim for herself a "deserved" place in academia. The tension between her origins and her ambitions makes her painfully alienated as she gradually finds herself feeling undeserving of either the warmth and support of her family or of a career in academia.

In "The Biography in the Shadow," Behar confronts her own feelings of inadequacy toward her profession as well as her right to be a member of the intellectual elite that makes up the world of academia. The politics of affirmative action, minority quotas, and hiring in the academic world prepares the author for her questioning of the true essence of her minority status: "If I'm going to be counted as a minority, if I'm going to be on the margin, then I'm going to claim that space and speak from it, but in the interest of a politics that challenges the language of authenticity and racial purity. I will no longer apologize and say, 'I'm a Latina, but don't worry, I'm not a real Latina, I don't need special privileges,' constantly feeling that I haven't passed 'the ethnic legitimacy test'" (339).

As indicated above, "The Biography" is interpolated in Behar's ethnographic treatise *The Translated Woman,* a study of a Mexican-Indian woman (Esperanza) from the small village of Mexiquitic. By serving as Behar's subject, Esperanza allowed the author to discover parts of her own self that needed to be explored. Writing of herself in the third person, Behar affirms, "I understand that . . . her desire to recognize Esperanza as a writer whose words are written in the sand of storytelling and conversation has to do with her own lack of language" (336).

If "The Biography" seems to give Behar enough authority to pursue her own heritage, the essay entitled "Juban" can be considered an extension of the first, for it sets out to clarify the relationships between the author's Jewish heritage and her Cuban heritage. The crisis of identity that had prompted Behar to confront the hypocrisy of affirmative action practices in academia now motivates her to search the issue of how her Jewishness fits in within her Cuban cultural background. In fact, Behar's autobiographical efforts in this essay are directed toward a discovery of self through family genealogy. As stated in her text, she wants to get at "the peculiar confluence of identity that is implied in the idea of being Jewish-Cuban."[23]

"Juban" centers on the transmigrated condition of Behar's grandfather Zayde. As a Russian Jew, the grandfather hardly dominated the structures of the Spanish language and as such becomes the embodiment of displacement for the granddaughter. In order to explain the displacement of the patriarch, Behar traces the fascinating history of how Jews came to settle in Cuba as a result of U.S. policy toward Jews in the 1930s. Yet what moves Behar's personal recollections of her grandfather's story are her own personal paradoxes: "it is not expected for a Jew to have Spanish as a mother tongue, nor for someone from Latin America to lay claims to a Jewish identity" (153).

The author's central quest of her heritage and origins ("how could I being Jewish claim to be Cuban?") is founded in her study of the Cuban nation and its heterogeneous cultural essence.[24] Behar considers herself a *mestiza* (person of mixed ancestry) and as such uses the genre of the autobiographical memoir to lay claim to an identity that she considers a composite of many strands from its very inception: "And yet, in the Cuban-Jewish case, there is a composite word 'Juban' which gets at a sense of '*mestizaje*' rooted in a creative amalgam that is different from assimilation. Such an amalgam is possible because of the criollism that is at the center of Cuban culture" (164). According to the author, the Jewish-Cuban community comes to be the present embodiment of both a "translated people" and a bicultural fluency. Because, in her words, Jews are "translated people," it is perfectly natural to claim for herself both her Cuban and Jewish ancestries.

Behar's most recent essays, gathered under the title *The Vulnerable Observer*, become an inseparable blend of her personal and professional concerns. These essays weave together the author's experiences as a Cuban-American Jew with accounts of her fieldwork in Spain, Cuba, and the United States and challenge the traditional ways in which anthropology looks at other cultures and minority groups. These personal narratives relate how crucial events in the author's life, such as the death of her grandfather or the crippling car accident she suffered as a child, deeply affected the author and made her quite vulnerable in her own practice as an anthropologist.

"Death and Memory," the centerpiece of the collection, relates Behar's memories of her Russian-Jewish grandfather's death, which took place when she was away in Spain doing field work on death and grieving practices in the lives of the Spanish villagers of Santa María del Mar.

Behar relates how her own personal experience of dealing with death profoundly affected the field work she was doing at the time, and how her writing about the mourning rituals of these Spanish peasants was modified by her own personal suffering:

> My conversations about death with people in Spain heightened my memory of my grandfather and the ways links to his past had been severed. And my preoccupation with the death of memory in Santa María provoked a resurgence of memory, for me, about my own Jewish heritage and how I had become alienated from it. In the course of these movements and shifts of perspective, the boundary between social realms that are purely personal and those that are part of ethnographic fieldwork became blurred. My grandfather was subjected to my anthropological gaze while I was drawn close personally to the people of Santa María. (82)

"Death and Memory" is a mournful, honest expression of a woman's personal pain, a text that by its contents becomes an example of the anthropological practice Behar advocates for her field of study.[25] By explaining how her perspective on scholarly research is rooted in her life experiences, Behar achieves a balance that allows self-understanding for this author.

In "Going to Cuba: Writing Ethnography of Diaspora, Return, and Despair," the author examines her intense involvement with creating a dialogue between Cuban writers in Cuba and those in the United States. Reflecting on her labor-intensive task of creating cultural bridges with Cuban intellectuals during the past decade, Behar's essay represents a hard examination of Cuban cultural life today. Here Behar questions if her efforts have been worth the personal sacrifices she has made: "return trips—for me and for all second generation Cuban Americans—are always about recovering our abandoned childhoods. My family left Cuba when I was almost five, and I return to Cuba in search of memories I never find. . . . Am I recovering my childhood at the cost of being absent from my own son's childhood?" (141). In this painful look at Cuba today, Behar becomes both observer and subject, and by doing so, she herself becomes vulnerable to her readers. Behar's personal writings provide a place from which she can speak as a woman, as a Jew, and as a Cuban. Resembling Pilar, the fictional character of Cristina García's *Dreaming in Cuban*, Behar searches for and reaches back to her mixed heritage in efforts to better understand herself.

The memoirs and personal essays analyzed above show male and female Cuban-American writers engaged in a construction of identity by means of confronting the present as well as the past. For some of the men, the past is a legacy that needs to be written down and preserved; for the women, the present becomes all important as they concentrate on issues of affirmation and advocacy. The personal essays of the diasporic experience of the women writers become self-affirming acts that assert a need to speak from the margins (Behar) or that seek to explain the condition of difference (Rivero). As simultaneous members of two cultures, these female authors sometimes place themselves outside American and Cuban culture and create new cultural definitions for other female Cuban Americans.

My analysis of these Cuban-American memoirs and personal narratives has sought to trace the dramatization of the Cuban-American autobiographical voice and has explored the solutions and substitutions these authors have devised in order to create a voice in a culture other than that of their country of birth. All authors have written about their experience of the diaspora from quite different perspectives, although each articulated important issues unique to their male and female perspectives. These are writers whose literary identity has been determined by history, and their narratives are representative of a pivotal moment in contemporary Cuban-American autobiographical writing. As a group, these authors exhibited a desire to communicate with their community in exile, to look at reality, and to seek the positive aspects of displacement in their individual lives. Rather than an indulgent activity, personal writing for these male and female writers becomes "an unending quest to replenish a lack,"[26] for their accounts raise questions about human dignity and about the tensions between assimilation and preservation of a culture.

PART 3

Encountering Others

Imagined U.S. Cuban Communities

All migrants leave their past behind, although some try to pack it into bundles and boxes but on the journey something seeps out of the treasured mementos and old photographs, until even their owners fail to recognize them, because it is the fate of the migrants to be stripped of history, to stand naked amidst the scorn of strangers upon whom they see the rich clothing, the brocades of continuity and the eyebrows of belonging.

Salman Rushdie, *Shame*

6   Contrasting Visions of Community

Truth may be stranger than fiction, but fiction is truer.

Frederic Raphael

So far we have looked at the Cuban-American poetic expression of the post-1959 diaspora through the prism of autobiography. The memoirs of Pablo Medina, Gustavo Pérez Firmat, and Virgil Suárez and the essays of Ruth Behar and Eliana Rivero highlighted authors who appeared as historians and witnesses of their own lives. These autobiographical works provided the reader with an awareness that there was a correspondence of identity between the authors and the narratives of their lives. The reading of such accounts appeared unmediated and provided the reader with the intimacy that characterizes confessional literature. These narrators shared a burden with the listener and sought in every case a reconciliation with their Cuban past. The reader, however, also knew that the success of these accounts was not based on the literal reproduction of facts but on the way in which these writers were able to pattern their experiences of the past into a meaningful narrative. In other words, the writers studied, arranged, and reordered their material in order to present a particular image of self.

Part 3 of this book explores the different ways in which the issue of community can be engaged by the Cuban-American writer. Rather than focusing on the individual, the novels analyzed in this section present a larger picture that addresses issues of acculturation and adaptation in today's dispersed Cuban-American communities. Fiction codes the experiences of these Cuban-American authors and allows them to conceal more of their personal lives, while at the same time permitting them to reveal more about the experiences of their family and their ethnic group. The fictional depiction of community in the novels of these Cuban-American writers can reveal to readers much about the experience of how a marginalized minority survives within a dominant culture.

Joaquín Fraxedas and Roberto Fernández seek to trace in broad strokes how the diasporic experience affects Cubans as a collective entity. Moving beyond the autobiographical "I," these writers have produced full-fledged fictions that portray the life of those who personally lived the diaspora of 1959. Their main concern is a depiction, not of their own personal suffering, but rather of how the trauma of displacement is portrayed in the literature of the Cuban-American story of transmigration. These writers produce a literature of mirroring communities in which members of the various generations inside and outside Cuba are given a voice in an effort to explain their place in Cuban history. The voices of these characters inspire Cuban readers to seek an understanding for themselves of almost forty years of exodus and diaspora in the history of Cuba.

In her recent book *All My Relatives*, Bonnie TuSmith indicates that, for the writers who identify with their ethnic cultures, "community is a continuously evolving possibility that they strive to capture in literary discourse." Adopting Thomas Bender's definition of community as a "network of social relations marked by mutuality and emotional bonds," TuSmith emphasizes the experiential level of this concept and points out that a particular ethnic writer's position regarding individualism and community stems from a combination of historical and social factors as well as from personal choice (22–24). For TuSmith, the notion of "community" calls attention to the positive values of close fellowship, social solidarity, idealism, and harmony. For an ethnic writer, the idea of community entails reuniting parts of a culture, asserting its identity, and mitigating the absence of culture by imagining it in literature.

Yet the idea of community can assume a less idealized understanding of the term. In "Différance and the Discourse of Community," Cordelia Chavez Candelaria expresses how both the ideal and the pragmatic concepts of community can exist in the depiction of community by ethnic authors: "In this conceptualization, the ideal of community competes with the individual's clear-eyed perception of the space and human relation that produced her/him" (187). According to Chavez Candelaria, community can be a source of tension for ethnic authors since its utopian connotations are far from the reality these authors must confront.

TuSmith's and Candelaria's findings on the subject of community are relevant to our reading of the novels of Fernández and Fraxedas, for in their narratives the reader can find radically different perspectives on the subject. Whereas Fraxedas devises an ideal community of Cuban Americans who are able to work together for the common good, Fernández offers a more somber picture. In fact, Fernández's protagonists are never insiders of Cuban or American discourse, for they always seem to yearn for a community that is always absent or beyond them.

J. Joaquín Fraxedas's *The Lonely Crossing of Juan Cabrera* (1993)

A moving portrait of a collective tragedy, *The Lonely Crossing of Juan Cabrera* is the fictional account of a treacherous raft journey from the island of Cuba to the Florida Keys. Depicting characters belonging to the various generations and migratory waves, Fraxedas seeks to reunite the ruptured parts of his own nation. Similar to Margarita Engle's *Skywriting,* this novel is explicitly didactic and uses character types in order to document the plight of the Cuban Americans and their Cuban counterparts. In *The Lonely Crossing,* plot, character, and metaphoric structures combine to produce the story of thirty-four years of exile for a community.

Born in Cuba and raised in Miami and Detroit, Joaquín Fraxedas came to the United States during the 1960s as a young boy. A lawyer by profession, he began to write fiction as a graduate student while he attended the University of Florida. *The Lonely Crossing,* published simultaneously in 1993 in English and Spanish editions, is Joaquín Fraxedas's first novel.[1] Centered on a *balsero*'s story, this novel precedes the mass exodus of August 1994 in which more than thirty thousand Cubans risked their lives in rafts and boats to cross the treacherous waters between Cuba and Florida. Fraxedas's focus on the *balsero* experience is prophetic, for this recent exodus has produced an unexpected bridge of compassion, with the Miami exiles welcoming this latest wave of escapees with open arms. According to recent reports, the *balsero* crisis has served to confront the generations that comprise the Cuban exodus in a way that had not been possible before.[2] Fraxedas captures this moment, for his story demands an understanding of both the Cubans in Cuba and the Cuban-American community in the United States.

From the start, Fraxedas's book pits humans against nature in a context quite reminiscent of Hemingway's sea adventures. The quotations from Cervantes and Homer set the poetic tone that frames this tragic saga: Three people set sail on a raft, yet only one will reach the other side. Indeed, the future of Juan's two companions seems bleak: Andrés, who had been Castro's political prisoner, was fifty-five years old and seemed too weak to make the crossing. Raúl, a poor farmer, was younger but did not seem to have enough balance between his physical abilities and his capacity to deal with the traumatic effects of the journey. Early in their tragic voyage, Andrés is killed by the crew of a Soviet gunboat. Soon after, Raúl loses his life during a shark attack. Only Juan is left and must make the crossing alone. It is during this perilous crossing that Juan Cabrera reflects on his past, and the reader learns about his life as a citizen of the revolution.

Fraxedas effectively depicts the three men's harrowing experience on the open seas as they confront sharks and hurricanes. Even if the descriptions seem hyperbolic at times, the documentary force of the text is undeniable and mirrors real-life accounts. Witness Rafael Lima's journalistic report of his experience as a *balsero* "spotter" for the Stock Island Refugee Center in Key West in 1994: "The impression one gets flying over the *balseros* at 500 feet is one of looking down at floating garbage. You cannot believe that people are crossing an ocean on these things. They are pieces of Styrofoam. Not blocks. Pieces. You lower to 200 feet and the garbage gets bigger, and then 100 feet and you see there are people dressed in rags standing on the garbage, and when you see the children being held up in the air for people in the plane to see, your heart breaks. We dropped survival packages with water and called the position in to the Coast Guard" (8).

In comparison to verifiable accounts such as Lima's, Juan Cabrera's meager transportation, as described in Fraxedas's novel, does not seem exceptional: "They brought the three deflated inner tubes . . . the nylon lines, the canvas tarpaulin, and the hand-operated Czechoslovakian air pump, along with a few personal items" (10). Yet if the life-and-death struggle of Juan and his companions constitutes the main narrative strand in this text, it is Fraxedas's skillful depiction of the various communities and migratory waves comprising today's Cuba that renders this novel a place in the imaginary trajectory of Cuban-American narratives of the aftermath of the revolution.

Together Juan Cabrera, Vivian, and Alberto encapsulate the generations and spaces that make up almost forty years of diaspora for the Cuban community. Vivian and Alberto's metaphorical crossings become central in the development of the novel, for each embodies a different generation and thus has a different perspective of the consequences of 1959 for the Cuban nation. Through their psychological crossings, the horrors of Juan Cabrera's ocean adventure are echoed in the North American space. It is these characters' questioning of their own role in the Cuban story that helps readers of Cuban heritage make sense of their own part as well.

Alberto's story enacts the plight of the first generation, as he typifies the lost idealism of the 1960s and the hopes of a quick return for the first generation of exiles. A veteran pilot of the failed Bay of Pigs invasion, Alberto earns his living as a flight instructor and devotes his spare time to spotting *balseros* off the Florida Keys. Exiles such as Alberto cannot stop feeling involved with the latest Cuban tragedy: "he usually started his days with a vague uneasiness, a lingering feeling that he should be opening his eyes in some other place, doing some other thing. . . . now in the sad light of the afternoon he felt a strange urgency, a powerful need, to use every last ray of light to search for these people" (108–9).

As a Cuban, Alberto is deeply devoted to his people. His job forces him to confront the daily tragedy of Cubans' crossing the ocean in rafts such as Juan Cabrera's. Life for exiles such as Alberto was forever linked with the news about and the responsibility for those still left in Cuba; it could never be otherwise: "It is very strange to be a Cuban exile in the United States, having gone through what you have gone through and knowing what you know and seeing what you see and hearing the stories you hear every day, and still go on living a normal everyday life as if nothing were happening around you, he thought. It is like living a double life, like constantly stepping out of one universe into another and back again" (100). A character drawn with authorial affection, Alberto is a man deeply involved with the tragedy of his community and fully devoted to helping his own people.

Vivian, on the other hand, belongs to the one-and-a-half generation and presents a perspective quite different from Alberto's. As the Cuban American in the text, Vivian is both Cuban and American, although not at the same time. Vivian's love/hate relationship with her own community is not atypical for her generation. She wants to be a source of pride for her people, while at the same time she recoils from the false promises and emotionalism of her parent's generation. Eventually, Vivian sees her fulfillment in helping her own, so she decides to stay in Miami working for the Coast Guard. Because Vivian has been raised in both Cuban and U.S. cultures, she has insight into both and thus can envision events from a more distanced perspective. She can also acknowledge flaws in her people, although she never forgets that she, too, is a member of her community.

One of the many children who were sent alone to the United States by their parents during the early 1960s as part of the so-called Operation Peter Pan,[3] Vivian resents not having had a say in her own future. As a child of the first exiles, Vivian expresses a sense of lost identity and feelings of not quite belonging anywhere: "But for us . . . for the Cuban Americans of our generation, for us who were plucked from our world as we slept . . . the transition was so sudden and the loss of innocence so abrupt, that in our memories the flight has assumed the trappings of a paradisiacal expulsion. And everything beautiful and distant that tastes of Paradise relates somehow to that flight. So we keep searching and waiting. For what? she thought" (124).

Ironically, Vivian's career in the Coast Guard has brought her face to face with the ongoing Cuban tragedy that started with her own life. When Vivian thinks of Miami Cubans and their constant promises and shouts of "*¡Volveremos!*" she seems repelled by the whole idea and wants to pretend she has nothing to do with these "emotional" Cubans. Yet, when asked by her friend Carmen why she did not stay in New England if she felt that way about Miami, she exposes her own contradictions: "*¿Qué iba a hacer allá arriba?* What was I going to do up there? It is not my home. This crazy place is. *¿Qué iba a hacer?* This is what I have to do. Besides, there was great pride in coming back after the academy" (126).

In keeping with Fraxedas's desire to create mirror images of the dispersed Cuban communities he depicts in the story, Juan Cabrera becomes Vivian's counterpart in Cuba. Juan is raised under the revolution and disappointed by it. His life in Cuba has been a struggle from the beginning. When he is only seven, his father is killed by the revolutionaries. In the years that follow, Juan survives the demands of the socialist government through hiding the fact that he himself is the descendant of wealthy Cuban landowners: "Making up stories to get ahead, telling everything except the truth: that he was born to a proud, respected family who owned vast tracts of land in Camaguey, that he had been a *latifundista*. . . . He felt embarrassed by his life, ashamed of hiding who he had been, of having accepted the unacceptable and serving the purposes of those who had killed his father and destroyed his own soul" (134–35). Juan Cabrera's interest as a character lies in his sense of his own vulnerabilities. In fact, many times in the book Juan feels shame whenever he thinks about the things that he has done because of his own cowardice in expressing dissent. Eventually, and due to the help he receives from his exiled counterparts, Juan can understand what has happened and can better assess the complexities of being part of a displaced nation.

By imagining the different fragments of his community and bringing them together in his fiction, Fraxedas wills an ideal community into existence. For this author, all Cubans (the exiles and those in Cuba) have a sense of shared history. By presenting to us the varied generations and communities that make up the Cuban nation today—from the newly arrived Juan to Alberto, the veteran soldier—Fraxedas implies that hope for unity is possible and desirable. Affirmation of Fraxedas's ethnic community relies on this author's desire to present a good face to the dominant society. The solutions to the problems in his novel can be solved if there remains a viable ethnic culture with which the individual can reconnect.

Roberto Fernández's *Raining Backwards* (1988)

Roberto Fernández's parodic portrayal of how a minority community reacts to displacement provides a critical perspective that differs widely from that of Fraxedas's account. Born in Sagua la Grande, Cuba, in 1951, Fernández arrived in the United States when he was ten years old. Between 1975 and 1985, the author published three works in Spanish: *Cuentos sin rumbo* (1975), a collection of short stories; *La vida es un special* (1982), a short novel that satirizes commercialism in the Miami Cuban community; and *La montaña rusa* (1985), a second collection of stories. All three texts could be considered preparatory to his more recent and mature novels written in English: *Raining Backwards* (1988) and *Holy Radishes!* (1995).[4] Fernández has been writing and publishing creatively for a longer time than any of the authors treated here. He is considered at the vanguard of Cuban-American literature because his thematics transcend the usual exile topics of displacement and nostalgia, centering instead on the world of post-exile.

Both *Raining Backwards* and *Holy Radishes!* challenge idealized notions of community through Fernández's humorous and at times mordant satirical style. These novels depict tensions between the characters' idealized past in Cuba and their bleak present as immigrants in the United States. Issues of racism and prejudice and the clash in values between Cuban and American cultures are also a central part of the world of these novels. Both works present characters who live in a chaotic world in which family members lack awareness and sensitivity toward each other and where each individual is trapped by his or her own ignorance. By constructing a fictional universe in which his characters appear as victims of historical events beyond their control, Fernández traces a parodic but also tragic biography of the Cuban community during the first wave of migration following 1959. Both *Raining Backwards* and *Holy Radishes!* seem to hold the view that connections to the group are not yet possible.

In *Raining Backwards,* a work that has received extensive critical attention,[5] the author's main focus is on the community of his parents, the first generation of exiles who came from Cuba during the early 1960s. Here the idea of community functions only in name, for the author is preoccupied with outlining the tensions between the older exiles and their children within the space of the United States. Fernández's characters—adults and adolescents—seem to be caught in a hostile environment, one that they do not understand or try to analyze. Because of the parallels in themes, many of the episodes in the novel become a critique of one another. These are stories that tell about isolated individuals who are at the mercy of events beyond their control and who in some cases are destroyed by themselves or by others. The novel develops in a cyclical manner, offering us vignettes in which the main characters and a supporting cast appear, disappear, and reappear. As the chapters develop, new information and different perspectives are reported to the reader.[6] The remarkable number of stories and the sad tales told to the reader constitute a metaphor for the cultural malaise of Cuban exiles.

An especially vulnerable character in the world of *Raining Backwards* is Mima Rodríguez, the entrepreneur who eventually succeeds with her plantain chips business, but who sacrifices her children to the corruption of the new society. Two of Mima's children, Connie and Keith Rodríguez, represent the children of exile, the first Cuban Americans, a generation that lives with the contradictions of straddling two cultures and two languages. Keith Rodríguez becomes involved in drug trafficking and ends up in jail. His sister, Connie, is trapped between her two cultures, has a torrid affair with the American captain of the football team, and winds up murdered by him. Mima's third child, Quinn, has the least tragic fate as he becomes a dubious religious leader for the Cuban community in exile. The grotesque stories of these Cuban-American children illustrate how difficult communication becomes between the various generations of immigrants and how the values of the native culture become obsolete for the children growing up in the adopted country.

Raining Backwards also presents in a laconic manner many sordid events without providing solutions to the dilemmas it poses, thus manifesting Fernández's desire to portray instances of friction between the two communities. In telling the stories of Keith and Connie, Fernández adopts a distant and almost indifferent narrative perspective, suggesting that their failures within American society were unavoidable. As the unhappy and confused Cuban American, Connie is a strong presence in the text. Her poems and letters to her brother Keith denote extreme loneliness as she straddles the world of her American high school and her mother's Cuban world. Keith is no better off, for it seems that life in exile has meant a different set of problems, ranging from troubles with the law to his fatal involvement with drugs. Fernández sees the members of his generation as caught between two cultural worlds that they do not fully understand and to which they do not fully belong. In keeping with the detached narrative perspective of satire, the novel refuses to theorize on the hostile reaction of the dominant members of the community toward the newly arrived exiles.

The Olsen family, who also appear in the author's most recent novel, *Holy Radishes!* represents the hostile "American other." Mr. Olsen is a bigoted, prejudiced man who finds it amusing to shoot at Cubans if they get anywhere near his property. Through the humorous yet sordid episodes of the Olsens, Fernández presents the open hostility of some members of the Anglo community of South Florida toward what they saw as the "Cuban invasion."[7] The presence of the episodes related to the "Tongue Brigade" denotes the author's own preoccupation with what was happening in Florida in the late 1980s as the "English only" laws were being hotly debated in that state. There was a clear threat to the survival of any non-English culture in southern Florida: "Do you realize my brother lost his job because he doesn't spica the spañol? In our own country and we're fired for not speaking spic. . . . Yes. The season is open. We're going to purify this land of dregs. You fucking Cubans!"[8] The satirical and sad episodes of *Raining Backwards* masterfully exemplify the differences between the children of exile and their parents. In an interview with critic Wolfgang Binder, Fernández expresses his own interpretation of the situation: "One thing is to welcome a few refugees, another is when the refugees take over. One says, hey, how can we get back at these people?" (Binder 110).

If Cuba is viewed by the second generation as a place that reminds them of their differences, the Cubans from Miami also become a world of the past, a world that admits only one political view and a single perspective of the Cuban tragedy. The episodes of Mirta Vergara demonstrate that, even though these immigrants have lived in Miami for more than three decades, their thoughts and memories are still very much rooted in the past. In fact, Mirta Vergara becomes the personification of a mentality that sought to preserve and reinvent Cuba in exile. On the other hand, her young boyfriend, Eloy, representing the second generation, cannot remember simply because he was too small to gather up any memories of the Cuba of his parents.

Mirta is engaged in seducing adolescent Eloy: "I pay him with memories. It's the best way to fight forgetting" (37). Mirta's memories of Varadero as an enchanted beach keep Eloy interested in coming back to see her: "In all the beaches in Cuba, the sand was made out of grated silver, though in Varadero it was also mixed with diamond dust" (12–13). Eloy's curiosity for Mirta's fabrications stem from his own need to keep his parents' memories alive. With these episodes, Fernández reminds us that the first generation's nostalgia for their lost Cuban world was indeed responsible for the Miami Cubans' unwillingness to adapt and confront their American present.[9]

Raining Backwards is a novel that demands a reader who can understand both English and Cuban Spanish. For instance, in the segment entitled "The Southern Pearl" (31–35), the author creates a parody of Cuban newspaper society columns and Cuban restaurant menus. The columns and the menus are in English, but they remain obscure to a monolingual reader since the humor originates in the assumption that a reader also knows the Spanish version of these items. Witness his parodic version of a menu featuring seafood dishes known to all who speak Spanish:

Shrimp at the little garlic.
Saw at the oven.
Chern at the iron.
Flour with Moorish crabs.
Seafood sprinkle.
Pulp in its own ink. (35)

These dishes, translated literally from their original Spanish, make absolute sense to the bilingual reader but lose all logical meaning for a reader who knows only English. Although Fernández writes in English, the audience preferred and perhaps intended for *Raining Backwards* seems to be readers who also know Spanish and who share with the author the experience of living between two cultures. Bilingual readers of *Raining Backwards* can enjoy the book at a different level than Anglo readers.

The cultural and literary strategy of using two languages simultaneously within a literary text has been referred to as *interlingualism* by critics of other bicultural literatures such as Chicano fiction. Interlingualism, according to Marta Sánchez, requires the reader to move from one language to another: "In an interlingual experience, the tensions in syntax, the connotations, the ironies, and the reverberations of words and images interlock, pulling in two directions at once."[10] Narratives written interlingually engage rival sets of reader expectations as they graphically enact on the surface of the page the conflicts and tensions between English-speaking and Spanish-speaking audiences. Fernández's particular use of English in *Raining Backwards* is at times interlingual, as this literary strategy serves as a metaphor for the divisions and separations between the Anglo and the Cuban exile communities.

According to critic Mary Vázquez, even if English is the language in which the book is written, native speakers of English who do not know Spanish will read things in English they cannot understand:

> the over-literal renderings of Spanish expressions into English become markers of cultural alienation and conflicting cultural values. . . . If the reader is a bilingual Hispanic comfortable in both Spanish and English, a distance is established between character and reader, with a measure of superiority perhaps accorded the bilingual reader. . . . For such a reader, both encoding and decoding of the message are shared. . . . If on the other hand, we are majority readers who do not know Spanish, the humor born of difference and surprise will remain, but that comedy based upon linguistic interchange is closed to us.[11]

Fernández's decision to write in English seems to want to create even further distance between *Raining Backwards* and the monolingual Anglo reader, as the author's coding and decoding of the novel's message becomes his own way to rebel against the language of the dominant culture.

An exception to Fernández's desolate episodes of the Cuban community in Miami appears in the vignette titled "Raining Backwards." Narrated by a young Cuban American named Miqui, the vignette tells of how Miqui's Cuban grandmother insisted on returning to Cuba in order to be buried with her family in Cuban soil. The grandmother is not afraid of dying, but she is terrified of dying in a country where technology reigns, a country that might not allow her to be buried next to her kin: "Once they get you, they plug you in and you just cannot die. Besides, I no want to be bury in this country. I will be the first one here and who knows where the next one will be, dead and all alone! The whole world gets scatter in America, even dead people" (142).

For the Cuban elderly, the idea of community is defined by conflict and sadness and becomes important not in life but in death. Here Fernández portrays with compassion the plight of the older refugees who, sensing their impending demise, only wish to return to their native land to be reunited with their loved ones. It is precisely their yearning for an absent community that allows these characters to become effective participants of their novelistic world. In *Raining Backwards,* the hope for the characters, young and old, resides not in how they live but in what they are able to imagine.

Roberto Fernández's *Holy Radishes!* (1995)

"We always want to forget something, so we create stories," says Delfina, the faithful servant in Roberto Fernández's most recent novel, *Holy Radishes!*[12] The story reaches back to Cuba's past as well as to the American present, depicting how the older exiles reacted to the trauma of displacement from Xawa, Cuba, to Belle Glade, Florida. Similar to the characters of *Raining Backwards,* those in *Holy Radishes!* also live by their imaginations, for they constantly fabricate stories in order to escape their cheerless present in their adopted land.

Holy Radishes! is a most successful fiction at the level of plot while simultaneously providing a comment about the ability and power of the human imagination in helping people cope with oppressive issues related to their conditions as immigrants in a new culture. Indeed, Fernández's novel is a deeply psychological expression of how individuals cope with extreme situations in their daily lives. Set during the early years of the Castro revolution and based on the author's family experiences of exile, the novel takes place in two places: the small town of Sagua la Grande, Cuba, and the rural community of Belle Glade, Florida. By offering us a mosaic of episodes both in Cuba and in the United States, Fernández produces a collective picture of a particular group of immigrants at a pivotal stage of their transition to a new environment. In so doing, the episodes transcend issues of ethnicity as they also speak to the reader's humanity.

Holy Radishes! narrates the fate of a group of *sagüeros* (in the text Fernández playfully uses the spelling *Xawa* instead of *Sagua*) as they tell the story of their community in Cuba and what became of it when many of its members settled in the small American town of Belle Glade. The structure of the novel is composed of a series of loosely connected episodes featuring four main characters: Nellie Pardo, Nelson Guiristain (Nellie's husband), Bernabé (Nelson's cousin), and Mrs. James B. Olsen. All the characters in the novel share a basic dislike of their present lives (be it in Cuba or in America) and are somehow involved in the process of reinventing a new life for themselves. The alternation of Sagua and Belle Glade as locations within the novel makes the two towns distorted mirror images of one another as sordidness and corruption become evident in both places.

The basic story of *Holy Radishes!* follows the misfortunes of Nellie
Pardo and her husband, Nelson, as they undergo the painful experience
of leaving their small town in Cuba. As members of the upper class, Nellie and Nelson's families suffer all kinds of humiliations when the Castro
rebels become the town managers and power mongers of the new society. Andrés Pardo, Nellie's father, dies in prison for having destroyed
his newly confiscated property. Nellie is taunted by the rebels as she tries
to visit her father in prison and is raped by one rebel before she is actually allowed to defect. Finally, Nelson is also harassed and humiliated before leaving the island. In narrating all these episodes, the author depicts
accurately the atmosphere of tension and the desire for reprisal that typ-
ically follow revolutions.

Undignified moments abound in the text as parody becomes Fernández's own way of coping with the somber reality he describes. Moreover,
the author's criticism does not spare the "xagüeros," as Fernández is
equally able to mock the pretense and grandiosity of old Cuban society
from small towns such as Xawa as well as the closed and xenophobic atmosphere of American small towns such as Belle Glade. In Xawa, Andrés Pardo seduces his women servants and uses his wealth and influence
in order to bribe others. Mr. Conway and other rich foreigners who
were part of Xawa's upper crust are portrayed as reckless and ambi-
tious, with very little interest in the welfare of the Cubans. Yet, if life after the revolution was untenable in Xawa, life in the United States offered these exiles a different set of problems.

In *Holy Radishes!* Fernández presents us with an immigrant community that is far from the assimilationist ideal of the American Dream.
In Belle Glade, the Cubans endure humiliation and prejudice as they are
attacked for being Catholics, for having a Spanish accent, and finally
"for taking away the jobs of others" (255). The women (rich, poor, and
middle class) all become workers in a radish packinghouse, where they
have to endure the abuses and prejudices of management as well as de-
plorable working conditions.

In Belle Glade, the ladies from the Xawa Tennis Club become the
ladies of the radish packinghouse, and the canasta parties they now hold
in Belle Glade become caricatures of the parties they held in Cuba. The
radish packinghouse episodes, according to the author, were based on
his own mother's working experiences when the family arrived in Belle
Glade in the early 1960s: "Then she went to work for a year or so in a
packing house. Radishes. And it was fine because all the Cuban bour-
geoisie was there, and they would work, picking the radishes from the

conveyor belt, and their hands would burn because of the Clorox. But they would work with all their jewelry and their bracelets on. They worked next to the rednecks and other people, but always with a sense of class."[13] Like the characters in *Raining Backwards,* the female characters in *Holy Radishes!* escape from their gloomy present by constantly fabricating and embellishing past events from their days in Cuba.

The reader encounters Nellie as a laconic, humble, and sometimes evasive woman who prefers to spend most her waking hours thinking of a mythical community (Mondovi) and a preferred companion (a pig named Rigoletto). The story portrays episodes of Nellie as an adult in Xawa trying to escape the country and suffering innumerable vexations from the revolutionaries who have taken over her town. Once in Belle Glade, memories of her beloved Mondovi and her pig friend Rigoletto, left behind in Cuba and eaten due to food scarcities, become Nellie's respite from her world of radishes. Yet things are not any better in the new country; in fact, they are worse. Nellie does not speak the language and hardly interacts with anyone in her new community. Her memories and her picture albums from Xawa sustain her, but even more importantly her cherished town of Mondovi and her piglet left in Cuba become a way of escaping the dire situation at home and the dismal working conditions at the radish factory. Hoping for a different reality, Nellie is always daydreaming of her idyllic town, Mondovi, in which "she was meant to be born."

Even if Nellie's exiled condition gives her reason for wanting to escape, Fernández broadens the exile context of his narrative by attributing psychological reasons to Nellie's unhappiness. For instance, the episodes that relate to Nellie's infancy tell us that her alienation and loneliness were present *before* she suffered the upheaval of displacement and were caused by upsetting events in her early life. In the segment entitled "Blue Moon," the reader learns how the traumatic loss of her mother during adolescence had been very difficult for the young girl. Rigoletto the pig becomes the girl's safe haven, a symbolic link to the mother whom she had lost and who had always been fond of piglets.

Nellie's best friend, Mrs. B. Olsen, an American native, shares with her an unhappy past and a deep desire to overcome the oppressive Belle Glade present. If for Nellie life at home was an indifferent husband who did not love her, Mrs. B. Olsen's situation was even more frightening since her alcoholic husband had made her a battered wife. Nellie becomes an inspiration for Mrs. B., who seeks to emulate Nellie's exotic ways of evading her everyday life. So much do these women have in common that Mrs. Olsen begins to invent a past for herself in order to compete with Nellie's picture albums from Cuba. Buying old pictures from the local pawn shop, Mrs. B. decides to create for herself an imaginary family, one that could provide her the same happiness Nellie experienced: "Mrs. James B. continued digging in the pile, at times feeling like an archaeologist. When she was finished, she had bought enough pictures to have a three-generational family, including a couple of very recent snap-shots of two children, a girl and a boy. The boy was dressed as a cadet. The girl, in a hoop-skirt and carrying a small parasol, was standing near the front entrance of a finishing school for young belles" (202). Nellie and Mrs. B. Olsen share family pictures with one another and together fabricate an ideal past through the memories evoked by these pictures. Their unhappiness becomes a source of closeness for the two women because they have in common both the dire working conditions at the packinghouse and male partners who are abusive to them. The two women are the victims not merely of an oppressive culture (in this case both Cuban and American cultures are viewed as oppressive) but also of their own husbands. Toward the end of the story, Nellie and Mrs. B. find the courage to leave Belle Glade as they set sail on their journey toward an ideal Mondovi.

Drawn with greater complexity than the other characters in the text, Nellie and Nelson display alienation and despair that can be attributed to a combination of psychological and political factors. Nelson's unhappiness, like Nellie's, is not rooted exclusively in his loss of a secure life in Cuba. In fact, for Nelson, the events surrounding the exodus become a kind of liberation from the pressure of succession of a family business he resented and did not want. Disposing with the family's fortune by throwing a suitcase filled with their assets into the ocean, Nelson demonstrates that he prefers the poverty of exile to the idea of remaining under the rigid grid of the family empire. Moreover, Nelson's fixation with "the Squirrel," a gum-chewing prostitute he met in Cuba, provides an outlet for this character not unlike Nellie's musings of Mondovi, as it reveals Nelson's own need for escaping his loveless marriage.

The story of another character, Bernabé, is a picaresque tale of greed and deceit that involves the invention of a past in the name of material gain: "This is America. Everything is prefabricated, even the past" (194), says Bernabé in order to explain why he invented for himself a Jewish identity. Bernabé lies, cheats, and steals in order to eventually gain access to old Stanley's savings from his pawn shop business. This *pícaro* eventually pays for his cruelty and greed when he finds out that

Stanley's fortune was limited to an old yellow picture of his deceased wife. Both Bernabé and his cousin Nelson are characters moved by their passions. Because of their dishonesty toward others, these men illustrate less than exemplary ways of overcoming their joyless American present.

Written in the same satirical vein as *Raining Backwards, Holy Radishes!* is critical of Fernández's own community and offers us an account that is humorous and grotesque at times. The Cuba of the past was no utopia, and at times the author's portrait of Xawa's upper classes clearly places responsibility on the Cubans themselves. At any rate, life in the United States is also presented as an unacceptable alternative for first-generation exiles who cannot be fully accepted into a society that is not theirs. At the story's conclusion, Nellie and Mrs. B. are able to escape and make Mondovi a reality, while Nelson and Bernabé learn a lesson when their schemes and false solutions backfire and eventually fail. A diasporic tale thus becomes a tale of greed, lust, and victimization. For the protagonists of *Holy Radishes!* a place in their ethnic communities is tangled by conflicting meanings of family and compounded by the hostility of the dominant American culture.

If the American Dream involves leaving the old country and reinventing a new story for yourself, the characters in *Holy Radishes!* enact a subversion of that dream. In both *Raining Backwards* and *Holy Radishes!* Fernández does not propose the possibility of harmony and trust between the first generation of exiles and the dominant U.S. majority. Rather, the author pictures a system that recognizes ethnic tensions and mutual distrust, a system of complexity and conflict. Throughout these narratives, the author maintains implicitly that community can come only from the recognition of difference. For Fernández, the future of the Cuban community in the United States can progress only by ongoing negotiations between Cuban and American communities since each has something the other needs in order to survive.

7 Gay and Lesbian Images
of Community

The art of memory recalls us not to the life we have lost, but to the
life we have yet to live.

Paul J. Eakin, *Touching the World*

THE NOVELS of Joaquín Fraxedas and Roberto Fernández
have shown contrasting perspectives and attitudes toward the concept of
community. These novels have presented visions of community that stem
from the varied spaces in which Cubans have chosen to live and interact.
Among these dispersed U.S. Cuban communities, gay and lesbian authors have also created their own stories of survival. The novels selected
in this chapter expound the complex relationship between the authors'
homosexual identities and their Cuban-American ethnic group. Does
Cuban-American gay and lesbian literature have something different to
say about the experience of being Cuban in North America? How does
being a homosexual interact with other factors of identity such as ethnicity and culture?[1]

Cuban-American gay and lesbian authors bring out ideas that are intimately bound to issues of ethnicity and the histories of their communities. Their accounts are significant because they dramatize the intersection of their sexual and cultural identities. These stories encompass
both the story of the diaspora and the stories of their gay and lesbian
selves since the possibility of being more than one self is real for these
authors.[2]

Both Achy Obejas and Elías Miguel Muñoz produce fictions in which
issues of sexual preference serve to unsettle rather than define identity.
Their novels narrate the trials and tribulations involved in growing up
gay or lesbian as well as Cuban. Because narratives of diaspora are
usually about crossings, it follows that many of the tensions felt by the
ethnic writer parallel in many ways the need of the gay and lesbian
writer to assert one type of identity over another. The story of exodus
appears in Muñoz's gay novels as an experience shared by male and fe-

male narrators who also recall the harshness of living within Cuban families that did not accept their sexuality. Obejas's lesbian protagonists, on the contrary, find safety and security in family and dramatize issues of the Cuban-American community as it interacts with other Latino communities in Chicago. These novels acknowledge the political and psychological importance of family and ethnicity within the gay context.

The fictions analyzed here, written by authors born within a year of each other (Obejas in 1953, Muñoz in 1954), would be expected to present similar concerns. Although the narratives do share the common ground of exile, these fictions represent surprisingly distinct perspectives of sexuality and ethnicity. Unlike Muñoz, Achy Obejas does not dwell in her Cuban past. In fact, her short stories and her most recent novel, *Memory Mambo* (1996), take place exclusively in the United States. Community, for Obejas, is a complex web of family histories, sexual preference, and Latino politics. Muñoz's narrative, on the other hand, begins in Cuba and concentrates on issues of homophobia in Cuban and Cuban-American families. Together, these narratives present different perspectives of how gays and lesbians live and cope within their Cuban-American communities.

Elías Miguel Muñoz's *The Greatest Performance* (1991)

Elías Miguel Muñoz was born in Cuba in 1954 and emigrated to the United States when he was fourteen years old. Like many of his peers from the one-and-a-half generation, he published his earlier narratives and poems in Spanish. In 1984, he published *Los viajes de Orlando Cachumbanbé* (The travels of Orlando Cachumbanbé), a novel that featured a protagonist who experienced a life divided between his Cuban and American selves. Like the *cachumbanbé* (seesaw) in his last name, Orlando is a conflictive and unhappy character who constantly wishes for balance in a life split between the demands of the Cuban and the American communities. In 1988, Muñoz published a bioliterary monograph, *Desde esta orilla* (From this shore), in which he examines the poetry of the one-and-a-half generation and comments on its nature and character. This critical but also personal essay, like his previous novel, expresses Muñoz's need for self-definition and his desire to have his literary work be recognized along with the writings of other U.S. Hispanics of Cuban origin. In 1989, the author also published *Crazy Love,* his first novel written in English. Both Muñoz's poetry and narratives elaborate on the dilemmas of a life divided between competing cultural identities.

Crazy Love (which is the title of a popular song from the late 1950s) is the story of Julian Toledo, a Cuban-American performer trying to cross over into the U.S. musical establishment. The challenge for this character is to position himself between the two cultures without giving up either. Julian is torn between two worlds that simultaneously make demands on him: his Cuban family (especially his oppressive grand-mother) and the American musical world in which he is trying to find a place. Julian realizes that if he is to forge his dream of success in America, he must live like an American and must resist the stifling demands of his Cuban family. The split between the Cuban and American worlds is also of a sexual nature since when Julian decides to create the kind of music that would satisfy the American market, he also gives up his gay relationship with Lucho, his Cuban partner. At the end of the novel, an unhappy Julian marries an American woman who will help him succeed in the U.S. musical world.

Muñoz's first novel in English rehearses many of the themes that appear later in *The Greatest Performance*. Commenting on *Crazy Love*, Muñoz indicates its importance in his trajectory as a writer: "I wanted to write about someone who would be forced to adopt another language, tempted by a Crossover Dream. Someone who would dare explore a way of being that wasn't his. . . . I was going to play the game by giving my protagonist a multiple ambiguity: sexual, ethnic, linguistic, and artistic."[3]

Although many of the themes found in *Crazy Love* appear in *The Greatest Performance*, the mood of the two works is drastically different. If the Cuban family and the demands of Cuban culture on the individual were viewed as stifling to the central character in *Crazy Love*, in *The Greatest Performance* the influence of family on the characters is even more damaging because it directly impacts on the characters' right to express their homosexual selves. In contrast to the festive tone and childish optimism in *Crazy Love*, the author's perspective in *The Greatest Performance* seems to have acquired a more somber mood. Images of death and sadness prevail in Muñoz's second novel. These images are not only literal (one of the main characters dies, a victim of the AIDS virus) but also represent a spiritual death for the central characters, young adolescents who are rejected by their families because of their sexual preference.

In "Political and Cultural Cross-Dressing," Flavio Risech explains the difficulties that Cuban-American homosexuals encounter in confronting the political complexities of their communities in exile. For the Cuban-

American gays of the second generation, community is a political and cultural cross-dressing act, a game that demands a variety of stances depending on the space in which the community is located. According to Risech, the intolerance of the Cuban community toward homosexuality creates identity problems for its gay members: "Each time we cross these boundaries . . . we must in an important sense 'cross-dress,' making coded decisions as to how to present ourselves, about what part of our identities to wear proudly or keep closeted" (527). Sharing with the reader his personal experience, Risech relates the rejection he has faced from family both in Cuba and in exile. Gay and lesbian Cubans, Risech adds, have to confront the discrimination and homophobia that prevail in their culture: "Hatred of homosexuality, whether dressed as Cuban *mariconería* or as American style queerness, pervades the Cuban communities on both sides of the Straits of Florida" (537). Risech concludes that, for himself, stepping outside the Cuban exile communities was all that he could do since he felt his sexuality and politics were better tolerated by the adopted culture.

The issue of homophobia is examined in *The Greatest Performance* as the story focuses on the ingrained *machismo* and community intolerance that have prevailed in Cuban culture both on the island and in exile. A poetic story of a close friendship between a gay and a lesbian protagonist, the narrative captures central moments in the lives of its characters: their sexual awakening and their exodus from Cuba. Because these sexual and cultural experiences come at a pivotal time in the maturation of the protagonists (that is, during their transition between childhood and adulthood), this novel invites a consideration of how sexuality and culture affect the manner in which the characters view themselves.

The novel is composed of fragments that deal mostly with the first-person memories of the narrators' childhood and early adulthood. Marito and Rosita tell their life stories in alternating chapters, and although their gay stories of diaspora are different, their memories merge in their sadness. These are the voices of Cuban preadolescents who recall discovering their homosexual selves during their childhood in Cuba. The stories of these children also recall with grief the homophobia of their families and peers both in Cuba and in the United States. Later, as young adults in the new country, these narrators also share with the reader their feelings of increased marginalization due to racial discrimination against them as Hispanics in Anglo America.

Rosita's memories begin in Guantánamo, Cuba. There is little idealization of her Cuban past as she describes her unhappy family as "stereotypical of Cuban culture: macho father, puppet mother."[4] It is in Cuba that Rosita discovers her lesbian sexuality and begins to suffer because of it. Her childhood friend, a boy who very much resembles the Marito she later meets in the United States, provides the emotional support Rosita badly needs. She tells Marito: "My father has forbidden me to hang out with you because you're obvious, Marito. . . . *Pájaro*. Bird. One of the words Cubans used in those days (still today?) to denigrate a gay man. What were some of the other ones? Ah yes, Duck, Butterfly, Inverted One, Sick One, Broken One, Little Mary, Addict, Pervert" (16).

During the mid 1960s, Rosita is sent to Spain by parents who feared for her safety and that of her younger brother under Castro's communist regime. Life in Madrid is hard for Rosa and her brother. Left in the care of distant relatives, Rosa is raped by an uncle in Madrid. This is a time of loneliness and resentment against her parents for deciding her fate without her consent. The pain and isolation are attested by the imaginary letters Rosita sends to Cuba: "This separation is becoming unbearable for us. We hate being alone and helpless. Why did you send us here?" (61). Eventually Rosita and her brother make it to the United States and are able to join their exiled parents in California.

Life in America presents a different set of obstacles for Rosita, who finds adaptation to the new land a struggle. Her affair with an American woman named Joan serves to bring out issues of cultural difference that eventually sour the relationship. Rosita describes her life with Joan and her search for assimilation into American culture as demanding that she erase her Cuban self: "Do you see her in the kitchen? She's really an average girl, this Rosita from Guantánamo. She never gets depressed. She doesn't ask existential questions, has no tormenting conflicts. . . . She thinks of herself as a renegade hedonist. She laughs at her family, she says they are a dying race, a soon-to-be-extinct species. She's playful and brutal, proudly and gladly unpatriotic" (117).

It is during this period of spiritual emptiness that Rosita meets Marito. His friendship and support allow Rosita to better understand and accept both her ethnic and sexual selves, and through Marito's acquaintance a more authentic way of living is possible for her. In fact, the only available respite to the sadness in Rosita's life is found in the friendship she has found with Marito: "After searching Heaven and Earth for a true love, for a generous homeland, for a family . . . who wouldn't betray our truest secrets, we found each other: A refuge, a song, a story to share" (149).

Marito's story is the more distressing of the two, for it describes memories of sexual prejudice and physical violence in graphic detail. The boy's story of exodus, like Rosa's, coincides with his sexual awakening. Marito's early sexual experiences in Cuba are traumatic and include being molested as a young child. Like Rosa, Marito suffers rejection from family and classmates in both Cuba and America. His father is a brutal figure who verbally and physically abuses the boy for the sole reason of his being gay. Memories of fatherly violence and rejection abound for the narrator: "The bean soup burns my tongue, I blow on it. Pipo tells me to stop and to eat it. 'It's not that hot,' he says. . . . He pulls the tablecloth and my soup spills. He throws a piece of bread at me. He pinches the inside of my thighs, hits my chest. He grabs me by the hair and pokes my stomach with his fingers. 'Men don't sit that way, shit!' he yells" (35). The rejection Marito suffers from his father deeply affects the child. The father's *machismo* and cruelty are ingrained in the memories of Marito, who, as a young adult, repeatedly shares his need for fatherly love with his friend Rosita.

In the United States, Marito seems to be just as unhappy. The Cuban community in general is seen as unfriendly (81–83); the other Latino homosexuals, especially Marito's Puerto Rican lover, do not appear to understand or care about the Cuban political story or the reasons for the narrator's exile (99). After leading a hedonistic life of multiple affairs, all equally disappointing, Marito realizes he has become infected with the AIDS virus. The novel's final chapter merges the voices of the two narrators in a dramatic dialogue that goes back to the past and serves to explain much of the pain in the life of the protagonists. Rosita and Marito are able to "perform" one more time, imagining a life that they never experienced but always wished for: "We were made in test tubes and we were able to choose, as adults, the identity and gender that we fancied. Then we were free, until the moment of our deaths (painless deaths) to change from man to woman, from woman to man, from tree to flower, from ocean water to ivy. Better yet we have existed from time immemorial as air" (150).

For Muñoz, the community of other homosexuals who are also Cuban provides the nurturing and affiliation that are vital to the survival of the group. Assimilation from Cuba to America becomes a context that echoes the sadness springing from the central issue of discrimination against gays and lesbians. *The Greatest Performance* presents Cuban and American life as a cruel farce imposed by parents and by a hostile society unaccepting of alternative lifestyles. As children, the narrators have their spirit broken by their parents' brutality and lack of approval; as adults, these narrators lead unhappy lives because they always have to hide their sexual selves, a problem compounded by the trauma of displacement. The book's ironic title is thus indicative of the lives of the protagonists: during childhood they are forced to seek evasion from prejudice and peer rejection in playful theater, in childhood "performance." This playful masking, however becomes a cruel way of life in adulthood since a more meaningful life is not possible for these characters. Sadly, for Muñoz's narrators, their lives as Cuban-American gays and lesbians are represented in this novel as a kind of punishment, only to be alleviated by death: "When the performance ends. And life begins" (151).

Achy Obejas's *We Came All the Way from Cuba So You Could Dress like This?* (1994)

Achy Obejas's fictions take up issues of lesbian identity in the context of the Cuban-American community in which the author herself grew up. Born in Cuba in 1953, Obejas came to the United States by boat as an exile when she was six years old, almost ten years before Elías Miguel Muñoz arrived. Obejas is a published fiction writer, journalist, and poet who currently works as a writer for the *Chicago Tribune*. In 1994, she published a collection of lesbian short stories under the title *We Came All the Way from Cuba So You Could Dress like This?* Two years later, Obejas published her first novel, *Memory Mambo* (1996). Both works indicate that for this author there is a need to confront the essential nature of an individual's sexuality as well as the controversial reality of the politics of being Cuban and lesbian in America.

Unlike Muñoz's novels, which take place both in Cuba and in the United States, Achy Obejas's fictions bypass the protagonists' childhood in Cuba and concentrate on the effects and consequences of displacement once the characters arrive in the United States. In both her short stories and in her recent novel, Obejas's view of her narrators' displacement is tinged with the protagonists' desire to assert their homosexual identities. In fact, the Cuban memories of Obejas's characters seem to be there as a point of departure for other issues of sexuality needing to be examined. For Obejas, the Cuban story of diaspora becomes a context that sometimes functions in a freeing manner for the protagonists, as the contact with the more liberal outlook of American culture is seen as a positive step in the construction of homosexual identities and communities.

In her short story anthology, *We Came All the Way from Cuba,* Achy Obejas collects seven narratives about lesbian and gay Latinos who have in common the experience of being uprooted. While in all the stories Obejas delves into her own memories of exile, one in particular takes up the theme of the Cuban exodus, linking it to issues of sexual identity. "We Came All the Way from Cuba So You Could Dress like This?" the title story, is a first-person account of a young lesbian girl's memories of exodus.[5] The story is a political statement of gender rights that connects the central character's past to her present but that does not remain nostalgic or even melancholic about what was left in Cuba. The narrative moves forward in time as it also tells a tale of growing to maturity and sexual awakening in a new culture. In so doing, it speaks of the first-person narrator's radicalization and of her breaking away from her Cuban parents' conservative politics as well as her coming to terms with her lesbian sexuality.

As is the case with the rest of the stories in this collection, the narrative is elliptical, packing many details and situations in a short prose span. In between the initial and final scenes describing her family's arrival thirty years ago, current events in the life of the protagonist are intermingled with the girl's Cuban past. It is precisely the reader's experience of witnessing both the present and the past of the narrative that adds significance to what is being read and renders poignancy as well as pathos to the events related. The content of the memoirs is then the interplay of past and present as the author makes the most of a narrative perspective that allows the reader to evaluate past events in terms of the present of the teller.

The narrative describes two central cores of action: the moment of crisis encapsulated in the unnamed female narrator's first day in the United States at the Key West immigration center when the protagonist was ten years old, and the future of the mature narrator in America as she becomes aware of her lesbian sexuality. The initial episode at the immigration center relates the earliest reaction of mother and daughter to their new status as poor immigrants. Obejas describes events in the processing center for refugees in Key West immediately following the girl's 1963 arrival by boat: the doll she held in her hand, the sweater she wore on the boat, the domineering Hungarian woman who took care of the processing of their documents. The trauma of arrival and the family's numbness before their own life-risking experience blend together with the narrator's remembrances of their first night in the country in a rundown motel in Key West.

The girl's first impressions as an immigrant are brilliantly captured in a scene where the narrator relates how the "the fat Hungarian lady with the perpetual smile" took them to a supermarket during their first hours after arrival. The narrator and her parents are "tired and bereft" but somehow go along with the schedule as planned: "The fat Hungarian lady pats [the father's] shoulder and says to the gathering crowd, Yes, he came on a little boat with his whole family; look at his beautiful daughter who will now grow up well-fed and free. . . . All around us people stare, but then my father says, 'We just arrived from Cuba, and there's so much here'" (123). By counterpointing the sordid events in her personal life with these painful details, the immigrant girl confronts the myth of the happy immigrant and America as the land of equality.

The unnamed girl's narrative stance is matter of fact, almost indifferent, and evokes a sense of inevitability and helplessness for the reader. In fact, she reminds the reader that not all is known about her story since "there are things that can't be told":

> Things like when we couldn't find an apartment, everyone's saying it was because landlords in Miami didn't rent to families with kids, but knowing, always, that it was more than that. . . . Things like a North American hairdresser's telling my mother she didn't do her kind of hair. . . . Like my father, finally realizing he wasn't going to go back to Cuba anytime soon, trying to hang himself with the light cord in the bathroom . . . but falling instead and breaking his arm while my mother cleaned rooms at a nearby luxury hotel. . . . Things like my doing very poorly on an IQ test because I didn't speak English, and getting tossed into a special education track, where it took until high school before somebody realized I didn't belong there. (123–24)

The father's dictum that "we came for her so that she could have a future" becomes ironic as the reader perceives that the future is not always happy and certainly not very ideal. Later, in a scene of physical violence between the girl and her father, the narrator challenges the notion that her father crossed the ocean "for her."

The present (and sometimes future) of the narration is more complicated because it relates how the narrator reaches maturity in the United States and how she learns to challenge the politics and life of the parents who brought her to the new country. It is the narrator's adoption of the radical ideals of the late 1960s that prompts her own father to ask the question leading to the title of the story: "We left Cuba so you could dress like this?" (121). The question is central to the meaning of this narrative, for it suggests the conflict between the girl's generation and that of her parents and introduces issues of difference between Cuban and American codes of behavior.

The author's strategies of fragmentation and play with temporal structures are tied to Obejas's own struggle of personal survival as a Cuban-American woman and also as a lesbian. In fact, the story uses the material experience of the construction of sexuality to add to the girl's diasporic memories. The protagonist's greatest challenge to the conservatism of her parents is thus connected to her own adolescent realization of her homosexuality.

In an episode that tells of a lesbian encounter between the narrator and one of her lovers, issues of sexual and political freedom seem to be one and the same: "The next morning, listening to her breathing in my arms, I will wonder how this could have happened, and if it would have happened at all if we'd stayed in Cuba. And if so, if it would have been furtive or free, with or without the Revolution" (126). Interpolating episodes that reflect the character's awakening and awareness of her lesbian identity, Obejas poses questions regarding sexual intolerance in Cuba and whether a gay life under communism would have ever been possible.

By using open-ended questions to preface some of the very personal details of her 1963 exodus from Cuba, Obejas's narrator renders her account a human dimension extending beyond her personal story. In addition, the narrative's moving questions structure a short but powerful tale that explores history, politics, and family relationships. The story's effectiveness has mainly to do with Obejas's expert handling of temporal structures and the impersonal, almost laconic manner in which the female narrator relates her personal tragedy to the reader. The story ends inconclusively as the young girl acknowledges the facts of her displacement: "I know we've already come a long way. What none of us can measure yet is how much of the voyage is already behind us" (131). Obejas's representation of displacement from her native Cuba is a loss that is mourned but quickly transcended.

Achy Obejas's *Memory Mambo* (1996)

Memory Mambo, Obejas's first full-length novel, reproduces a rhythm that is both Cuban and American, a life of a community marked by immigration and exile. In this novel, the protagonist's self is defined by the expectations that her family and the other women in her community have of her. Juani, the fictional "I" of this narrative, is a twenty-four-year-old lesbian who defines herself through a web of women: blood cousins but also female "cousins in exile": "I know a lot of people think cousins in exile are really random relationships, links forged out of loneliness and desperation. And that's kind of true, I admit, but there's more: We have an affinity, a way of speaking that's neither Cuban nor American, neither genetic or processed. There's a look, a wink, the way we touch each other. We communicate, I suspect, like deaf people—not so much compensating for the lost sense, but creating a new syntax from the pieces of our displaced lives."[6] Family and community are inextricably linked in this novel since community here happens to be family, too.

Memory Mambo is a narrative of maturation and growth in which the first-person narrator seeks self-understanding and appears to have gained some by the end of the book. When the story begins, Juani is trying to get her life together after ending a particularly tortuous relationship with Gina, her Puerto Rican lover. At the center of the tormented and failed relationship is a particularly ugly incident in which Juani and Gina hurt each other physically and emotionally. The couple decide to separate, and Juani begins a long healing process entailing much support from the women in her family. It is during this period of healing that the tale begins, and it works itself back to the episode of battery and emotional injury between Juani and Gina. When the book ends, Juani has grown in self-knowledge, and thanks to her supportive clan of women cousins, she is now better equipped to go on in life. The novel does not center on issues of the first Cuban exile generation; rather, it explores how the experiences of the first generation affect their children. In the meantime, the reader also learns about how several communities of Spanish heritage live and interact in a Latino neighborhood of Chicago: first- and second-generation Cubans, Puerto Ricans, and, finally, the lesbian group of which Juani is a part.

The book begins with the self-questioning of Juani as she poses the problem of factuality. What does it mean to remember, and is what she remembers reliable? Are the memories Juani has from Cuba her own, or are these the memories of her parents? What about the claims her father makes of his own talents and success as an inventor? While these issues never achieve centrality in the telling of the novel, they do much to add to the uncertainty that consumes the central character, who thinks about these issues often: "And I realized that I'd left Cuba too young to remember anything but snatches of color and scattered words, like the cut-out letters in a ransom note. And what little I could put together had since been forged and painted over by the fervor, malice, and nostalgia of others. What did I really know? And who did I believe? Who *could* I believe?" (133). The power of remembrance unifies this tale, for not only will Juani question factuality regarding her family's memories of their Cuban past, but she will also question events in her own life as ever having happened. While the narration begins with a Juani who very much wants the truth but deeply fears it, the novel ends with a Juani who has learned about accepting and coping with life's uncertainties.

For Juani, who came from Cuba as a child, Cuba is a place others have interpreted for her. Similar to the characters in Roberto Fernández's *Raining Backwards,* the Cubans in Juani's family live on the memories of their past. In fact, the parents' stories, their exotic pictures, and their idealization of their former lives in Cuba are totally obsolete for children like Juani, who have spent most of their adult lives in the United States: "Right now, I hold on to myself, sometimes literally. I hold on to my sides, my arms, my stubborn ankles, because in this house of nostalgia and fear, of time warps and trivia, I'm the only one I know about for sure. I keep my own space, a journal with the right dates, photographs with names and places written on the back" (79). Juani's role is to sort out the truth of her family's remembrances so that they can also become part of who she is.

Paradoxically, while the narrator-protagonist seeks the truth in the memories of her Cuban parents, she refuses to see the truth in her own life. Juani's doubting of her own reality becomes a shield that allows her to hide moral issues from herself that she must confront. For instance, she refuses to analyze the events and reasons that led to the breakup with Gina, and she is also unable to face the violence that she inflicted upon Gina. In another instance, when Jimmy, her cousin's husband, sexually molests her young niece, Juani wants to think that she is not remembering the facts correctly (234). Thus the narrator's willful denial of the veracity of events in her own life functions as a way to avoid facing up to the truth of those events.

For Achy Obejas, the ideal community is female, lesbian, and tolerant of the politics of the different Latino nationalities from which the members originate. In fact, in Obejas's novel the male characters are weak and only contribute to the narrative in negative ways—Juani's father lies about who he was in Cuba; her uncle cheats constantly on his wife; Jimmy, her cousin's husband, is a wife batterer and a sexual predator. Women like her sister Nena and cousin Patricia allow Juani to confront emotional issues and move beyond the unfortunate events in her personal life. In fact, it is through the support of her extended female family that Juani comes to know herself. She can find a source of strength in her family, a support that was absent in the narratives of Elías Miguel Muñoz.

Cuba and the Cuban story of diaspora enter in Obejas's narrative as factors that condition the image that other members of the community have of her protagonist. In fact, being Cuban seems to be a cross to bear socially since there is no political sympathy for Cuban exiles among Juani's circle of friends. Juani's Latino friends (mostly Puerto Ricans) have already decided that the Cubans in the United States are "worms" since they left a regime that in her friends' eyes was more equitable to minorities than current U.S. society. Moreover, Juani's Cuban background is one of the reasons that her love relationship with Gina eventually comes to an end—Gina is the object of racial "Puerto Rican jokes" among Juani's family; Juani, in turn, is the center of "Cuban exile jokes" among Gina's friends (122). Both women feel unfairly treated, yet neither does anything to remedy the situation.

Juani fares no better with Gina in the area of sexual politics. In contrast to Gina, who wishes to remain in the closet, Juani sees it as her right to express her lesbian self as part of who she is. Gina, an ardent advocate of Puerto Rican independence, is of a different mind when it comes to lesbian and gay rights: "'Look, I'm not interested in being a *lesbian,* in separating politically from my people,' she'd say to me, her face hard and dark. 'What are we talking about? Issues of *sexual identity?* While Puerto Rico is a colony? While Puerto Rican apologists are trying to ram statehood down our throats with legislative tricks and sleights of hand? You think I'm going to sit around and discuss *sexual identity?* Nah, Juani, you can do that—you can have that navel-gazing discussion'" (77). Whether it is the Puerto Rican activists who hover around Juani's lover Gina, or the government in Cuba that does not let her cousin Titi lead an open lesbian lifestyle there, the novel raises issues of acceptance concerning the sexual politics of progressive groups.[7] Thus the events in the life of the protagonist make Juani skeptical of ideologies. Gina's politics are problematic for Juani since she feels that neither the activist groups in the United States nor the communists in Cuba are yet ready to open their arms to a lesbian lifestyle: "I know all too well how the world of politics, with its promises and deceptions, its absolute values and impersonal manifestos, can cut through the deepest love and leave lovers stranded" (87).

By introducing sexual preference into the Cuban story of diaspora, Obejas speaks from a position that demands tolerance and recognition from her own ethnic community. Choosing as a protagonist a twenty-four-year-old Cuban, the author makes a concerted effort to put distance between her own life and her literary rendition of the story of exodus. Moreover, the protagonists' concerns in this novel are meant to appeal to younger Cuban Americans who are also lesbian. The novel thus provokes the reader (lesbian or otherwise) into thinking that the issue of sexual identity is fraught with complexity, and that it cannot be understood without first taking into account other factors of identity such as ethnicity and culture and the relations in between.

In her essay "Women's Autobiographical Selves: Theory and Practice," Susan Stanford Friedman establishes a workable theory that is useful for the explication of fictional autobiography in Anglo-American and European women's texts and also in the work of minority writers such as the ones examined here. Friedman studies the reigning attitudes toward autobiography in contemporary theory and questions "the individualistic concept of the autobiographical self" as it has been proposed by well-known scholars of autobiography such as Olney and Gusdorf. Friedman argues that for the "marginalized cultures," a definition of autobiography that stresses interdependent identification within a community is a much more useful tool of analysis. The autobiographical consciousness of marginal groups, according to Friedman, results in autobiographical forms that are not only individualistic but also collective (35). Listening to the stories of her cousins in exile binds Obejas's protagonist into a relationship with a community of tellers. Fictional autobiography functions in her text as a "community binding ritual" (50) in her search for the Cuban-American voice.

The novels of Achy Obejas and Elías Miguel Muñoz exhibit an affirmative as well as a critical relationship to questions of identity and self-definition. According to critic Diane Martin,[8] "self worth, identity, and a sense of community have been fundamentally connected with the production of a shared narrative and the assimilation of an individual's story and the history of the group" (83). As Martin explains, the many coming-out stories in lesbian and gay literature are there to respond to what it means to be a lesbian and what it means to come out. These writings are accounts of the process of becoming conscious of homosexuality and about accepting and affirming that identity against the odds of societal and family pressures. In many cases, Martin adds, a lifestyle based on gender preference becomes a central moment around which the lives of these authors are reconstructed: "by rendering their sexual selves as self evident and natural these gay and lesbian narratives contest heterosexual life accounts" (85).

Achy Obejas's narrative has gone beyond the trauma of displacement, tackling instead issues that have to do with the internal politics of lesbian communities that are also ethnic. Juani does not experience the rupture of a Cuban childhood and American adulthood; in fact, in many respects this narrator is much more American than she is Cuban. Life in the United States has meant for Obejas an opportunity to explore political and personal perspectives far away from her family's Cuban conservatism. Nostalgia is not allowed, for this author knows that today's and yesterday's Cuba would not have been as tolerant of her ideas and of her sexuality. With a perspective that focuses on the United States, Obejas as author can tackle issues that consume her present rather than her past: the politics of Latino and lesbian communities in Chicago and how Cuban Americans interact and are received by other immigrant nationalities of Spanish heritage. Finally, Obejas's protagonist can also challenge U.S. Latino–activist groups to truly accept the homosexuality of their members.

Muñoz's narrative, on the other hand, is closely tied to the moment of exodus for both protagonists. *The Greatest Performance* begins in Cuba and ends in the United States, thus keeping the trauma of displacement and discovery of sexuality closer in chronology for the central characters. The thematic conflicts for this author are related to being gay within a culture that very much rejects gayness. Muñoz's perspective on the story of exodus is that of protagonists who remember Cuba for themselves, and who underwent an experience of cultural adaptation in their lifetime (their language, their cultural mores, their music). In contrast to Obejas's work, Muñoz's text offers a dark picture of what it means to be gay and Cuban in both countries. For this author, family is not supportive; in fact, no one in the community seems to care. Community for Muñoz is reduced to the friendship of those who are alike in their marginality.

Even if Obejas and Muñoz are chronological peers, their perspective on the story of the Cuban diaspora very much separates the way they view the experience of displacement. Are Muñoz's and Obejas's versions of diaspora different because these authors left Cuba at very different stages of their maturity? Obejas was only a six-year-old girl when she left, but Muñoz was a fourteen-year-old adolescent. Are these narratives different because they each represent female and male perspectives? I believe these factors cannot be ignored. Muñoz's characters reflect the sensibility of the one-and-a-half generation, and as such their experiences are those of discontinuity and rupture of cultures and languages. Obejas, on the other hand, looks at Cuban reality as very much the concern of her parents' generation. Similar to the autobiographical essays of Eliana Rivero and Ruth Behar, the writings of Obejas feature characters who look ahead to bettering the future of their ethnic community. What is evident for both Obejas and Muñoz is that the idea of gays and lesbians living openly and forging for themselves a new community in the midst of America's melting pot is an issue that competes with and at times takes priority over issues of culture and nationality. If Muñoz's characters do not transcend the past and the prejudices of their Cuban culture, Obejas's protagonists make a clear effort to do so.

8 Collecting the Tales of the Community
From Person to Persona

> All that non-fiction can do is answer questions.
> It's fiction's business to ask them.
>
> Richard Hughes

LITERALLY A mask, the term *persona* is used in the criticism of fiction in order to refer to a "second self" created by the author and through whom the narrative is told.[1] As we have seen in our study of self-narratives and novels, the persona in Cuban-American texts has operated in both literary and psychological contexts as it illuminates the writers' perceptions of their Cuban past and cultural identity. These fictional protagonists have provided the reader with a close, intimate look at how Cuban-American writers go about piecing together identities shattered by the 1959 revolution and its aftermath.

The novels in this chapter, written by older and younger members of the second generation, feature *writers within the fiction* whose task is to collect the memories of their Cuban communities in exile and in Cuba. In all the novels, the narrative strategy of the metatext—that is, the presence of a text within the fictional world of the novel—becomes central in these fictional writers' recovery of their fragmented lives. These narratives make use of embedded texts and fictional authors in order to dramatize language shifts and to show the function of literature in healing the wounds of displacement. Some of the writers analyzed in this section imitate the autobiographical model by creating a first-person perspective for these fictional writers; others write in the third person; still others present a combination of points of view in order to construct community within their narratives. For all narratives in this last chapter, the emphasis is on how the fictional "I" interacts with his or her fragmented community.

The presence of embedded texts, interior writers, and fictional readers within the world of these Cuban-American novels is indeed significant, for it focuses our attention on issues of language as translation and on the complex circuit of communication within a given work. In addition, the introduction of interior texts and writers in these novels increases their complexity since it can become an extended metaphor for the task of inventing and reconstructing a life in words, a life that the writers can control and arrange, unlike their real lives. These fictional strategies are quite useful for Cuban-American writers since the "narrators within" are able to clarify and avoid misinterpretations from readers who might or might not understand Cuban culture. Finally, metafictional literary strategies enhance our understanding of the Cuban-American predicament by presenting us with a dramatization of the actual process of recording the memories and traditions of a community *within* the world of the text.[2]

As Naomi Schor indicates, narratives that feature readers and writers within their fictional world are concerned with the act of making meaning: its scope, its necessity, and the frustrations that might accompany this task. Schor emphasizes the concept of the *interpretant,* a term that she acknowledges was originally coined under a different context by Charles Peirce. Schor defines *interpretants* as "the fictional characters that make sense of meaning within the fictional world" (Schor 168). These interpretants do not exist as images of us, the readers; rather, they function to acquaint us about the various notions regarding the acts of perception and interpretation. The works of the writers examined here can be studied as autobiographical fictions of interpretation, for they all exhibit a need to make meaning from both experience and the stories of others. How the story of the Cuban diaspora is addressed by the readers and writers within these representative texts illuminates the perceptions of self that inform Cuban-American fictions.

I have chosen to examine the novels of Pablo Medina, Omar Torres, Margarita Engle, and Cristina García because they illustrate simultaneous but different stages in the evolution and dramatization of a Cuban-American writer's persona within these authors' fictional worlds. Pablo Medina's *The Marks of Birth* (1994) is a fictional account extending from 1949 to the present and describing the impact the revolution has on three generations of a Cuban middle-class family when they are forced to abandon their country. In this novel Felicia, the matriarch, writes a "biography" that eventually helps her grandson Anton (also a writer) overcome the difficulties involved in adapting one cultural perspective to another. Omar Torres's novel *Fallen Angels Sing* (1991) is a fictional autobiography of a young Cuban-American poet who is very much engaged with his Cuban past and whose writings are misused by the exile communities in Miami and New York as well as by the government in Cuba. Margarita Engle's *Skywriting* (1995) relates how an American woman of Cuban heritage visits the Cuba of the 1990s and becomes involved in the release of her half brother from a Cuban prison. Her task is to bring out of Cuba a four-part manuscript detailing the history of both the family and the country. In Cristina García's *Dreaming in Cuban* (1992), the protagonist, Pilar, is a Cuban-American ethnic who grows up in New York desperately searching for her Cuban roots. When she finally reaches Cuba, Pilar is able to write down for posterity the memories of her Cuban grandmother and her other Cuban relatives. Finally, García's most recent novel, *The Agüero Sisters* (1997), also features a narrator within the text. The memoirs written by the patriarch Ignacio Agüero, buried in his hacienda in Camaguey, contain not only the details of his wife's murder but also the history of Cuba and the many dictatorships that plagued the republic since its birth in 1902.

Unlike Engle, whose ties to Cuba are those of an outsider, García is the daughter of exiles of the first generation and was two years old at the time of her departure from Cuba. Medina and Torres, on the other hand, were young Cuban boys of twelve and thirteen when they left the country and as such experienced a Cuban childhood. All four write in English about stories that took place in Spanish.

Pablo Medina's *The Marks Of Birth* (1994)

The Marks of Birth is a novel about the acquisition and loss of languages through the crossing of places and cultures.[3] It is also a novel about the process of gaining coherence by writing down and reordering events that in real life have been outside the writer's control. As opposed to Medina's memoir *Exiled Memories* (analyzed in chapter 5 of this book), which relied on the security of a happy childhood, Medina's latest story of the 1959 exodus is an autobiographical fiction successfully using a genealogical framework and embedded texts to tell both a political and a literary tale. The two dimensions of the story do not remain separate, for if the political tale is about the immense losses of the 1959 diaspora, the literary tale dramatizes the writing and reading of that experience by the characters themselves. Writing and reading about the aftermath of 1959 becomes the healing ground that restores the losses common to exile. Through a creative use of his sense of language loss, Pablo Medina poses ways in which he might reconcile his past and present.

Autobiographical material serves a dual function in this text. First, it is the source for the mimetic plot since Medina personally experienced the 1960 exodus. In fact, there are many biographical coincidences in this text between Anton, the character, and Pablo Medina, the author.[4] Autobiography, the experience of writing down a life, is utilized here as a crucial narrative strategy that serves to blend the book's aesthetics with the political story of exile. Fictional autobiography functions for Medina as an analytical tool providing him with the forum to examine the trauma that his family members underwent and his own experience of biculturality.

The Marks of Birth is a novel about family and origins but also about the function of literature in helping people lead their lives. From the beginning of the book, several strands of action are developed simultaneously: the story of the family (which includes Anton's development as a writer), the story of the diaspora of the 1960s and the tragic consequences it had for a nation, and the story of Felicia, the matriarch, as she assumes the role of historian through the writing of a legacy she terms her *biography*.

The novel is divided into three main sections corresponding to three decades of Cuban history. Part 1 provides the context for the 1959 Cuban diaspora—it describes the fairly quiet and affluent life of middle-class families such as the García-Turners during the decade preceding the 1959 revolution. Part 2 provides a detailed account of the splintering of the García-Turner family due to the exodus after the revolution of 1959. This segment provides details of the radical changes that occurred in the life of many middle-class Cubans as they were forced to abandon their country, leaving careers and possessions behind. Part 3 begins fifteen years later and shifts its focus to Anton, the family's youngest member, and his adjustment to life in the United States two decades later. The book concludes as Anton flies to Cuba in defiance of Castro's air space in order to fulfill his grandmother Felicia's wish to have her ashes disseminated over Cuban soil.

Soon after Anton's birth, Felicia becomes ill and loses her speaking voice. Feeling that there is a link between her illness and her unexplained rebuff of grandson Anton, Felicia decides to write a text, her biography, in order to atone for her rejection of the youngest member of the García-Turner family. Once the matriarch begins to write, her speaking voice returns. This initial episode illustrates the curative power of writing, as the task of reproducing history in words becomes a metaphor for the grandmother's spiritual healing. In fact, it is Felicia's writing of the biography that allows the matriarch to survive the initial years of the 1960 exodus and the emigration from Cuba of most of her kin: "Had it not been for

that exercise, she would not have survived her tribulations" (183). If Felicia's Spanish voice had been silenced by repression in her country and
later by exile in the United States, her decision to write this biography
serves to repair the loss. Moreover, the act of writing down her life becomes the way in which Felicia overcomes the silence of political repression in Cuba as well as the loss of her native language once she reaches
America, for "the world in English was not a world to her at all" (183).

As the text progresses, Felicia thinks seriously of her biographical
task, which now has expanded beyond the life of her grandson to include the story of the family. In fact, the matriarch even becomes self-
conscious of her own style and begins to censor her earlier versions:
"Could she, even in the depths of her guilt and expiation, ever have
written such drivel?" (179). Felicia, as author within the text, realizes
the limitations of capturing life's experiences in words. Thus she now
strives to write with more honesty, keeping in mind that "the most important things about someone's life can never be recorded" (180). Once
her family has left the island, "she would give herself the freedom to
speculate in order to cover the blank spots . . . keeping the despair that
stalked her everywhere at bay" (178–79).

Felicia's own speculations about Cuba and about her family become
important in Medina's assessment of cultural differences and challenges.
Above all, the voice of Felicia provides a strong dose of political theory,
which she records in her biography, hoping to allay the harshness of her
present: "If we had no memory, there would be no history, and without
history there would be no guilt or regret. . . . But we have consciousness,
and history, and regret, and the only way to cope with them is to place
one's faith in God, trust that He is merciful and caring and not a tyrant"
(193–94). The biography Felicia writes becomes a platform for philoso-
phizing and theorizing about Cuba's complex history. By choosing to tell
the story of the first generation of exiles from the viewpoint of the
family's matriarch, Medina distances himself from the events of 1959
and introduces in his narrative a variety of perspectives regarding the
historical events that changed his nation. The voices filtered through Felicia's narrative perspective include those of her brother, Antonio, and of
the longtime family friend José María Unanue.

Antonio's story establishes the political dimension of the text as his
own case becomes an example of the injustices perpetrated by the revolution on the individual. Reminiscent of one of Novás Calvo's tales of
the revolution, Antonio becomes a victim of the thirst for retribution
that was so prevalent during the first months of Castro's regime. Soon

after Castro gains power, Antonio begins to have doubts about the new regime and the radical changes it announced to the country: "Antonio called Campión [Castro] the most dangerous ruler in the history of the island, not really explaining his statement but adding that every promise he made was not to the people but to himself and that he was turning the country into a monument to Nicolás Campión" (116).

Predictably, Antonio's skeptical stance lands him in trouble with the revolution. Early during the first year, he is accused of counterrevolution, given a summary trial, and imprisoned. His spirit, however, remains unbroken as he fearlessly stages his own defense at his trial, fully knowing that it would be of no use: "So we are all victims: I of injustice, you of a will much greater than your combined ones can ever be" (120). He eventually dies in prison. Later in the narrative, Felicia's perspective adds context to her brother's unjust murder: "He died in hell without a loved one to bring dignity to his last moment. Though the authorities brought misery to him, they never broke him" (193). Antonio's memory, lessons, and philosophy of life remain present throughout the novel, as they become vivid memories for Anton, the child. In fact, the great-uncle's skepticism seems to be a trait eventually inherited by Anton: "The world would be a grand place without religion or politics. It would be like heaven, like Detroit, Michigan" (108).

On the other hand, family friend José María Unanue, the mysterious Spaniard, twice an immigrant, who came to Cuba from Spain at the age of fifteen, tempers the illusion of an ideal life in the United States and brings out the perils of leaving one's soil. Unanue's philosophical meditations about the fate of Cuba includes his own version of how countries and forms of government develop:

> Jose María once told me that the United States was created out of a refusal to pay taxes. . . . A man's home was his kingdom and he made his own laws and lived in balance with nature. . . . Without this understanding . . . there can be no progressive society. . . . He claimed that we would not have that understanding in our country because it was too small, and whatever good land there was had been taken by the rich long ago and the only thing for the rest of us to become was merchants. . . . The merchant does not respect the land. . . . That is why there was a revolution, and we are paying the consequences. (186–87)

José María's assessment of the essential differences between the fates of Cuban and U.S. histories is persuasive since as a non-Cuban who has suffered himself the ravages of immigration, he provides a needed distance from the events he discusses. Unanue's and Antonio's voices stand in counterpoint and bring out crucial issues in the ideological wars and positions held across the years by Cubans who live on the island and those who live elsewhere. By means of their stories, Medina engages the reader to consider and balance the variety of perspectives regarding the sad fate of Cubans as a people and as a nation.

In addition to giving a voice to the exiles of the first generation who experienced the onset of the revolution firsthand, the matriarch's narrative also serves as a useful narrative strategy since the embedded biography provides a link between the politics of the text (the stories of Antonio and José María Unanue) and the story of Anton, Medina's fictional persona. In fact, both the grandmother and the grandson suffer from their initial efforts to deny themselves: Felicia by initially rejecting her own grandchild, Anton by creating for himself an American mask that eventually suffocates him.

For Anton, language loss is real, and his solutions are related to the phenomena of displacement. As the child of exiles who comes to the United States in his eleventh year, Anton exemplifies the one-and-a-half Cuban American in this novel. Anton's immediate solution is to create a mask, a persona that would allow him to function in the new society: "It became his obsession to eliminate Spanish from his consciousness and make English the language of his thoughts and dreams. He whittled away at his accent and toned down his mannerisms so that they were controlled and Anglicized. . . . By the time he entered college, two years later, he was signing his name as A. G. Turner, speaking accentless English and behaving as if he had never heard of the island, let alone been born on it. . . . He had surged into a present that could be his only in proportion to how fully he erased his old self" (212–15).

Throughout the narrative, Anton appears as a mixed-up figure who has fumbled along from job to job and who is intrinsically unhappy about his present. Described through the distance of a third-person narrator, this character remains an elusive figure within the text. However, Anton's unhappiness is evident: a failed marriage, a teaching job he does not like, a writing career that does not seem to be going anywhere.

Although much attention is given to the child's literary aspirations in the text's initial chapters, Anton's writing vocation becomes only one of the many goals that were never attained nor fulfilled by this unhappy character. The childhood stories told to Anton by Munda, the servant, were imaginary tales filled with blood and violence, which fired the boy's imagination. Munda's stories, some of which appear interpolated within the narrative, were countered in turn by those tales Anton himself invented and told in confidence to his trusted servant. In addition, the diverse literary readings prescribed for Anton by his great-uncle equally stimulated the child's imagination, even if, at the time, these readings seemed to be far beyond his age. Finally, the fantastic tales of the lives of saints that were part of his grandmother's repertoire also contributed to the boy's interest in listening to and creating stories about imaginary beings and strange events. Unfortunately, Anton's initial talent seems lost by the time the child reaches maturity in the United States. When his estranged wife throws paint on his manuscripts, he seems relieved to lose his writings, for he has no faith in his own talent: "All these years he had been languishing as a writer who has had many more dreams than publications, Alice had . . . freed him with a gallon of red paint" (234).

Through Anton we can see the dilemma of the false solutions assumed by Cuban Americans in order to cope with dislocation and loss. Upon reaching maturity, the protagonist finds that his strategies for survival do not work, that he has somehow ignored his true self in his search for total assimilation (213). Anton, the would-be author, becomes despondent and adopts an indifferent attitude toward his own life: "Neither the past nor the family held anything for him" (196). Eventually, this unhappy character divorces his unfaithful wife and decides to join a group of anti-Castro guerrillas training in the Everglades. But once again Anton feels out of sorts, for he did not share the group's convictions and had no trust in what they were doing: "Every night he came home with his heart weighed down and his head ringing with the bickering of two demons: the demon of self-doubt, low and obese-sounding, and the demon of mortification, shrill and implacable" (207).

Medina's fictional rendering of a Cuban-American writer in this novel strives to explain the difficulties involved in adapting one cultural perspective to another. Anton is simultaneously dealing with two ways of seeing the world; he has had to replace his language and culture, and the process has not been easy. Yet life in the United States is not hopeless for this character, if he is willing to look at things in a different manner. Accepting change and adapting to it are essential lessons contained in the grandmother's written legacy. By reading the pages of her biography, Anton finds relief for his lack of purpose and anxiety: "They contained his life, to the merest detail, from the instant of his birth to the moment of his reading. They spoke of all things and of nothing, of the family, of his power, of the need to accept his reality" (270). Reading the legacy of the grandmother has a curative power[5] for this character because it provides him with the clues he needs to understand his situation. At the end of the text, Anton is not any happier, but he is certainly more cognizant of why his own life turned out the way it did and how history affected his own destiny. The writings of the grandmother provide the means by which this character can obtain an understanding of self.

The themes and narrative strategies of *The Marks of Birth* provide Medina with an original response to the dilemma of authority facing a bicultural author. As a Cuban American, Anton is "marked" by family ties (212) as well as by destiny (247). The "mark," which stands for Anton's essence as a Cuban American, is neither positive nor negative but instead is there to be confronted and assumed. Anton is different even if his condition does not necessarily yield any advantages ("In El Norte no one is special or marked" 187). The novel lacks closure—as the book ends, the reader sees Anton disappear into Cuba's forbidden air space. Yet it is clear that, even in the face of possible death, Anton is now open to the possibilities of change. Writing the story of the post-1959 diaspora becomes a needed exercise for author Pablo Medina as he joins and explores simultaneously the aesthetic issues of writing as well as his own bicultural status.

Omar Torres's *Fallen Angels Sing* (1991)

As in Medina's case, the resulting diaspora of the 1959 revolution becomes the structural and thematic core of Omar Torres's narrative *Fallen Angels Sing*.[6] Similar to Medina's novel, Omar Torres's version of his present in the United States requires the distance of fiction because it conveys the existential anxiety of the divided self. Omar Torres, who was born in Cuba in 1945 and who emigrated as a young boy, is a novelist, poet, and playwright. A version of *Fallen Angels Sing* (1991) was published in Spanish in 1981 under the title *Apenas un bolero*.[7] Both narratives imitate the structure of autobiography via a protagonist who seeks the capacity to tell his own story.

The story takes place in the United States and concentrates on the present of a thirty-three-year-old exiled poet as he copes with the shattering experience of dislocation. As was the case with Medina's text, there are coincidences between the life of Miguel Saavedra, the protagonist, and the life of author Omar Torres. Like Torres, Saavedra was born in Victoria de las Tunas in 1945; both were poets who left Cuba for Miami at the age of thirteen and eventually settled in the New York City area. Both were thirty-three years old at the time of publication of the Spanish version in 1981.

The reader meets protagonist Miguel Saavedra on his way from Miami to New York City as he agonizes about his frivolous life and the need to become more involved in the political future of his country: "I had been a Philistine, living on the periphery of my convictions about Cuba. I had dodged the issue, but it was in vain. Cuba was embedded in me; I had to harvest my involvement anew" (78). In New York, Miguel finds himself caught between pro- and anti-Castro groups that wish to use him as a symbol to further their political causes. Yet, the protagonist's inability to decide between these factions contributes to his deep anxiety: "The exiles admired my work, but distrusted me. Now it happened that those in Cuba also admired me, but I distrusted them. They were clearly wanting to use me, but I didn't know for what" (97). In his search for meaning and commitment, Saavedra attends university poetry readings and *santería* churches, which combine elements of African and Catholic beliefs and rites. He visits gay bars and finally travels to Cuba, where he dies in a failed attempt to assassinate Castro.

The hybrid structure of Torres's novel and his use of metafictional devices provide a potential avenue for the understanding of the protagonist's evolving self. The mixing of the genres of theater, poetry, and narrative in the telling of Saavedra's tale parallels the protagonist's anxious and undecided condition as Miguel flounders between the Cuban communities of New York and Miami. A section entitled "Memories of my Father's family" is narrated as a play within the narrative; another segment entitled "We interrupt this program" takes on the shape of a long poem. The protagonist's dilemma is well articulated when, in a play that is interpolated within the text and acted out by Miguel and his friends, Torres's one-and-a-half generation confronts the values of his parents' generation: "The question is not to forget, Dad. Take me or my friends; you have a life to remember, but in that life we are nothing, we don't belong, because we have nothing to share with you in that life. We don't belong there, and we don't belong here; we just don't belong. We're not Cubans and we're not Americans" (111). Miguel Saavedra does not achieve a coherent sense of self, for he is too involved in the reality of his elders and thus paralyzed in his attempt to reconstruct his own story. Some of this same conflict is demonstrated by the fact that the novel appeared first in Spanish under the title *Apenas un bolero* back in 1981 and then in English as *Fallen Angels Sing*. Torres's decision to publish an English version of the same novel in 1991 points toward the ambiguity and unresolved pull felt by the Cuban-American writer regarding his likely audience.

Early in the novel, Saavedra addresses his potential reader: "You are what you read, but you are also what you write. I was part of this story, even though it's not autobiographical. I wrote it on my Smith-Corona. How would non–Latin Americans react to this story?" (27). The protagonist's frequent dialogues with his readers as well as with his author are examples of the many self-conscious narrative devices used by Torres and denote anxiety and uneasiness between writer and audience. Saavedra engages the "non–Latin American" reader as an outsider, as someone to be instructed about the details of a country in crisis. Digressions by the narrator about specific events in Cuban history abound in the narrative and become a way to inform and instruct the English-speaking reader about Cuban history (33, 83, 123).

A central issue in the novel is literature, since Saavedra's writings become the source of his own exploitation by factions from the right and the left. As an artist, Saavedra is pictured as a vulnerable element and as a likely victim of the politics that divide Cubans and Cuban Americans: "You are the Cuban exile; you're all of us with your longing and your endless nostalgia" (131), writes a friend to Miguel as the protagonist sets off to Cuba to meet his death. In the last pages of the book, a figure of the author appears in the text and states his intention to travel to Havana, ostensibly to meet the same deadly fate as his protagonist Miguel.

The use of embedded texts and metafictional devices in Omar Torres's novel is central to the fate of his main character, Miguel Saavedra. As a poet, Saavedra is most vulnerable since it is his writing that victimizes and eventually dooms him. Writing within this novel does not illuminate or alleviate Saavedra's search for identity; instead, it becomes the source of his problem. Saavedra becomes caught up in the reality of his elders and thus paralyzed in his attempt to tell the Cuban-American story. Although Torres's protagonist fights to be different from the Miami Cubans, he does not achieve this goal. If Saavedra rejects the Cuban community in Miami, it is because he fears that he is in fact a little bit like them. Even though what he most desires is to forget Cuba, he is basically unable to do so.

Miguel Saavedra typifies the split self of the one-and-a-half generation, writers who can opt to make the best of the split between childhood and adulthood but who at times can become paralyzed by the dualities inherent in their bicultural lives.[8] If the metatext is in fact a dramatization of the construction of the self as the pieces of writing come together within the fiction, in the case of Torres these interior texts seem dooming rather than redemptive. Saavedra never acquires control over his experiences because he cannot achieve the needed balance to overcome his fear of not really belonging in America or Cuba. To the central question asked by this novel—Where does a Cuban American really belong?—Torres's answer would be, "nowhere."

Margarita Engle's *Skywriting* (1995)

Similar to Pablo Medina's and Omar Torres's narratives, Margarita Engle's first-person tale of exodus weaves autobiographical details into the plot of her fiction. As a child, the author had spent many summers in Cuba until political events on the island made it impossible for her family to stay there. Margarita Engle returned to Cuba in the early 1990s with a journalist's visa and happened to be there when her distant cousins set sail for the United States on a makeshift raft. It was this experience that fueled the writing of Engle's second novel about the Cuban diaspora.[9]

In the creation of Carmen Peregrin, the narrator-protagonist in *Skywriting*,[10] Margarita Engle assumes her hybrid heritage as she envisions a story from the perspective of a North American, not a Cuban or Cuban American. Like her protagonist, Margarita Engle, daughter of a Cuban mother and an American father, was born in Cuba and raised in Los Angeles. In *Skywriting* she tells the story of Carmen Peregrin, an American woman of Cuban ancestry who returns to Cuba in order to meet her half brother, Camilo. Carmen and Camilo share a father who dies during the first years of the revolution, and they correspond with one another during childhood. From the start, Carmen assumes an outsider's perspective: "Camilo said that the library commemorating *balseros* should include at least one North American female point of view, my own. He asked me to write this history with the heart of a mother, from my refuge of imagined Northern safety" (279). Moreover, Carmen often reflects on the radically different but parallel lives that she and her half brother Camilo have led: "Somehow it's deeply disturbing to be born across the sea from a sibling. . . . To claim a different nationality, different liberties, sorrows, rules-of-conduct, a different sense of humor" (193).

As a first-person narrator, Carmen Peregrin is tied to the issues at hand by coincidence—she happened to be in Cuba when Camilo defected via a raft—and by duty since she is asked by Camilo to smuggle the vast document that becomes the center of the text. Documenting the crisis from the inside, Carmen Peregrin first lives the anguish of Camilo's mother at not knowing where he is and then experiences the mother's resignation and sadness when she realizes her son has become a prisoner. During Carmen's stay in Cuba, Camilo escapes the island on a raft, and Carmen is left to experience the anguish of her relatives and to share with them the uncertainty of Camilo's whereabouts. Eventually, the family discovers that Camilo has been found by the Castro police and is being held prisoner in Villa Marista, a well-known prison destined for dissidents. Faced with the unexpected, Carmen returns to the United States and from abroad tries to effect Camilo's release. In the meantime, Camilo has asked that Carmen take back with her a mysterious package that she later finds out is a manuscript containing an important legacy for the family and for Cuban history.

The manuscript, which Carmen is to take to the outside world, is in reality three documents in one: the father's account and history of human rights violations throughout Cuban history; a chronicle of Carmen's ancestors (Vicente, the Spaniard, and Siren, the native islander); and a *balsero*'s manifesto explaining how the dire conditions imposed on Cuban citizens caused Camilo's desire to leave the island. For Engle, the manuscript within the text is used to inform the reader about Cuban political realities. Carmen, as the bearer of these documents, becomes a political interpreter of the contents of this document for the outside world. In the narratives of Medina and Torres, interior texts and the act of writing itself served as a mechanism for personal healing and for piecing together shattered identities. In *Skywriting,* the literary device of the metatext becomes a document bearing testimony of injustices throughout the history of Cuba, including injustices under Castro's dictatorship.

Engle's novel stands alone among Cuban-American narratives of her generation in its attempt to describe in detail the situation inside Cuban prisons and the tactics of repression used by the Castro regime inside Cuba today: "North Americans . . . possess no framework for understanding what it's *really* like to be locked up inside secret police headquarters for any crime of any nature, but especially for one as innocuous as trying to float away from an island kingdom imagined by its ruler. . . . We're like different primitive tribes. . . . We're related but separate. Our languages branch away from each other, with only a few words shared" (193–94).

The narrator also includes a desire to discuss openly the *balsero* crisis as well as to include the activities of the Brothers to the Rescue (Hermanos al Rescate), who risk their lives to save Cuban rafters lost at sea.[11] Engle's denunciation of U.S. policy toward the *balseros* becomes prophetic, for her text was written and published during the exodus of 1994, a crisis culminating in the creation of *balsero* tent cities on the U.S. base at Guantánamo and in a change in President Clinton's policy toward accepting *balseros* in the United States.[12] "It was a year when the *balseros* who survived their ordeal at sea could still hope to be granted political asylum in the U.S., when the eyes, hearts and doors of *los Estados Unidos* had not yet slammed shut, when *balseros* did not yet fear the barbed wire of foreign detention camps but only the Viper's [Villa Marista's] entrails" (248).

As the bearer of her half brother's manuscript, Carmen Peregrin becomes a central link in denouncing human rights violations in today's Cuba. Engle's efforts in depicting the contemporary realities of Cuba and the United States within the world of this novel and in connecting the two represent an important dimension in the trajectory of the fictional story of 1959. Engle's protagonist becomes a mediator between the Cubans in Cuba and those in the United States and provides an outsider's perspective on the Cuban crisis: "Camilo says it is essential to view each sliver of history from many sides, as if the past were a hologram, or a fire opal or star sapphire, reflecting different shapes and hues when viewed from different angles" (279).

Of the novels examined in this segment, *Skywriting* portrays a perspective that is more distanced from Cuba and from things Cuban than the other narratives. Throughout the text, Carmen Peregrin's descriptions of Cuban culture seem to adopt a *costumbrista* tone as the protagonist wants to explain to the reader the differences between American and Cuban humor and even reflects on the meaning of certain words and idiomatic expressions from the perspective of someone who is primarily North American. Yet Margarita Engle's work shares the generational anguish that plagues her Cuban-American half brothers and sisters. In fact, her psychological distance from the story of 1959 is sometimes helpful, for she brings to bear aspects that take into account a reader not fully aware of Cuban history.

Cristina García's *Dreaming in Cuban* (1992)

In a 1993 interview with the *Boston Globe,* Cristina García, author of *Dreaming in Cuban,* made the following statement: "In terms of the Cuban experience, the Revolution is 34 years old—as old as I am. We're in a unique position to tell the story of exile in a way our parents couldn't because they were too scarred and busy remaking their lives."[13] García's reference to her age indicates that she feels part of a new generation of

Cuban-American writers, writers who left their country as infants following the 1959 revolution or who were born in the United States of parents in the first exile generation. Her comments also speak of a thematics linking her group to the writers that came before: "the story of exile." But it is her reference to being "in a unique position" that points to the complex dynamics of the extraterritorial Cuban narrative because it exposes all that is common in the age-old story of exile and all that is unique to the literary production of Cubans in America.

Dreaming in Cuban is significant because it treats the experience of exile from the perspective of an ethnic writer.[14] Through her protagonist, Pilar, Cristina García dramatizes the anxieties felt by an ethnic writer about the issues of voice and identity. Nominated for the National Book Award in 1992, this novel is one of the best-known Cuban-American works written to date. Like Pilar, García was born in Havana in 1958, came to the United States when she was two years old, and grew up in New York City. García has worked as a journalist and has been a reporter and bureau chief for the *New York Times* and for *Time* magazine. *Dreaming in Cuban* was García's first novel.

At the beginning of *Dreaming in Cuban,* the protagonist formulates the question of belonging that she pursues throughout: "Even though I've been living in Brooklyn all my life, it doesn't feel like home to me. I'm not sure Cuba is, but I want to find out. If I could only see Abuela Celia again, I'd know where I belonged" (58). Pilar is the daughter of exiles, a kind of skeptical punk who dabbles in art and *santería*. As narrator of and participant in her own story, Pilar believes that, if she can get to Cuba, she will be able to reconstruct the puzzle of her fragmented family and thus recapture a missing part of her life. The stories of *abuela* Celia and *tía* Felicia provide Pilar with a context within which her life can be assumed.

In her narrative, the author examines three important dimensions of Cuban exile: the story of the Cubans who remained in Cuba (exemplified in the book by *abuela* Celia and *tía* Felicia), the story of the Cuban exiles who came to America in the 1960s (the story of Lourdes, Pilar's mother), and, finally, the story of the children of exile (that is, Pilar's story). The narrative is told mostly in the first person of Pilar (when she narrates events related to her own life in the United States) or filtered through Pilar's omniscient voice (when she relates the stories of Celia, Lourdes, and Felicia). When Pilar visits Cuba, the reader also hears the first-person voice of Ivanito, Pilar's Cuban counterpart. García's skillful use of point of view provides the reader with a variety of perspectives from members of the various generations and migratory waves and produces a panorama of Cuban history that transcends the story of 1959. The novel's fragmented structure focuses on two moments in time: a Cuban past (which goes back to the beginning of the century and presents us with the poverty and corruption under which Celia, the matriarch, grew up) and the American present (which takes us all the way to Pilar's visit to Cuba during the early 1980s). While there are contradictions in how each character views events, virtually all the stories from the past of these characters help explain present circumstances and demonstrate the links of past and present.

As with the other novels analyzed in this chapter, metafictional narrative strategies are central to the search undertaken by Pilar, the narrator-protagonist. Pilar records her family's stories in a journal she keeps in the lining of her winter coat. Her notes and recordings eventually become the reader's text. As an embedded text within the novel, Pilar's diary functions as a repository of stories that will help her piece together her life.

The stories Pilar compiles in her diary describe a family split between two countries due to the harsh realities of the Castro regime. These tales seem to fall into two categories: those in which language loss is directly related to the exile experience and those in which loss of voice transcends exile and becomes a metaphor for existential alienation. For Pilar herself, language loss is a given. As a Cuban American who grows up in the United States, Pilar has grown up speaking English, and English is the language in which she writes and records the tales of the Del Pino family. Thematically, Pilar's own anxiety about losing the language of her culture is manifested through her obsession with painting and in her ruminations about visual texts. To the dilemma of language loss, Pilar finds that visual images communicate meaning much more effectively than language: "Painting is its own language. . . . Translations just confuse it, dilute it, like words going from Spanish to English" (59). She asks, "Who needs words when colors and lines conjure up their own language?" (139).

In terms of the text's narrative process, Pilar uses telepathy rather than Spanish to communicate with her grandmother. Celia, the Cuban matriarch, becomes Pilar's inner voice, and their frequent exchanges help Pilar cope with her daily existence: "I feel much more connected to Abuela Celia than to Mom, even though I haven't seen my grandmother in seventeen years. . . . Even in silence, she gives me the confidence to do what I believe is right, to trust my own perceptions" (176).

Pilar is a collector of the stories of others, and her omniscient voice inverts the relationship to figures of authority that have dominated her in the past. Lourdes, her mother, does not fare well in Pilar's narrative. A representative of the first exile generation that left Cuba in the 1960s, Pilar's mother is ridiculed in the text. Her politics are wrong, she is overweight and unbecoming, and, worst of all, she is totally unable to understand her daughter. García does not shy away from the diversity and differences that separate Cubans from Cuban Americans, yet she understands the challenges common to both groups. Like most of the characters in García's narrative, Lourdes is tormented by feelings she does not confront. Her anxiety about her own displacement is evident when she passes the Arab shops in Brooklyn, which make her reflect on her condition as an exile. "What happens to their languages?" she asks herself. "The warm burial grounds they leave behind?" (73).

Not surprisingly, when Lourdes visits Cuba, the language she speaks cannot be understood by the Cubans in Cuba: "Mom is talking louder and louder. . . . Four or five people gather at a safe distance. It's all the audience she needs. . . . *Oye!* she calls out to the bystanders. 'You could have Cadillacs with leather interiors! Air conditioning!' . . . Then she turns to me, her face indignant. 'Look how they laugh Pilar! Like idiots! They can't understand a word I'm saying!' . . . I pull my mother from the growing crowd. The language she speaks is lost to them. It's another idiom entirely" (221).

For the women living in the United States, the loss incurred by exile is clearly expressed through the metaphor of language loss. Pilar knows Spanish but does not use it. Her telepathic conversations with Celia and her obsession with painting become the bridge that connects her two cultures. Lourdes, on the other hand, speaks in Spanish but seems unable to communicate in that language, as becomes evident during her visit to Cuba.

In an interview with Iraida H. López,[15] Cristina García asserts her feminist objectives in writing the novel: "I wanted to very specifically examine how women have responded and adapted to what happened to their families after 1959. . . . Traditional history, the way it has been written, interpreted and recorded, obviates women and the evolution of home, family, and society and basically becomes a recording of battles and wars and dubious accomplishments of men. You learn where politics really lie at home" (609–10). From the perspective of gender issues, García's text is indeed unique because it becomes a pioneering voice in telling the story of the Cuban diaspora from the point of view of Cuban women.

The female characters left in Cuba experience a loss of voice that can only be understood in terms of gender and political history. Both Celia and Felicia are products of male-dominated Cuban society. García establishes a definite connection in this text between the oppressed situation of women and Cuban *machismo*: Celia's husband tries to punish her for having had a lover before she met him; Felicia's husband abandons her as soon as they are married. Their poverty, their unhappy childhood, and their lonely existence are indirectly tied to events that have rendered them powerless.[16]

Celia, the matriarch, is a case in point. She is a strong woman of deep beliefs, although somehow she feels she has failed her own children. Her childhood is ravaged by poverty and devoid of love; she is abandoned by her own mother and raised by her aunt. As an adult, she suffers from acute depression, which is connected to the men in her life. When her lover, Gustavo, leaves for Spain, she becomes inconsolable—in the words of Pilar, "a housebound exile" (117). If there is meaning in Celia's life, it is her magical link with her granddaughter, Pilar. Celia will pass on to Pilar the family history contained in the unmailed letters she writes to her lover during the twenty years she stays married to Jorge Del Pino. When Pilar visits Cuba, Celia will give her the letters, and these "texts within the text" will become part of Pilar's diary. In one letter, Celia summarizes how she views her own situation: "If I was born to live on an island, then I'm grateful for one thing: that the tides rearrange the borders. At least I have the illusion of change, of possibility. To be locked within boundaries plotted by priests and politicians would be the only thing more intolerable. Don't you see how they're carving up the world, Gustavo? How they're stealing our geography? Our fates? The arbitrary is no longer in our hands. To survive is an act of hope" (99).

Felicia, Celia's daughter, does not fare any better. In fact, Felicia remains a stranger to the rational world due to her own real dementia: she suffers from acute syphilis, which eventually robs her of her own mind. Felicia's madness isolates her, and only her interest in the practice of *santería* rites seems to provide some solace for her solitary existence: "She opens her mouth but her thoughts erase themselves before she can speak. Something is wrong with her tongue" (83). Felicia's religious practices, her shells, and her coconuts seem to be the only comfort available in her sad and distraught life. When she finally takes her own life, her friend Herminia, a *santería* priestess, is the only one who seems to understand her predicament. One of the saddest characters in the novel, Felicia suffers from profound unhappiness born out of her inability to share her joy with others (119). Hers is the silent world of inner exile.

Toward the end of the novel, Pilar has an opportunity to visit Cuba and to see Celia, the grandmother she left behind when she was only two years old. Her encounter with the Cuba of her parents produces a variety of feelings that she seeks to unravel and hopes to understand (236). If reconstructing a legacy was the task of Medina's matriarch in *The Marks of Birth,* for Cristina García's matriarch the task is to communicate with her American granddaughter and pass on the family's stories. For Pilar, on the other hand, the task of collecting the stories her grandmother tells and writing them down stems from her archaeological need to recover a past that was already there and needed to be recovered: "Every day Cuba fades a little more inside me, my grandmother fades a little more inside me. And there is only my imagination where our history should be" (138).

Dreaming in Cuban ends fittingly with one of Celia's letters to her lover Gustavo in which she designates Pilar as a keeper of the family's legacy: "The Revolution is eleven days old. My granddaughter, Pilar Puente del Pino, was born today. It is also my birthday. I am fifty years old. I will no longer write to you. . . . She [Pilar] will remember everything" (245). This last segment, which appears in the text's last pages, is chronologically out of sequence, for the readers of *Dreaming in Cuban* realize they have been reading the contents of Pilar's diary all along. The vignette, however, is aesthetically significant, for here author Cristina García identifies Pilar as the inner narrator of her novel. At the story's end, Pilar leaves the reader with the conviction that the double consciousness of being both narrator and participant in her own story has enabled this protagonist to find that part of her own identity she knew was missing. Through Pilar's diary, García builds a psychological bridge back to Cuba.

In *Exile and the Narrative Imagination,* Michael Seidel has stated that an exile is "one who inhabits one place and projects the reality of another" (1). Ethnic writers such as García have lost not just the reality about which they write but also the language upon which this reality is construed. However, for Cristina García, language loss need not be regarded as detrimental to her creative identity because she has preserved a poignant vision of Cuban culture in English. The following passage, which narrates Pilar's impressions of her homeland upon her visit to Cuba, reveals García's gift with poetic language, her ability to write in English yet speak to Cubans of her generation: "Until I returned to Cuba, I never realized how many blues exist. The aquamarines near the shoreline, the azures of deeper waters, the eggshell blues beneath my grandmother's eyes, the fragile indigos tracking her hands. There's a blue too, in the curves of the palms, and the edges of the words we speak, a blue tinge to the sand and the seashells and the plump gulls on the beach. The mole by abuela's mouth is also blue, a vanishing blue" (233). The pictorial way in which Pilar's perceptions of her homeland blend with the grandmother of her dreams allow Cristina García to express her Cuban vision in English. Furthermore, in her lyrical writing, she displays an ability to speak to two audiences at once.

Cristina García's *The Agüero Sisters* (1997)

Cristina García's most recent novel, *The Agüero Sisters*,[17] tells the story of two half sisters, one in Cuba and the other in exile in the United States, whose common tragedy is the murder of their mother in 1948, when they were young children. Set in Havana and Miami in the early 1990s, the novel also narrates the past of the Cuban nation since the birth of the republic in 1902, through the narrative voice of Ignacio Agüero, the father of one sister. Also referred to as his "memoirs," the patriarch's narrative allows the reader to gain an understanding of the family's Cuban past and its relationship to the present. Moreover, the sad story of the sisters cannot be comprehended without the context provided by Ignacio Agüero's embedded narratives.

As in *Dreaming in Cuban,* the use of a multiple narrative perspective allows García to tell the story from the point of view of various generations and provides the author with a way to examine Cuba's history of injustice and repression. The story is a murder tale in which the perpetrator of the murder, Ignacio Agüero, is known from the very first pages. Thus the novel does not present a search for the identity of the murderer; rather, the narrative's central concern is to examine the reality that would allow such a heinous crime to take place. The context is Cuban history, as the past is explored from the sisters' present in the 1990s.

Ignacio Agüero's murder of his wife deprives his young daughters of growing up with their mother. Traumatized by their loss, the two women spend their lives dealing with the real and psychological consequences of their mother's murder. As in *Dreaming in Cuban,* the women in this text appear as victims of male-dominated Cuban society. Agüero's narrative of the Cuban past reveals the sad lives of his own mother and grandmother, and the present of the sisters relates an equally sad story for them and for their female children. Dulce, Reina's daughter and a product of the revolution, becomes a *jinetera,* a prostitute who eventually leaves the island for a sordid life in Madrid with one of her richer clients. Constancia's daughter, Isabel, a Cuban-American sculptor, is betrayed by her lover and is left alone to have their child at her mother's house in Miami.

Born two years apart during the early 1940s, Reina and Constancia have little in common because they were raised apart as children. Constancia, the older sister, is twice an orphan since her mother, Blanca, abandons her when she is a few months old. When Blanca returns (pregnant with Reina by another man), she continues to reject Constancia until the little girl is sent away to live in the Cuban countryside with relatives. During the 1960s, Constancia leaves Cuba for the United States while Reina remains in Cuba during the first thirty-four years of the revolution. In exile, Constancia leads a financially successful but unhappy life married to a man she does not love.

Reina, on the other hand, seems to be the luckier of the two. Raised and educated in her own country, this sister also has the love and care of her mother until Blanca is murdered in 1948. Reina is beautiful and sure of herself, a kind of amazonic superwoman who is afraid of nothing and who feels she can accomplish the impossible. When Reina eventually goes into exile in the early 1990s, she joins Constancia in Miami. Together, they find out that they are both haunted by the fragmentary memories surrounding their mother's death. It is their common need to search for the truth that eventually brings the two women to confront each other and to face the consequences of a life of silence and geographical separation.

In keeping with the magical setting of Cristina García's first book, the lives of the protagonists in her second novel are filled with coincidences, strange happenings, and omens. Through her use of *santería* rituals, García skillfully weaves these magical realistic features into her tale as all of her characters seek help from *santero* priests during hard times and seem to be able to obtain some answers from Afro-Cuban religious practices. In fact, it is on the advice of a *santero* that Constancia eventually goes to Cuba in order to rescue her father's memoirs buried in his Camagüey hacienda: "Papi's papers are buried there, under the Mestre farmhouse. The house in which our mother was born, the house of the grandmother who'd been pig-trampled to death. Tío Dámaso wrote that he'd concealed Papi's memoirs in a copper chest lined with yellow felt. Every few years he would dig up the chest and read them again" (283). Agüero's first-person narrative is not fully disclosed as coinciding with the reader's text until the last pages of the novel, when Constancia reaches Cuba.

The facts Constancia recovers from her father's memoirs are indeed sad—they do not exculpate the father from having killed the mother. However, difficult as they are to accept, Agüero's memoirs help Constancia understand the unhappiness and unexplained sorrow that have prevailed in her life. As in Pablo Medina's *The Marks of Birth,* García's embedded narratives are in direct dialogue with the work of Gabriel García Márquez.[18] Also, like Medina, García uses these interior texts as documents that her characters need to read in order to learn from their past and to confront their present.

At the level of plot, Agüero's memoirs establish his involvement in and responsibility for his wife Blanca's death, a fact he tried to keep away from the family. Agüero's story also narrates the birth of the Cuban republic, a tale fraught with violent dictatorships that did much to weaken the fiber of the country. In fact, through the recollections about the patriarch's childhood and adolescence, author Cristina García seems to draw a parallel between the sad events in Agüero's family history and the violence and repression of the first years of the Cuban republic. A son of Spanish immigrants, Agüero represents Cuba's first *criollos,* those who in fact created the country that became today's Cuba. Born in 1904, Agüero portrays in his narrative the violence of Cuba's most repressive tyrannies, in particular that of Eduardo Machado, which corresponded to the years Agüero spent at Havana University: "It was 1931, a dreadful year. Thousands of students were rounded up and many murdered in cold blood" (151–52). Thus the patriarch's writings provide a sociohistorical link to Constancia's unhappiness first in Cuba and later in exile in America.

Agüero's interior texts are also tied to the novel's main effort of pondering about what it means to be human. Agüero's vocation, that of a naturalist, provides him with the opportunity to reflect on what it is that separates humans from lower forms of life in an effort to consider the most human aspects of our lives: "It is my conviction that to our dying breath we have a will, diminished though our range of possibilities may be. Even a man condemned to death can shout one last obscenity. This is our grandeur, what separates us from the lesser creatures of the planet. What then could be more wretched than its voluntary surrender?" (263). Throughout the text, Ignacio's reflections between our humanity and the rest of the species centers on our ability to exert our freedom to choose good over evil and on our vulnerability as human beings. Unfortunately, for Ignacio Agüero himself, his ambition prevails over his better instincts when he carelessly decides to sacrifice his wife's life in order to possess a valuable specimen of a rare hummingbird.

Through Agüero's embedded narrative, the reader also learns about Cuba as a physical wonder of nature, about its flora and its fauna, and about the myriad natural species found therein. The final passage of the novel, which eerily confirms Agüero's responsibility for his wife's murder, also depicts for the reader the beauty of the Cuban landscape: "The day stole past in an hour. Clouds scrolled by, dragging their shadows across the watery land. I heard Blanca's voice in the stirring of grasses and reeds, in the crisscrossing cranes overhead, in the swaying clumps of cow-lily leaves. All afternoon the Zapata clicked and rustled, clicked and rustled its fatal chorus, until a lone red-tailed hawk soared above us. . . . Then, in the broken violet light of dusk, I carried her seventeen miles to the nearest village and reluctantly began to tell my lies" (300). Reminiscent of the last vignette in Guillermo Cabrera Infante's *View of Dawn in the Tropics*, García's novel leaves the reader with only the permanence of Cuba's physical reality and makes no predictions about the future of its unhappy characters. At the end of the novel, the mothers and daughters remain alone and countryless to solve their fates. In fact, within the novel's Darwinian perspective, Reina, the most Cuban character in the novel, seems to have the best odds for survival since she has had to give up little compared to the others.

The Cuban-American writers we examine in chapter 8 exhibit a desire to connect with a larger community of Cubans as well as Cuban Americans in the process of telling their life stories. These novels have made use of narrative strategies such as interior texts and were set in magical realistic contexts in order to construct their different versions of community. But if these narratives looked for answers through the artistic use of metafictional narrative strategies, the process has yielded different results in each case.

The findings of James Ruppert and Reed Way Dasenbrock on the subject of monocultural versus bicultural audiences are pertinent in the assessment of the translatability of these Cuban-American autobiographical fictions.[19] Ruppert coins the term *mediation* to designate the act of negotiation by the writer between two cultural codes. According to Ruppert, the bicultural writer must be free to use the epistemology from both cultures as a way to strike what he calls a "dynamic confluence of values and expectations" (210). The ideal writer of any bicultural text would be able to speak to two audiences at once. Dasenbrock states that "multicultural works of literature are multicultural not only in their subject matter but also as far as how they allow readers into the text" (18).

In the case of Torres and Engle, their texts seem to be directed first to readers who are steeped in either the Cuban culture (Torres) or American culture (Engle). Torres writes his story in English, but there is a reluctance to allow the English reader into the world of the text. In fact, Torres's protagonist agonizes over the possible reaction of the "non–Latin American reader" to his narrative. *Fallen Angels Sing* is the most hopeless of the four versions of diaspora analyzed here, for when Miguel Saavedra looks at his community for acceptance and rediscovery of his identity, he is unable to find much positive to incorporate into his own story. Margarita Engle's text, like Torres's, remains on a cultural periphery although for vastly different reasons. Engle's version of the aftermath of 1959 looks at Cuban culture (in the United States and in Cuba) from the perspective of English. The author's vision of Cubans and of their history comments on the issues of the aftermath of 1959 with affection but also from the distance of someone who is an outsider to the crisis described.

Rather than questioning the idea of belonging to one or two cultures, Pablo Medina's *The Marks of Birth* devotes itself to confronting the inevitability of living in a second culture. The metatext for Medina serves as a document that is drafted by the first generation of exiles (the matriarch Felicia) and that needs to be read and interpreted by the children of these exiles. Anton, Medina's fictional persona, is not given a voice within the text, which is significant. However, he is given the ability to read and interpret the text of the grandmother. Medina's text ends not unlike that of Torres, for both protagonists seem to be doomed to die on Cuban soil. Yet there is a difference between the way Medina and Torres envision the Cuban predicament. For Torres, change is simply not an option. For Medina's character, on the other hand, reading the biography of the grandmother represents a possibility for change or at least for confronting change. *The Marks of Birth* challenges the English reader by questioning the values and differences between Cuban and American cultures.

Finally, Cristina García's novels engage the U.S. experience with self-assurance. In *Dreaming in Cuban*, it is precisely the pull between two places that motivates Pilar's actions. The questions posed by this ethnic version of the Cuban-American condition are directed to the issue of heritage and to reconstructing an identity that very much belongs in the United States but that needs Cuba in order to be complete. Pilar needs Cuba as a context to assume her life because she needs to complete the puzzle of her heritage. By going back and collecting the tales of the women in her family, Pilar will gain the knowledge that she needs about her origins. The stories Pilar collects become the bridge she wishes to make with her relatives in Cuba.[20]

In *The Agüero Sisters,* Constancia's search for the truth about her mother's death is also a search for her understanding of Cuba's unhappy history. Like Pilar, Constancia goes to Cuba in order to collect the lost pieces of her unhappy past. Unlike the young Cuban American in García's first novel, Constancia belongs to an earlier exile generation. She is sure of her Cuban heritage but needs to know more about her country's history in order to understand the roots of her permanent exodus. As one of the first ethnic Cuban-American writers, Cristina García envisions questions of identity, heritage, and history with less anxiety and thus greater distance from her material. Her novels belong to the Cuban exile tradition, but for this author exile has had a different meaning than it had for the Cuban-American writers of the one-and-a-half generation.

Through the study of these fictional stories of geographical and historical crossings, we have seen a divergence in the concerns of contemporary Cuban-American writers. All novels studied in this chapter included both Cubans in Cuba and Cubans abroad in depicting their splintered community. For some, Cuba was the community left behind; for others, Cuba is the unavoidable present, as the *balsero* crisis has indeed shown us. Clearly the work of younger writers of Cuban heritage is separated from the tradition of Cuban letters by much more than language choice. The stories analyzed here serve as reminders of how different in perspective and literary sensibility these versions of diaspora have become.

A Conclusion in Progress

> There are Cubas in many places: on the inside and on the outside, in Havana and in Miami, in bunkers and in dispersion, in little and intransigent cenacles and in large groups, in the ideological storm clouds of "isms" and in the heart of those wandering throughout the world with the deep blue imprinted in their memories.
>
> Joseph Ramoneda, *Cuba la isla posible*

In CUBAN-AMERICAN literature, we are witnessing a field very much in the process of being delineated and discovered. This is attested to by the number of anthologies and creative works that have been published in only the last five years. The almost simultaneous appearance of these novels and anthologies, reviewed here in chapter 4, points toward the idea of the birth or emergence of a new tradition. This publishing boom also leads us to ponder the relationship of Cuban-American literature in English to peer communities of writers publishing in the United States today—namely, the Cuban Americans who have opted to publish in Spanish while residing in America and that amorphous grouping constituted by other Latino/Hispanic writers living in this country.[1]

My study argues that the Cuban-American literary expression is firmly grounded in the experience of exile. Given the separate histories and diverse experiences of Mexican Americans, Puerto Ricans, and Cuban Americans—to name only the three major groups of writers of Spanish heritage residing in the United States today—it is not surprising to find that each represents quite a distinct literary expression. Since the terms *Hispanic* and *Latino* ignore significant political, historical, cultural, and economic differences, I have sought to approach the Cuban case through a manner of exegesis that considers the Cubans' unique history and immigration patterns since 1959.

In her recent study on ethnic labels, Susan Oboler suggests that both *Latino* and *Hispanic* blur the cultural distinctions of writers who can be of at least eighteen different Spanish-speaking countries.[2] *Hispanic,* according to Oboler, is a U.S. government–created distinction that can permit electoral coalitions to be built or census figures to be calculated. *Latinos* is the preferable term, Oboler tells us, since it speaks to a shared cultural dimension that is the Latin culture as well as the Latin roots of the Spanish language. Yet, according to a recent article in the *Miami Herald,* the U.S. government and most of mainstream America's institutions see *Hispanics* as a national category of people.[3] Whether we agree or not, this merging of the various nationalities is quite permanently engraved in U.S. official categorizations.

If asked about personal identity, few Cuban-American writers would identify themselves as Latino or Hispanic writers. The dilemma of labeling these writers as Latinos or Hispanics runs deeper than mere pride of origin. When Latinos or Hispanics look at each other they see Chicanos, Puerto Ricans, Cubans, Dominicans, and so on. Gustavo Pérez Firmat summarizes some common objections that writers of Spanish heritage have to the idea of labels: "Latino is a statistical fiction, a figment of the imagination of ethnic ideologues, ad executives and salsa singers. I am not a Latino. I am Cuban . . . to me a Latino is an empty concept. Latino doesn't have a culture, a language, a place of origin. How do you eat Latino? You can dance Cuban. You can dance rancheras, but how do you dance Latino? And if you drink a rum and Coke, it's a Cuba Libre not a Latino Libre."[4]

In a recent article, Pablo Medina explains how ethnic labels are used and misused in order to classify writers and literatures: "When I became a writer and started publishing my work . . . I was called a Hispanic-American writer or a Cuban-American one, or occasionally, a Latino writer. . . . I had the distinct impression that I was somehow being manipulated. I wanted to be known simply as a writer, a good writer preferably, and all other labels seemed to detract from and diffuse that ambition."[5] Medina's essay is significant because it expresses a common concern of minority authors writing in English today. For this author the important aspects of his literature, or any literature for that matter, lie in its ability to communicate its human content to the reader, and labels, of any kind, are seen as a restrictive influence on the creative act.

How *Latino* or *Hispanic* is the Cuban-American text? Cuban-American literature seems to be less concerned with issues of political advocacy than its Mexican-American or Puerto Rican counterparts. Writers of Spanish heritage raised in the United States, such as Chicanos and Puerto Ricans from New York, write a literature of political engagement, speaking of issues in their lives as minority groups within American society.[6] Compared to the ideological dimension historically associated with these literatures, the Cuban-American corpus *as a whole* has not displayed a clearly delineated political stance. Nevertheless, the writings of Cuban-American males have concentrated mainly on issues of self-understanding rather than political activism, whereas the fictions and personal writings of Cuban-American women such as Cristina García, Ruth Behar, and Eliana Rivero consistently include issues related to minority politics, gender issues, and women's rights. As writers, these women have had to reckon with the patriarchal antecedents of their culture and deal with *machismo* as a transplanted value here in the United States. The same can be said for the lesbian narratives of Achy Obejas, a writer who brings to her texts issues of sexual identity and tolerance within the context of her Cuban-American community in exile.

In addition, if Cuban-American narratives in English have not been more engaged in minority politics to date, it is quite possible that this situation might change. Current events such as the anti-immigrant sentiments in certain states and Washington, D.C., the immigration and welfare reforms of Congress, and the downing of the Brothers to the Rescue planes by the Cuban government in February 1996 (an incident in which three of the killed crew members were American citizens)[7] may impact the splintered politics and ideologies of Cubans residing in America. Events such as these have forced the members of the Cuban communities in Florida and other parts of the country to unite in protest and to find commonalities in order to achieve political gain.

With regard to literary aesthetics, Cuban-American writing in English opts for a more traditional expression than its other Latino/Hispanic counterparts. Unlike Chicano and Puerto Rican narratives, which often mix languages or create combinations of English and Spanish within the literary work (especially in their poetry), the Cuban-American narrative is usually either in English or in Spanish.[8] The Cuban Americans' preferential use of traditional English in their literary works could be attributed in part to the fact that a Cuban-American literary expression in Spanish also exists in the United States today.

The Spanish Tradition

The presence of a Spanish corpus in Cuban-American letters is a unique phenomenon that responds to the existence of Spanish-dominant exile enclaves such as Miami and the cultural influence that the frequent immigration patterns of Cubans as a group have had on the enclave within the last forty years.

David Rieff and Mark Falcoff tell us that the constant migrations and the geographical proximity between Cuba and the United States provide the populations in exile as well as those on the island with a constant source of vitality and creativity.[9] According to Rieff, the recent improvement of phone communication and the more open travel policies of the last few years have made contacts with the island almost commonplace. If this is the case, it is most likely that the tradition of writing literature in Spanish rather than the English tradition will be influenced most by these new and more frequent associations with the national culture.

Writers of Cuban heritage from a variety of generations and migratory waves continue to publish and thrive in Spanish, especially among the U.S. Cuban communities of Miami, New York, and Los Angeles. In addition, a loyal readership in Spanish seems to be holding strong, especially in South Florida.[10] In the Miami area alone, the production of literary works in Spanish in the area of poetry and theater is extremely prolific. Theater (texts and dramatic productions) and poetry (readings and collections) are most popular among Spanish-speaking Cuban audiences. Most Cuban-American works written and published in Spanish remain unexamined today and are in need of careful study and analysis from scholars and literary critics. Like other literatures in Spanish available in the United States, the dissemination of these works owes most of its vitality to the minority publishing venues that have sprung up in the last two decades, such as Ediciones Universal in Florida, Bilingual Press in Arizona, and Arte Público in Texas.

Among the Miami writers producing in Spanish, we must mention Hilda Perera.[11] By chronology, she would be best placed with the first exile generation, but she has written most of her mature work in the United States. Uva Clavijo and Ileana Fuentes Pérez of the second generation and Carlos Victoria and Jesús Barquet of the Mariel migratory wave are also well-known local literary figures who continue to write in Spanish about issues of Cuban culture from an exilic perspective. Most important due to their high visibility, Cuban playwrights such as María Irene Fornés, Matías Montes Huidobro, José Triana, and Pedro Monge continue to enjoy a great deal of popularity among Spanish-speaking audiences in South Florida. In the Northeast, the narratives of Antonio Benítez-Rojo and the poetry of Heberto Padilla,[12] both first-generation writers who arrived from Cuba in the 1980s, as well as the poetry and prose of one-and-a-half generation authors such as Maya Islas, José Kozer, Emilio Bejel, Lourdes Gil, Alberto Chiroldes, and Flora González Mandri, among others, continues to be published in Spanish.

In addition to the prolific work by Cuban writers in the various literary genres in Miami and New York City, other Cuban-born novelists write in Spanish from other parts of the globe. For instance, Mireya Robles and René Vázquez Díaz visit Miami periodically but permanently reside in South Africa and Sweden, respectively. These writers have created their Spanish works in isolation from Cuban communities, even if some, like Mireya Robles, have been away from the national soil for as much as thirty-seven years. Others, like Zoé Valdés, have recently become exiles, and their writings have become instant best-sellers in France and Spain.[13] Many of these writers fight to preserve the cultural traditions that existed in Cuban letters before the revolution.

Among this multifarious group of Cuban-American writers producing in Spanish, poet-essayist Lourdes Gil stands out, for she has contributed to her one-and-a-half generation with her poetry and with some insightful essays on the predicament of writers such as herself (see chapter 4 of this book).[14] The choice of language is crucial for a writer, although in the case of Lourdes Gil the choice of Spanish assures her a place in the margins of the Anglo intellectual community. Most of Gil's creative and scholarly writings have sought to explain her need to continue to write in Spanish. Her latest book of poems, *El cerco de las transfiguraciones,* features a poem entitled "Reincidencia en la tierra," which suggests a possible dialogue with Pablo Neruda's *Residencia en la tierra* since both Neruda and Gil wrote their poetry away from their native countries. In this poem, Gil expresses a sense of dislocation toward her creative task as well as the anxiety of a writer who knows the consequences of writing in a tongue alien to her adopted space: "If all writing is a search / where is this search leading us?" (3; my translation; "*Si toda escritura es una búsqueda / ¿por qué veredas caminamos?*"). Many of the poems included in Gil's latest collection denote the anxiety of a writer aware of creating in Spanish while residing in the space of English. Indeed, as Lourdes Gil explains in her recent piece "Against the Grain: Why I Write in Spanish," writing her poetry in Spanish becomes a need and a form of resistance: "Holding on to one's old identity in the face of the new can be an obstinate, fearsomely barren gesture of defiance. There is also an innate complicity in the act of choosing a language over another—a form of loyalty, perhaps, loyalty to the well-worn frame of reference where the self has been, up to that time, contextualized, an attachment to one's past, a devotion" (371). For Gil, Spanish means a link to her roots and to the traditions of the culture of her nation. She and the others who have chosen to continue to write in their native tongue feel that their literary production very much belongs to the tradition of Cuban letters and therefore want to be a part of this canon. In other words, their identity as writers neither comes from nor belongs to North American letters.

Interestingly, many writers publishing in Spanish are now beginning to translate their works into English in order to acquire a wider readership. Others, such as writer-scholar Benítez Rojo, have translated their Spanish works into English since coming to the United States. It is important to emphasize, however, that the literature written originally in Spanish and now being translated into English in order to reach both English- and Spanish-reading audiences responds to essentially different aims and perspectives than the Cuban-American production in English analyzed in this study.

The Spanish and English traditions of Cuban writing in the United States have in fact two different functions. The English branch seeks to create a distinctive culture of Cuban roots, whereas the Spanish branch wishes to preserve Cuban culture and seeks affiliation with the canon of Cuban and Latin American letters. Indeed, writers who prefer to use Spanish feel that their choice of language maintains a needed link with their Cuban culture and with the traditions of Spanish and Latin American letters.

Writing Cuban Culture in English

In a panel discussion on Cuban-American literature held in Orlando, Florida, in 1996, author Roberto Fernández was asked by a member of the audience why he had decided to publish his last two novels in English. He replied, "I write in English so that the future generations of Cubans in the U.S. can read me."[15] In my mind, what Roberto Fernández said had to do with his intense need to know that if his literature was not going to be part of Cuban letters, his work had to survive somehow for the community that will always live abroad. For this author, as well as the others I have analyzed in this text, the tradition of Cuban writing in English serves an important function of mediation between the Spanish and the English worlds by explaining one to the other. By choosing to write and publish in English, writers like Fernández face the challenge of educating the younger members of their community as well as the dominant culture about what it means to be a Cuban in North America.

As with all ethnic literatures in English, a key issue in the study of these English narratives of Cuban heritage has to do with the English tradition itself and with the interactions between ethnic literatures and

American culture. In *A Double Exile,* West Indian scholar Gareth Griffiths asserts that writers writing in a language other than their own have two traditions in their background: the poetic tradition of their native countries and the tradition of their language of choice. In order to achieve an individual style, the writer must balance the problems of both linguistic traditions (57). According to Griffiths, ethnic writers can borrow from more than one tradition, and this borrowing itself renews the possibilities of English (145). He further points out that any writer who is totally fluent in two languages and two cultures has the potential to change the perception of the one culture's reality by writing in the language of the other culture. Thus, when a non-English culture and the English language combine, the possibility of changing the perception of reality as experienced by English native speakers occurs. Griffiths points out, "although the language employed is English, the experience recorded is not, and that new experience may profoundly alter the language and the form employed" (141).

Has the Cuban culture as portrayed in our texts been translated into forms comprehensible to American readers? Is the literature of Cuban heritage produced in English distinctive? Cuban-American writers have incorporated social and aesthetic aims into their fictions that have resulted in distinctive versions of conventional genres: bicultural memoirs and novels of historical and geographic crossings. In very different ways and with different results, the novels we examine here have introduced techniques and contents that are the product of a merger of both the North American and Latin American traditions of letters. These fictions are very much tied to issues that pertain exclusively to Cuban historical realities but that in some cases reflect aesthetic influences associated with Latin American or North American literature.

Works such as *The Marks of Birth* by Pablo Medina and Cristina García's *Dreaming in Cuban* and *The Agüero Sisters* bear the imprint of the magical realistic tradition of García Márquez and Isabel Allende. These novels have shown us that the Cuban-American production at its best is a mix of Latin American and North American literary traditions, a production that borrows from both, a writing of Cuban culture in English. Such works have merged the Cuban culture and the English language, and in some cases, the writings produced have contributed to an English writing with a Latin American spirit. On the other hand, Roberto Fernández's *Raining Backwards* and *Holy Radishes!* and Achy Obejas's *Memory Mambo* seem to be grounded away from the context of magical realism and toward a tradition rooted in the direct, popular style more commonly associated with today's North American writing. The style of Fernández and Obejas sometimes evokes the sad, sordid realities of North American streets, although it never loses the self-directed humor and compassion that render these works their particular Cuban flavor. Both writers, by virtue of their bicultural perspective, display a unique Cuban and American consciousness.

In the same vein, the bicultural memoirs produced by Gustavo Pérez Firmat, Pablo Medina, and Virgil Suárez evolve from an autobiographical style that responds to needs outside the mainstream tradition of American immigrant autobiography. Their memoirs align themselves with a current wave of ethnic autobiographical writing that does not so much aspire to achieve the traditional idea of the American Dream but that uses autobiographical writings to "talk back to this American Dream."[16] In fact, rather than seeking to call American society "home," Cuban-American autobiographical writing attempts to redefine and expand just what being Cuban in America really means. Similar in some respects to other autobiographical narratives produced today by other ethnic immigrant writers, these autobiographical texts propose a different image from what had been known traditionally as American immigrant autobiography.

Cuban writing in English today owes much of its originality to its link to a unique event in history—the revolution of 1959. The stories of that event, as analyzed in this text, have shown how the reality of these writers and their memories of incidents that occurred in Spanish have effectively and dramatically communicated a Cuban vision through the linguistic medium of English. Exile has indeed proved to be a positive experience for the members of the second generation as the physical distance from their original geography and culture has led these writers to look anew at the values and traditions of Cuban culture. English, as used by these writers, serves to validate the experiences of their group. As they incorporate their Cuban selves into their English selves, the writing of these authors becomes enriched, and therefore their ability to create is magnified.

Because my study concentrates exclusively on the prose writings of representative authors, many Cuban-American ethnic writers of promise are not included. A useful point of departure for readers who wish to study these emerging writers is to examine the anthologies mentioned in chapter 4, especially Virgil Suárez's *Little Havana Blues,* the contributors to which are authors who write and reside in the United States. It should also be noted that these anthologies incorporate selections of theater and poetry,[17] also fertile areas of literary activity in English that remain outside the boundaries of my study.

This examination of the English versions of the story of exile by several generations of authors writing outside Cuba shows how these writers have had to rely on their own experience as inspiration for their writings, hence the predominance of autobiography and autobiographical fictions tracing these writers' struggle to understand themselves. Because of the loss of community and culture inherent in the exile experience, the Cuban-American writers' attempt to replicate their community in their works is based on their individual experience. To a large extent, the Cuba that these writers have discovered is really the Cuba within themselves.[18]

A literature born of exile is a literature that by force has to rely on memory and imagination more than any other since the cultural reality of an exiled writer is no longer available to fuel his or her creativity. Perhaps a fitting way to end this study is to return to scenes taken from three narratives that feature divergent sensibilities toward the story of the diaspora. In all three, the characters involved reflect on their lack of ability to imagine and to dream. I read these scenes as metaphors of the authors' concerns about their ability to function as writers outside their native country. These narrative instances can readily demonstrate the aesthetic transformation of an exiled literature.

In *The Doorman*, the challenge for Reinaldo Arenas was to be able to create and imagine away from his Cuban homeland. During one of his many sad meditations, Arenas's doorman-protagonist refers to the United States as "this other place where we now survive, but where we don't exist because we no longer dream" (168). Arenas perceived his literary task in terms of the space lost and from the spaces and the geraphy he could no longer see. Arenas's posthumously published short story entitled "Final de un cuento" (End of a story), dated 1982 but available in print only recently, also gives us evidence of what writing in exile meant for him.

In "Final de un cuento," narrated as a letter to a lover who stayed in Cuba, the author mixes chronology and geographical spaces. Arenas begins by describing the northern geography of New York State and abruptly takes us back to his dear Cuba, his Havana streets and the Cuban countryside. In this tale, the Hudson River breaks against the walls of the Cuban Malecón, and the Calzada de Jesús del Monte blends with Lincoln Center. This mixing of landscapes, Key West and Havana, the streets of New York and the Cuban countryside, becomes a background for the words of Arenas, the wounded writer, who seeks to explain himself to a lover he will probably never see again: "Listen to me: Nostalgia can also be a kind of consolation, a sweet kind of pain, a way of seeing things and even a way to enjoy them. Our triumph is in our resistance. Our revenge is to outlive ourselves" (156).[19] Reinaldo Arenas lived within his nostalgia, and in a way nostalgia fueled his writing. The United States as an adopted homeland becomes a necessary evil that must be accepted, since it is the only place for the exile writer who knows that a return to the native land would never be possible. In a poetic dialogue with nineteenth-century exiled poet José María Heredia, Arenas's antidote to exile becomes his ability to blend the Cuban and the American landscapes.[20]

Like Arenas's doorman, Felicia, the matriarch in Pablo Medina's *The Marks of Birth,* reflects her doubts and anxieties regarding imagining and creating in a new or adopted land. But there is a difference. In the following scene, Felicia listens to the advice of a friend who wishes to alleviate her pain: "This is the land of waking. . . . Ours was the land of dreaming. Here, people matter in relation to their objects; there, we mattered in relation to the people who dreamed with us. Our objects died when our dreams did. That is why we need inner light to illuminate our path" (246-47). For Medina, a writer of the one-and-a-half generation, understanding what has happened in order to go on is crucial. Creation in a new space cannot occur unless there is first a recognition of self. In this novel, Medina's task is that of coping, but he must also assess issues of dislocation and look toward new manners of reconstructing a life in exile.

The trajectory of creating and imagining can only be completed when the ability to dream and to imagine in both languages is possible. In the work of Cristina García, the experience of exile is described from a distance, which allows García the freedom to once again imagine. In order to fully dream, Pilar, the protagonist in *Dreaming in Cuban,* needs Spanish even if her dreams are to be expressed in an English destined to validate the experiences of her group: "I've started dreaming in Spanish, which has never happened before. I wake up feeling different, like something inside me is changing, something chemical and irreversible" (235). Even though Cristina García, as an American writer of two cultures, knows that Spanish is essential in her need to understand the strands of her heritage, English is the language that gives life to her work as a writer, the language that stimulates her creative dreams.

In a text such as this, I have approached the extraterritorial narratives of the aftermath of the revolution of 1959 and have pursued their aesthetic transformation. I have read books that define an English literature of Cuban heritage. The path this text has taken displays a trajectory of a specific literature that has evolved from the personal injury of exile to the creation of fictions that allow their authors to make sense of events in a way they could not in their real lives.

Central to this process of aesthetic distancing is also the issue of choosing the best critical practice in order to approach this literature. Behind all literature, especially a literature rooted in exile such as I have examined. there is always an "I" that insists on perduring by narrating himself or herself. In like manner, criticism is also a way of narrating the self through the writings of others, a way to ask questions through the artistic works of others. As a critic who is also a Cuban American, I too have faced the task of separating the personal from the critic's persona. In my readings of these works, I have looked for the distinctive characteristics of each writer in relation to the others and for their points of convergence, with the goal of understanding each text and not merely classifying them under any specific rubric. Hopefully, the Cuban-American story of exile has also taught readers something about their own humanity.

This book deals with a living and evolving literary expression, which makes any predictions and conclusions tentative because every one of the writers analyzed in parts 2 and 3 continues to grow and develop their own vision of community away from Cuba. What shape the future of Cuban-American writing in English will take is hard to predict, although a few paths seem to have been traced already. A very promising literature will continue to be produced by Cuban-American women who are introducing in their fictions both the concerns of biculturality and the gender issues common in the literature of other Latina writers living in the United States. In addition, as long as new waves of immigration from Cuba continue to occur, carrying with them would-be writers of all ages, a literature displaying divided selves due to a rupture of languages and cultures will continue to be created in English. This literature will carry a different yet similar story of rupture than the one experienced by the writers of the one-and-a-half generation. If these future writers preserve their Cuban culture in their works, Cuban-American letters will be guaranteed a place in today's American ethnic literatures.

Notes

Introduction

1. "The culture of a people is an ensemble of texts, themselves ensembles, which the anthropologist strains to read over the shoulders of those to whom they properly belong . . . societies, like lives, contain their own interpretations. One has only to learn how to gain access to them." Geertz, "Deep Play," 412–53.

2. White, *Tropics of Discourse,* 121–34.

3. For a panoramic view of exile in Cuban letters see Luis, "Latin American Literature," 526–57. Also see Souza, "Exile," 1–5; for a valuable overview of exile in Latin American letters see González Echevarría, "Literature and Exile," 124–36.

4. See Falcoff, "Cuban Diaspora," 1, 4.

5. M. C. García underscores the importance of looking at the various waves of migration that have comprised the 1959 diaspora in order to fully understand the historical complexity of the last Cuban exile. For a complete account of the Mariel exodus see "The Mariel Boatlift of 1980: Origin and Consequences," in *Havana USA,* 46–80.

6. For a look at the impact of the Mariel exodus on Miami see Portes and Stepick, *City on the Edge,* 18–38.

7. In recent years there have been various attempts to classify the writings of Cuban Americans according to their different waves of migration. Eliana Rivero, in particular, makes useful distinctions between the concerns of exiles and ethnic writers. See Rivero, "From Immigrants to Ethnics," 189–200, and "Cubanos y Cubano Americanos," 81–101. Also see Burunat, "Comparative Study," 101–23; Hospital, "Los hijos del exilio," 103–14, and her introduction to Hospital and Cantera, *Century of Cuban Writers,* 1–26; see also Figueredo, "To Be Cuban," 18–23.

8. Hospital, "Los Atrevidos," 22–23.

9. Pérez Firmat, *Life on the Hyphen,* 136–53.

10. Paul J. Eakin reminds us that recent work in cultural anthropology and linguistics has deepened our understanding of the ways in which culture and language shape the ideology of identity that informs autobiography: "if the self . . . is so deeply implicated in the emergence of language, then . . . a recreation of the dramatization of the self can occur in autobiographical discourse" (*Fictions in Autobiography*, 213). Eakin's second study, *Touching the World*, continues his exploration of autobiography, providing a wealth of insights into the relationships of autobiography and culture. My study of Cuban-American narratives of autobiography owes much to Eakin's findings on this subject.

11. Kristeva, *Nations without Nationalism*, 1–47.

12. Antonio Vera León applies Kristeva's insights to his discussion on the nature and essence of extraterritorial Cuban literature. See his "Bilingual Writings," 243–45.

1. Exile and Retribution

1. Kavolis, "Women Writers in Exile," 43–46.

2. Gass, "Philosophical Significance of Exile," 1–8.

3. Cabrera Infante, "Invisible Exile," 34–41.

4. Ugarte, *Shifting Ground*, 3–31.

5. Novás Calvo, *Maneras de contar*. All stories and quoted passages come from the Las Américas edition. The translations are mine.

6. Of the eighteen stories in this volume, thirteen were written after the author came to the United States. The other stories in the collection are earlier pieces from different periods of his career. For a full evaluation of all the stories in this volume as well as Novás Calvo's complete works see Souza, *Lino Novás Calvo*, and Roses, *Voices of the Storyteller*.

7. Novás Calvo, "Nadie a quien matar," in *Maneras de contar*, 75–90 (written in 1968).

8. Desnoes, *Inconsolable Memories* (*Memorias del subdesarrollo*, 1965), trans. by the author. In 1968, Desnoes's novel was also made into a well-known film, *Memories of Underdevelopment*, directed by Gutiérrez Alea.

9. Novás Calvo, "Fernández, al paredón," in *Maneras de contar*, 153–71 (written in 1961).

10. Novás Calvo, "Un buchito de café," in *Maneras de contar*, 209–25 (written in 1961).

11. Novás Calvo, "Un bum," in *Maneras de contar*, 281–95 (written in 1964).

12. Novás Calvo, "La noche en que Juan tumbó a Pedro," in *Maneras de contar*, 263–80 (written in 1964).

2. Challenging History from Exile

1. Cabrera Infante, "Viaje verbal," interview by Isabel Alvarez Borland, 58–59. The translation is mine.

2. Cabrera Infante, *View of Dawn in the Tropics*. All page references come from the Creative Arts edition.

3. Peavler, "Cabrera Infante's Undertow," 125–45. Also see Souza, "Images of History," in *Guillermo Cabrera Infante*. According to Souza, Cabrera Infante was "reassembling a fragmented memory, an essential step on his own personal road to recovery" (124).

4. Key dates in the history of Cuba can be deduced from historical details provided within the vignettes: discovery to independence (1492–1898), 1–48; Machado's years (1925–33), 60–66; Batista's dictatorship (1952–59), 66–116; the revolution (1959–72), 116–41. For an earlier reading of *View of Dawn* based on its generic features see "La viñeta" in my *Discontinuidad y ruptura*, 33–59.

5. Hutcheon, *Poetics of Postmodernism*, 92. According to Hutcheon: "Historiographic metafiction refutes the natural or common sense methods of distinguishing between historical fact and fiction. It refuses the view that only history has a truth claim, both by questioning the ground of that claim in historiography and by asserting that both history and fiction are discourses, human constructs, signifying systems, and both derive their major claim to truth from that identity" (93). *View of Dawn* can be considered a historiographic metafiction because it dramatizes the process of historical reconstruction by means of a fictional historian who confronts the process of how official history is created. Hutcheon's model is applicable to other contemporary Latin American novels, such as García Márquez's *El general en su laberinto* and Vargas Llosa's *La Historia de Mayta*, among others.

6. Studying the influence of other painters on Goya, Sara Symmons explains that "Goya found two qualities in John Flaxman's work which became fundamental to the evolution of *The Disasters*: a story linked through pictures and compositions stripped of all detail to make the narrative clear" (83). See Symmons, *Goya*.

7. See Foster, "Hacia una caracterización," 5–13.

8. Ong, *Orality and Literacy*, 170–90. Also see his "Writer's Audience," 9–21.

9. Vargas Llosa, "Is Fiction the Art of Lying?" 40.

3. Existential Exile

1. Arenas, *The Doorman*. All quoted passages come from the Grove Press edition.

2. Arenas, interview by Francisco Soto, "Conversación con Reinaldo Arenas," 47. The translation is mine.

3. For the most complete study on Reinaldo Arenas's life and works see Soto, *Reinaldo Arenas*.

4. The published works in Spanish by other members of the Mariel generation, such as Carlos Victoria and Roberto Valero, will be deserving of critical attention. For a brief overview see Bertot, *Literary Imagination*.

5. The French novelist-philosopher Jean Paul Sartre has done the most to give existential criticism and philosophy its present form. While Arenas introduces Sartre's *Being and Nothingness* as one of the books read by his protagonist doorman (151), his character has much in common with Sartre's Roquentin, the protagonist of *La Nausée*. "The existentialist's point of departure is the immediate sense of awareness that human beings have of their situation. A part of this awareness is the sense they have of meaninglessness in the outer world; this meaninglessness produces in them a discomfort, an anxiety, a loneliness in the face of human limitations and a desire to invest experience with meaning by acting upon the world, although efforts to act in a meaningless, 'absurd' world lead to anguish, greater loneliness, and despair." For a complete definition see Holman, "Existentialism," in *Handbook to Literature*, 176–78. For contemporary discussions of existentialism see Baker, *Dynamics of the Absurd*, and Wolin, *Terms of Cultural Criticism*.

6. Kristeva, *Strangers to Ourselves*, 1–41.

7. Illie, *Literature and Inner Exile*, 1–35.

8. Soto, "*El Portero*," 106–17.

9. In *Of Grammatology*, Jacques Derrida tells us that "Written discourse is born out of a primary expatriation, condemning it to wandering and blindness, to mourning" (39). Derrida's critique of language focuses on the privileging of the spoken word over the written word. Writing, being the representation of speech, is removed from meaning in a way that speech is not.

10. Derrida, "Edmond Jabès." For an adaptation of Derrida's insights on writing and the literature of exile see Incledon, "Parricide and Exile," 169–81.

11. Arenas, interview by Perla Rozencvaig, "Last Interview," 81.

12. As quoted in Souza, Review of Reinaldo Arenas's *Before Night Falls*. Also see González Echevarría, "Outcast of the Island," 1, 24.

4. Issues and Patterns

1. Pérez, "Unique but Not Marginal," 258–71. Also see Alejandro Portes's recent study, *New Second Generation*.

2. Most of the Cuban-American writers studied here began their English writing careers as poets. See the authors' bibliography for a listing of their publications. Also see Caufield, *34th Street* and *Angel Dust*; Curbelo, *Geography of Leaving*; Pau-Llosa, *Bread of the Imagined, Cuba,* and *Sorting Metaphors*; and Martínez, *History as a Second Language* and *Bad Alchemy*.

3. Please note that Achy Obejas's *Memory Mambo* is reviewed in chapter 7, Cristina García's *The Agüero Sisters* in chapter 8, and Virgil Suárez's *Spared Angola* in chapter 5.

4. *Contra viento y marea* is an anthology of anonymous contributions by second-generation Cuban Americans who decided to return to Cuba for the first time since their families left in the early 1960s. The collection is significant because it pioneers a literature of exile. The contributors, most of whom were born

in Cuba between 1945 and 1955, grew up in the United States and returned to Cuba as young adults either through the Antonio Maceo Brigade or through the flights established after 1979 in order to rediscover their place of birth. In 1978, Cuba awarded this anthology its most distinguished literary award, the *Premio Casa de las Américas*. Among the editors of *Contra viento y marea* is Lourdes Casal, who is considered one of the major poets in modern Cuban-American literature. Casal died in 1979.

5. Representative pieces in *Bridges to Cuba,* such as those by María de los Angeles Torres and Esther Shapiro Rok, express the difficulties of the second-generation Cubans in negotiating their culture of origin and their native community in exile. For Torres, her parent's politics become obsolete; for Shapiro Rok, emotional issues need to be confronted. See Torres, "Beyond the Rupture," 419–37, and Shapiro Rok, "Finding What Has Been Lost," 579–90. The publication of *Bridges to Cuba* was also observed with a two-day conference held in Michigan during the fall of 1994 at which many of the contributors were present.

6. At present, Carolina Hospital is associate professor of writing and literature at Miami-Dade Community College and was resident scholar for the Florida Humanities Council in 1994. For additional bio-bibliographical details see Kanellos, *Hispanic Literary Companion,* 138–42.

7. My thanks to Lourdes Gil for allowing me to read some of the essays that are included in her as yet unpublished collection "Viaje por las Zonas Templadas."

8. Pérez Firmat, "Transcending Exile," 1–13.

9. Gil, "Conjugar los espacios," 86–96. The translations are mine.

10. For additional perspectives on the role of extraterritorial Cuban cultural production and the Cuban homeland see Behar, "Cuba y su Diáspora," 7–14; Vera León, "Bilingual Writings and Bicultural Subjects," 243–45.

11. Eakin, *Touching the World,* 117–18. Here Eakin applies his insights on how language is related to the structures of identity to his discussion of Mexican-American writer Richard Rodríguez's *Hunger of Memory*. His findings are relevant to the autobiographical writings of the Cuban Americans discussed in my text.

12. Weiss, *On the Margins,* 1–15.

13. Eakin, *Fictions in Autobiography,* 9.

5. Autobiographical Writing

1. According to Phillipe Lejeune, an autobiographical pact occurs between reader and writer only when the latter discloses his or her identity as that of the person who authors the autobiography. See Lejeune, "Autobiographical Pact," 3–30.

2. Olney, *Tell Me Africa,* 3–26. Olney's classic treatise on African literature written outside Africa as well as V. Smith's study on Afro-American narratives were quite helpful in my own conceptualization of the Cuban-American case.

3. Research in the theory of autobiography has approached the problem from very diverse angles. Olney's *Metaphors of the Self: The Meaning of Autobiography* and de Man's essay "Autobiography as Defacement" have become classic texts arguing contrasting positions on the subject. Paul de Man, drawing from the poststructuralism of Lacan, Foucault, and Derrida, argues that the question of autobiographical truth is not a question at all since the identity that the text seeks to represent is originally constituted as a fiction. Moreover, de Man's writings sustain that the concepts of subject, self, and author collapse into the act of producing a text. James Olney, on the other hand, asserts the informing "I" behind the autobiographical act as indispensable to the significance of this genre. For a concise review of these opposing views of the self see Gunn, *Autobiography,* 5–8, and Eakin, *Fictions,* 188–91.

4. Although Molloy's study concentrates on nineteenth- and twentieth-century Latin American literary figures, her observations regarding these writers' perceptions of self are relevant to contemporary Cuban-American autobiographical narratives as well. See Molloy, introduction to *At Face Value,* 1–13.

5. Under "Operation Peter Pan" more than fourteen thousand children boarded planes and left Cuba between 1961 and 1963. The experience of being uprooted and sent alone to a different country with a new culture and language was extremely traumatic for these children. As María Cristina García recounts, "Thirty years after the fact, the views of the now grown children of Operation Peter Pan vary: some are grateful for the care they received, while others remember those years with bitterness." See her *Havana USA,* 23–26. Also see Armengol Acierno, *Children of Flight Pedro Pan.*

6. Medina, *Exiled Memories* (1990). All references are to the University of Texas Press edition. Portions of my analysis of *Exiled Memories* previously appeared in my "Displacements and Autobiography," 43–49.

7. Pascal's classic study of autobiography makes useful distinctions between autobiography and memoir according to whether the focus is primarily inward, on the development of the self (autobiography), or more external—on others, on events, and on deeds (memoir). See Pascal, *Design and Truth,* 54, 132.

8. Bruss, *Autobiographical Acts,* 1–31.

9. Said, "Reflections on Exile," 157–75. In this essay, Said distinguishes between exiles (those prevented from returning to their homelands) and refugees (those who made a conscious choice to leave their homelands).

10. Renza, "Veto of the Imagination," 271.

11. Pérez Firmat, *Next Year in Cuba,* 8. All quoted passages come from the Doubleday-Anchor edition.

12. See Eakin, *Touching the World.* Using a series of texts from Henry Adams to Howard Fraser, Eakin demonstrates how autobiography functions as a way for the individual to come to terms with history and how the writing of autobiography itself can function as the instrument for this negotiation (144).

13. For definitions of *machismo* from a Latina perspective, see del Castillo Guibault, "Americanization Is Tough," 163–66; for a Cuban woman's view see Fuentes Pérez, *Cuba sin caudillos*, 55–101.

14. Just as the community in Cuba has changed from what these writers knew in their infancies, the adopted community of Miami has also become something else for those who grew up there. For a perceptive look at change in Miami see Grenier and Stepic, *Miami Now!* Portes and Stepic, *City on the Edge;* and Rieff, *Exile*. These texts try to interpret the lives of Cubans in Florida for the American reader. For a summary of different perspectives on the city of Miami see León, "Connecticut Yankee," 690–701.

15. Shapiro Rok describes a systemic theory of family development that "redefines the individual as collaborative creation." As she explains, her work on this theory stems directly from the personal circumstances of her life, "from my need to create coherence out of a shattering personal and family legacy of politically motivated traumatic immigration." Shapiro's insights on the psychology of immigrants are extremely helpful in the understanding of Pérez Firmat's personal traumas in the United States and his own recognition of the amnesiac effects he suffers when trying to recall aspects of his Cuban childhood. See Shapiro Rok, "Finding What Has Been Lost," 570–89. On the psychological implications of exile also see Espín, "Roots Uprooted," 151–64.

16. See Virgil Suárez, *Latin Jazz* (1989); *The Cutter* (1991); *Welcome to the Oasis* (1992); *Havana Thursdays* (1995); and *Going Under* (1996). Suárez has also edited two anthologies, one of which is *Little Havana Blues,* reviewed here in chapter 4. For bio-bibliographical details see Kanellos, *Hispanic Literary Companion,* 323–26.

17. See Suchlicki, "The Decade of Institutionalization," in *Cuba,* 173–202.

18. Suárez, *Spared Angola,* 11. All quoted passages come from the Arte Público edition.

19. For an overview of Chicana literature see Rebolledo and Rivero, *Infinite Divisions.*

20. Rich, "Notes towards a Politics of Location," 210–31.

21. Rivero, "'Fronteraisleña,' Border Islander," 669–75; "Of Borders and Self," 1–25.

22. As Homi K. Bhabha indicates, the paradigm of hybridity entails the formulation of a border subject, basing this construction on multiple rather than unified identities. See Bhabha, *Location of Culture,* 171–211.

23. Behar, "Juban," 151–70. My thanks to Ruth Behar for sharing with me the galley proofs of this essay.

24. In the construction of her own theories regarding Cuban Jews as "translated" people, Behar refers to Pérez Firmat's treatise on the heterogeneity of Cuban culture. See Pérez Firmat, *Cuban Condition.*

25. In her introductory essay ("Vulnerable Observer," 1–34) and concluding

essay ("Anthropology That Breaks Your Heart," 161–78) in *The Vulnerable Observer,* Behar advocates changes in the methodologies of anthropological research.

26. Eakin, *Touching the World,* 136.

6. Contrasting Visions of Community

1. Joaquín Fraxedas's *The Lonely Crossing of Juan Cabrera* and the Spanish edition, *La travesía solitaria de Juan Cabrera,* were published simultaneously by St. Martin's Press. All quoted passages come from the English version.

2. The 1990s has been a tragic decade for the *balseros.* See M. C. García, *Havana USA,* 78–80; also see Balmaseda, "Appalling, Outrageous"; and Pérez, "Viewpoint."

3. For Operation Peter Pan, see note 5, chapter 5.

4. See Fernández's bio–bibliographical entry in Kanellos, *Hispanic Literary Companion,* 83–93.

5. Among recent studies examining *Raining Backwards* see Vázquez, "Parody, Intertextuality," 92–102; Ibieta, "Transcending the Culture," 67–77; Deaver, "Structure, Theme, Motif," 100–112; and Deaver, "Colonization and the Death," 112–18.

6. The episodic and cyclical structure of Fernández's novel resembles that of G. Cabrera Infante's *Three Trapped Tigers.* Fernández has favored this episodic structure in most of his works, including his latest novel, *Holy Radishes!*

7. Sadly enough, the xenophobia that worried Fernández almost a decade ago has become a reality in the 1990s as Hispanic immigrants in the United States have become a political football for both Republicans and Democrats. See Cornelius, "Latin American Presence," 4–6.

8. Fernández, *Raining Backwards,* 107–8. All quoted passages come from the Arte Público edition.

9. When asked about this subject, Fernández points out what he sees are the flaws of his own community: "I thought they were taking themselves too seriously. . . . People should learn to laugh about themselves. And I thought it was time to get a little humor and a little satire here and there and let this people relax from this euphoria—the anti-Communism, the anti-this and the anti-that, Castro, and all the campaigns." Binder, "Interview with Roberto Fernández," 117.

10. Sánchez, *Contemporary Chicana Poetry,* 21.

11. Vázquez, "Parody, Intertextuality and Cultural Values," 100–101.

12. Fernández, *Holy Radishes!* 140. All quoted passages come from the Arte Público edition.

13. Binder, "Interview with Roberto Fernández," 107–8.

7. Gay and Lesbian Images of Community

1. Hispanist critic Paul Julian Smith's prolific work in the area of gay and lesbian studies reflects the increasing concern of today's critics with issues of

gender, class, sexuality, and nationality. Smith's texts, especially *Laws of Desire* (1992) and *Representing the Other* (1992), and the anthologies he has recently edited, such as *New Hispanisms* (1994) and *Entiendes? Queer Readings* (Bergmann and Smith, 1995), have influenced the way Hispanic critics look at gay and lesbian writing today. My reading of gay and lesbian Cuban-American texts is informed by the above texts.

2. Diana Fuss's *Essentially Speaking* (1989) theorizes on the various critical positions regarding homosexual representation in autobiographical texts. According to Fuss, homosexuality in autobiography has been viewed from two perspectives: a "constructionist" or discursive position and an "essentialist" or personal identity position. Fuss adds that a discursive interpretation of the homosexual self entails a view that homosexuality is a cultural construction; on the other hand, a view of homosexuality as essence is based on the view that homosexuality is the innermost truth of a subject and the center of individual identity. Fuss proposes a more complex approach to these positions stressing a tension between "an identity that has been repressed and an identity that is still to be developed" (100).

3. Muñoz, "Todos los que son," 46. The translation is mine.

4. Muñoz, *Greatest Performance*, 16. All quoted passages come from the Arte Público edition.

5. Obejas, "We Came All the Way from Cuba So You Could Dress like This?" in *We Came All the Way from Cuba*, 113–31. All quoted passages come from the Cleis edition.

6. Obejas, *Memory Mambo*, 13. All quoted passages come from the Cleis edition.

7. The well-known anthology *This Bridge Called My Back: Writings by Radical Women of Color* (1981), edited by Cherríe Moraga and Gloria Anzaldúa, is a pioneering text seeking to move the questions of homosexual identity away from exclusively psychological grounds. The articles included in this collection serve as a point of departure for a challenge by Chicana lesbians to the politics of identity of white lesbian feminists. Also see Moraga, *Loving in the War Years*, and Anzaldúa, *Borderlands/La Frontera*.

8. Martin, "Lesbian Identity," 77–103.

8. Collecting the Tales of the Community

1. "The persona may be a narrator. The persona can be not a character in the story but an implied author . . . a voice created by the author and through which the author speaks." See Holman, *Handbook to Literature*, 327. For specific studies on the subject see Olshen, "Subject, Persona, and Self"; and Elliott, *Literary Persona*.

2. In using the term *metatext*, I allude to the general subject of metafiction and reflexivity as it appears in contemporary narrative. Among many basic studies on this subject see Alter, *Partial Magic*; Scholes, *Fabulation and Metafic-*

tion; and Dällenbach, *Le Récit speculaire.* Specific studies on embedded texts, readers, and writers within fictional narratives have also influenced my investigation. See Prince, "Introduction a l'étude du narrataire," 178–96.

3. Medina, *Marks of Birth.* All quoted passages come from the Farrar and Straus edition.

4. Like Anton, Medina was born in 1948 and has lived in the United States since 1960. Medina is a writer and a college professor, as is his character Anton. For coincidences regarding biographical details, see Fitchner, review of *The Marks of Birth,* by Pablo Medina.

5. Reminiscent of García Márquez's *One Hundred Years of Solitude,* Medina's tale of generations includes an embedded text (Felicia's) that mirrors the reader's text. Anton's need for self-understanding through reading and interpretation of his family's story is clearly in dialogue with the prophetic reading of Márquez's protagonist Aureliano Babilonia at the end of *One Hundred Years.*

6. Torres, *Fallen Angels Sing.* All quoted passages come from the Arte Público edition. Portions of my analysis of Torres's text and Cristina García's *Dreaming in Cuban* appeared in Alvarez Borland, "Displacements and Autobiography," 43–49.

7. Torres's Spanish original *Apenas un bolero* and its English version, *Fallen Angels Sing,* are separated by ten years, but their content is essentially the same. Notable differences in the English version are the absence of a table of contents and slightly longer discussions by the narrator regarding Cuban history.

8. Both Pascal in *Design and Truth in Autobiography,* chapters 2–4, and Renza in "The Veto of the Imagination," 1–26, study the idea of the split self as it applies to autobiography. On the essential division of the narrating subject see Rimmon-Kenan, *Narrative Fiction,* 71–106. In addition, Feldhay Brenner's discussion on the interaction between the "formative" and the "present self of the autobiographer" is relevant to my work on Cuban-American writers. See Feldhay Brenner, "In Search of Identity," 431–45.

9. Engle's first novel about the diaspora, titled *Singing to Cuba,* also features an American protagonist who returns to Cuba in order to find information about Cuba's concentration camps.

10. Engle, *Skywriting.* All quoted passages come from the Arte Público edition.

11. Brothers to the Rescue (Hermanos al Rescate) is an emigré organization founded in 1990 specifically to patrol the Florida Straits by helicopter and planes and to alert and assist the Coast Guard with rescue missions. This group received international attention on 24 February 1996 when four of their crewmen were killed in what was believed to be Cuban air space. See Balmaseda, "Appalling, Outrageous." The activities of this organization have been severely curtailed since changes in U.S. law require that *rafters* be returned to Cuba.

12. The most complete accounts of the latest *balsero* exodus of 1994 are contained in the frequent and almost daily reports found in the *Miami Herald* during the weeks and months of August and September 1994. For excellent sum-

maries see articles by Lisandro Pérez and Sebastian Arcos in "Viewpoint," *Miami Herald,* 28 August 1994.

13. Patricia Smith, "Interview with Cristina García," 26.

14. C. García, *Dreaming in Cuban.* All quoted passages come from the Knopf edition. For bio-bibliographical details on this author see Kanellos, *Hispanic Literary Companion,* 93–99.

15. Iraida H. López, "Interview with Cristina García," 605–18.

16. In her review of this novel, Rosario Ferré remarks, "As women, Celia and Felicia have been victimized by their men, as Cubans, their history has not served them well." See Ferré, Review of *Dreaming in Cuban,* by Cristina García. For other reviews of *Dreaming in Cuban* see Davis; Kakutani.

17. See C. García, *Agüero Sisters.* All quoted passages come from the Knopf edition. For book reviews of *The Agüero Sisters* see Fitchner; McNamer; Pollack.

18. In addition to creating a magical yet realistic context of surreal happenings and omens in this novel, Cristina García makes ample use of hyperbole and suggestive nonsequiturs, all trademarks of the playful Spanish of Nobel Prize winner García Márquez.

19. Ruppert, "Mediation and Multiple Narrative," 209–25; Dasenbrock, "Intelligibility and Meaningfulness," 10–19.

20. The way García's and Medina's protagonists envision themselves in relation to New York City as an adopted space offers a useful contrast between an "exilic" and an "ethnic" perspective of life in the United States. Anton, Pablo Medina's quiet and unsure character in *The Marks of Birth,* looks at living in New York as something inevitable. Moreover, Anton must call his adopted space home since nothing else seems closer to that feeling: "If there was any place he might call home, it was New York. . . . If New York wasn't home, nothing was" (229). In contrast, Cristina García's protagonist in *Dreaming in Cuban,* Pilar, is certain New York is home even though she needs to go back to Cuba in order to gain this perspective: "sooner or later I'd have to return to New York. I know now it's where I belong—*not instead* of here, but *more than* here" (236).

A Conclusion in Progress

1. The bibliography of Latino titles has dramatically increased in the last few years. For general overviews see Heyck, *Barrios and Borderlands;* Stavans, *Hispanic Condition;* and Luis, "Latin American (Hispanic Caribbean) Literature." In addition, *American Journey: The Hispanic American Experience,* a CD-ROM publication, offers excellent overviews of the various Latino literatures. For the Cuban-American segment see Alan West, "Cuban-American Presence"; Kanellos, *Hispanic Literary Companion,* is a useful bio-bibliographical dictionary that includes entries of selected prominent Latino writers of today. In addition, recent texts, available after the completion of my study, are Luis, *Dance between Two Cultures;* Christian, *Show and Tell;* and West, *Tropics of History.*

2. Oboler, *Ethnic Labels, Latino Lives,* 1–17.

3. Santiago, "People Ask," 1A.

4. Pérez Firmat, as quoted in Santiago, "People Ask."

5. Medina, "Literature and Democracy," 1–2.

6. This political advocacy is easily understood when we consider that the literature of Mexican Americans, for example, was born out of conflict with its northern neighbors: "When the borderlands were forcibly annexed, Anglo culture was officially imposed, but Mexican patterns of culture remained deeply embedded throughout the Southwest." In a similar manner, the Puerto Rican history, although very different from Mexican history, shares the common experience of discrimination and isolation from the mainstream. A colony of Spain until 1898, Puerto Rico was "given" to the United States after the Spanish-American War. "What followed has been a history of economic disappointment and cultural confusion. Thus the greatest challenge for the Puerto Rican migrants has had to do with cultural identity: Puerto Ricans arrive in the mainland already having experienced serious loss, no so much economic loss like the Mexicans, or political like the Cubans, but rather, severe cultural deprivation and loss of community and family coping mechanisms." See Heyck, introduction to *Barrios and Borderlands,* 1–15.

7. The death of the Cuban-American pilots had a curious effect on the Cuban community living in the United States. For the first time, Cubans of a variety of political persuasions and ideologies were united in considering this incident an injustice and in agreeing that the U.S. government had not reacted sufficiently toward the Cuban government. Elaine de Valle and Manny García, of the *Miami Herald,* reported the sad events on 26 February 1996: "Cuban MiG fighters streaking over the Straits of Florida shot down two single-engine planes belonging to Brothers to the Rescue, U.S. officials said. Four crewmen were missing and presumed dead. . . . U.S. officials told *The Herald* that the planes apparently were shot down over international waters but in an area under the jurisdiction of Cuban air traffic controllers" (1A).

8. A clear exception are the earlier narratives of Roberto Fernández, which show evidence of some interlingual punning. See his *La vida es un special* and his English novel, *Raining Backwards.*

9. See Rieff, *Exile,* and his "Cubans in America"; also see Falcoff, "Cuban Diaspora."

10. Cuban authors have been writing in Spanish in Florida since the beginning of the twentieth century, as Hospital and Cantera's anthology *A Century of Cuban Writers in Florida* well demonstrates. Among the outstanding Cuban writers who settled in Miami in the early 1960s but who are now deceased, we must mention Lydia Cabrera (1899–1992), Cuba's foremost folklorist; vanguard novelist Enrique Labrador Ruiz (1902–91); and poet and essayist Eugenio Florit (1903–94).

11. Hilda Perera was born in 1926, left Cuba in 1964, and has had a prolific

career as a novelist in South Florida. Between 1972 and 1993 she published six novels and several collections of short stories, all of them in Spanish. She has been the recipient of various literary awards. See the bibliography for a listing of specific titles.

12. Considered by anthologists "the best short story writer of the Revolution," Antonio Benítez Rojo was born in Cuba in 1931 and began his literary career there in 1967. Exiled in 1980, he published his first novel, *El mar de las lentejas* (*Sea of Lentils*) in Cuba in 1979. This novel and a collection of stories, *Estatuas sepultadas y otros relatos* (*The Magic Dog and Other Stories*), have been translated into English. Heberto Padilla was born in Cuba in 1932. One of Cuba's leading poets, he is best known for the political controversy caused by the publication of his award-winning book of poetry, *Fuera del juego*, in 1968. Padilla, who knew Fidel Castro at the beginning of the revolution, was given a cultural post in the Foreign Commerce Ministry. Because *Fuera del juego* openly criticized the regime, Padilla was incarcerated for several weeks in the cells of the Cuban state security police. He lived in Cuba in virtual ostracism until he was finally able to leave in 1980. Since his exile, he has published novels and several poetry collections in Spanish, some of which have been translated into English (*Poetry and Politics* and a novel, *Heroes Are Grazing in My Garden*). Padilla's memoir, *Self-Portrait of the Other*, was published in translation in 1990.

13. Mireya Robles was born in Cuba in 1934 and came to the United States in 1957, but she has resided in South Africa most of her life. To date, she has published several collections of poems and narratives, all in Spanish. Her best-known work, *Hagiografía de Narcisa la bella*, has recently been translated into English as *Hagiography of Narcisa the Beautiful*. René Vázquez Díaz was born in Cuba in 1952 and left his homeland in the mid 1970s. He has since published several novels, plays, and short story collections, all in Spanish. Zoé Valdés left Cuba permanently in 1994 and now resides in Paris and Madrid. Her novel *La nada cotidiana* was translated into English in 1997 as *Yocandra in the Paradise of Nada*.

14. Lourdes Gil has published seven poetry collections to date. See the authors' bibliography for a listing of her publications.

15. Remarks by Roberto Fernández, member of a panel on the topic "Self and Community in Today's Cuban-American Literature," with Gustavo Pérez Firmat and Isabel Alvarez Borland, at the annual meeting of the American Association of Teachers of Spanish and Portuguese, Orlando, Florida, 6–10 August 1996.

16. Jones, "Desi Chain," 34–36.

17. Among contemporary playwrights is Dolores Prida, whose most recent play is *Botánica* (1990). Prida, who left Cuba shortly after 1959, has published in English, in Spanish, and in bilingual mixtures. She is ranked among the most important playwrights of the contemporary Hispanic theater in the United States and is quite popular among New York Hispanic audiences. Other well-received

plays by Prida are *Coser y cantar* (1981) and *Beautiful Señoritas* (1977). Eduardo Machado's six-hour immigrant epic, *Floating Islands,* was produced in Los Angeles in 1994 and received national attention. A second production, *Once Removed,* was produced in 1995. There are numerous contemporary poets. As indicated in the analyses of individual authors, most writers of the second generation included in this book began their literary careers as poets and continue to publish poetry to this day (see the authors' bibliography). See also the work of Carlotta Caufield, Silvia Curbelo, Ricardo Pau-Llosa, and Dionisio Martínez. These poets are not included in this study, but their works are listed in the bibliography.

18. As indicated in chapter 4, the dispersion and isolation of Cuban writers of the post-1959 exodus was the primary reason behind the compilation of *La isla posible.* See Ballester, Escalona, and de la Nuez, "La isla posible," 11–17.

19. Arenas, "Final de un cuento," 149–75. The translation is mine.

20. José María Heredia (1803–39) was born in Cuba and resided for periods of his life in the Dominican Republic, Mexico, and Venezuela. In his famous poem "Niágara," Heredia merges Cuban and North American landscapes as he laments his exile from his native Cuba.

Bibliography

Alter, Robert. *Partial Magic: The Novel as a Self-Conscious Genre*. Berkeley: Univ. of California Press, 1975.

Alvarez Borland, Isabel. *Discontinuidad y ruptura en Guillermo Cabrera Infante*. Gaithersburg MD: Hispamérica, 1982.

———. "Displacements and Autobiography in Cuban American Fiction." *World Literature Today* 68, no. 1 (1994): 43–49.

———. "Readers, Writers, and Interpreters in Cabrera Infante's Texts." *World Literature Today* 61, no. 4 (1987): 553–59.

Anzaldúa, Gloria. *Borderlands/La Frontera: The New Mestiza*. San Francisco: Spinsters, 1987.

Arcos, Sebastian. "Viewpoint." *Miami Herald*, 28 Aug. 1994, sec. L, p. 1.

Armengol Acierno, María. *The Children of Peter Pan*. Needham MA: Silver Burdett Ginn, 1996.

Baker, Richard E. *The Dynamics of the Absurd in the Existential Novel*. New York: Peter Lang, 1993.

Ballester, J. P., M. E. Escalona, and I. de la Nuez, eds. *Cuba la isla posible*. Barcelona: Destino, 1995.

Balmaseda, Liz. "Appalling, Outrageous—But Not Surprising." *Miami Herald*, 25 Feb. 1996, sec. A, p. 1.

Barquet, Jesús. *Las peculiaridades del grupo Orígenes en el proceso cultural cubano*. Miami: Letras de Oro, 1992.

———, ed. *Puentelibre: Más allá de la isla* 2, nos. 5/6 (summer 1995). México: Puentelibre Editores, 1995.

Benítez-Rojo, Antonio. *The Magic Dog and Other Stories* (translation of *Estatuas sepultadas y otros relatos*, 1984). Hanover NH: Ediciones del Norte, 1990.

———. *Sea of Lentils* (translation of *El mar de las lentejas*, 1979). Amherst: Univ. of Massachussets Press, 1990.

Bergmann, Emilie, and Paul Julian Smith, eds. *¿Entiendes? Queer Readings, Hispanic Writings*. Durham: Duke Univ. Press, 1995.

Bertot, Lillian D. *The Literary Imagination of the Mariel Generation.* Miami: Cuban American National Foundation, 1994.

Bhabha, Homi K. "Difference, Discrimination, and the Discourse of Colonialism." In *The Politics of Theory,* ed. Francis Barker, 194–212. Colchester: Univ. of Essex, 1983.

———. *The Location of Culture.* New York: Routledge, 1994.

———. "The Other Question." *Screen* 24 (1983): 18–36.

Bruss, Elizabeth. *Autobiographical Acts: The Changing Situation of a Literary Genre.* Baltimore: Johns Hopkins Univ. Press, 1976.

Burunat, Silvia. "A Comparative Study of Contemporary Cuban-American and Cuban Literature." *International Journal of the Sociology of Language* 84 (1990): 101–23.

Casal, Lourdes, Roman de la Campa, and Vicente Dopico, eds. *Contra Viento y Marea.* La Habana, Cuba: Casa de las Américas, 1978.

Caufield, Carlota. *Angel Dust. Polvo de ángel. Polvere.* Madrid: Betania, 1990.

———. *34th Street and Other Poems.* San Francisco: el Gato Tuerto, 1987.

Chavez Candelaria, Cordelia. "Différance and the Discourse of Community in Writings by and about the Ethnic Other(s)." In *An Other Tongue,* ed. Alfred Arteaga, 185–203. Durham: Duke Univ. Press, 1994.

Christian, Karen. *Show and Tell.* Albuquerque: Univ. of New Mexico Press, 1997.

Clavijo, Uva de Aragon. *El caimán ante el espejo.* Miami: Ediciones Universal, 1993.

———. *Entresemáforos.* Miami: Ediciones Universal, 1981.

———. *Ni verdad ni mentira y otros cuentos.* Miami: Ediciones Universal, 1977.

———. *Tus ojos y yo.* Miami: Ediciones Universal, 1985.

Cornelius, Wayne A. "The Latin American Presence in the U.S.: Can Scholarship Catch Up with the Immigration Backlash?" *Journal of the 19th Congress of the Latin American Studies Association,* 4–6. Washington DC, 1995.

Curbelo, Silvia. *The Geography of Leaving.* Eugene OR: Silverfish Review Press, 1991.

Dällenbach, Lucien. *Le récit spéculaire: Essai sur la mise en abyme.* Paris: Seuil, 1977.

Dasenbrock, Reed Way. "Intelligibility and Meaningfulness in Multicultural Literature in English." *PMLA* 102 (1987): 10–19.

Davis, Thulani. Review of *Dreaming in Cuban,* by Cristina García. *New York Times Book Review,* 17 May 1992, 14.

Deaver, William. "*Raining Backwards*: Colonization and the Death of a Culture." *Américas Review* 21, no. 1 (1993): 112–18.

———. "Structure, Theme, Motif, and Dialogue in *Raining Backwards*." *Chattahoochee Review* 4 (summer 1996): 100–112.

del Castillo Guibault, Rose. "Americanization Is Tough on Macho." In *Ameri-*

can Voices, ed. Dolores la Guardia and Hans P. Guth, 163–66. Mountainview CA: Mayfield, 1993.

de Man, Paul. "Autobiography as Defacement." *Modern Language Notes* 94 (1979): 919–30.

de Valle, Elaine, and Manny García. "MiGs Blast 2 Exile Planes." *Miami Herald,* 25 Feb. 1996, sec. A, p. 1.

Derrida, Jacques. "Edmond Jabés and the Question of the Book." In *Writing and Difference.* Trans. Alan Bass. Chicago: Univ. of Chicago Press, 1978.

———. *Of Grammatology.* Trans. Gayatri Chakravorty Spivak. Baltimore: Johns Hopkins Univ. Press, 1976.

Desnoes, Edmundo. *Inconsolable Memories* (translation of *Memorias del subdesarrollo,* 1965). New York: New American Library, 1967.

Eakin, Paul J. *Fictions in Autobiography.* Princeton: Princeton Univ. Press, 1985.

———. *Touching the World: Reference in Autobiography.* Princeton: Princeton Univ. Press, 1992.

Elliott, Robert C. *The Literary Persona.* Chicago: Univ. of Chicago Press, 1982.

Espín, Oliva M. "Roots Uprooted: Autobiographical Reflections on the Psychological Experience of Migration." In *Paradise Lost or Gained? The Literature of Hispanic Exile,* ed. Fernando Alegría and Jorge Ruffinelli, 151–64. Houston: Arte Público, 1990.

Falcoff, Mark. "The Cuban Diaspora: Beyond the Stereotype." *Miami Herald,* 11 June 1995, sec. C, pp. 1, 4.

Feldhay Brenner, Rachel. "In Search of Identity: The Israeli-Arab Artist in Anton Shammas's *Arabesques.*" *PMLA* 108 (1993): 431–45.

Ferré, Rosario. Review of *Dreaming in Cuban,* by Cristina García. *Boston Globe,* 23 Feb. 1992.

Figueredo, Danilo. "Ser Cubano/To Be Cuban." *Multicultural Review* 6 (1997): 18–28.

Fitchner, Margaria. Review of *The Agüero Sisters,* by Cristina García. *Miami Herald,* 18 May 1997, sec. I, pp. 1, 2.

———. Review of *The Marks of Birth,* by Pablo Medina. *Miami Herald,* 26 July 1994, sec. E, pp. 1, 5.

Foster, David William. "Hacia una caracterización de la escritura de *Vista del amanecer en el trópico.*" Caribe 2 (spring 1977): 5–13.

Friedman, Susan Standford. "Women's Autobiographical Selves: Theory and Practice." In *The Private Self,* ed. Shari Benstock, 34–63. Chapel Hill: Univ. of North Carolina Press, 1988.

Fuentes Pérez, Eliana. *Cuba sin caudillos.* Princeton: Linden Lane Press, 1994.

Fuss, Diana. *Essentially Speaking: Feminism, Nature, and Difference.* New York: Routledge, 1989.

García, María Cristina. *Havana USA.* Berkeley: Univ. of California Press, 1996.

Gass, William. "The Philosophical Significance of Exile." In *Literature in Exile,* ed. John Glad, 1–8. Durham: Duke Univ. Press, 1990.

Geertz, Clifford. "Deep Play." In *The Interpretation of Cultures*, 412–53. New York: Basic, 1973.

González Echevarría, Roberto. "Literature and Exile: Carpentier's Right of Sanctuary." In *The Voice of the Masters*, 124–37. Austin: Univ. of Texas Press, 1985.

———. "An Outcast of the Island." Review of *Before Night Falls*, by Reinaldo Arenas. *New York Times Book Review*, 24 Oct. 1993, pp. 1, 32–3.

Grenier, Guillermo J., and Alex Stepick III. *Miami Now!* Gainsville: Univ. Press of Florida, 1992.

Griffith, Gareth. *A Double Exile*. London: Marin Boyars, 1978.

Gunn, Janet Varner. *Autobiography: Towards a Poetics of Experience*. Philadelphia: Univ. of Pennsylvania Press, 1982.

Gusdorf, George. "Conditions and Limits of Autobiography." In *Autobiography: Essays Theoretical and Critical*, ed. James Olney, 28–49. Princeton: Princeton Univ. Press, 1980.

Hall, Catherine. "Histories, Empires and the Post-Colonial Moment." In *The Post-Colonial Question*, ed. Iain Chambers and Lidia Curtis, 65–78. New York: Routledge, 1996.

Heyck, Daly Denis, ed. *Barrios and Borderlands: Cultures of Latinos and Latinas in the United States*. New York: Routledge, 1994.

Holman, C. Hugh. *A Handbook to Literature*, 4th ed. Indianapolis: Bobbs Merrill, 1980.

Hutcheon, Linda. *A Poetics of Postmodernism: History, Theory, Fiction*. New York: Routledge, 1988.

Ibieta, Gabriela. "Transcending the Culture of Exile." In *Literature and Exile*, ed. David Bevan, 67–76. Amsterdam: Rodopi, 1990.

Illie, Paul. *Literature and Inner Exile*. Baltimore: Johns Hopkins Univ. Press, 1980.

Incledon, John. "Parricide and Exile: Tracing Derrida in Augusto Roa Bastos's *Yo el supremo*." In *The Literature of Emigration and Exile*, ed. J. Whitlark and Wendell Aycock, 169–81. Lubbock: Texas Tech Univ. Press, 1992.

Jones, Malcolm. "The Desi Chain." *Newsweek*, 10 July 1995, 34–36.

Kakutani, Michiko. Review of *Dreaming in Cuban*, by Cristina García. *New York Times*, 25 Feb. 1992, C17.

Kanellos, Nicolás, ed. *The Hispanic Literary Companion*. Detroit: Visible Ink, 1997.

Kavolis, Vytautas. "Women Writers in Exile." *World Literature Today* 66, no. 1 (1992): 43–46.

Kristeva, Julia. *Nations without Nationalism*. New York: Columbia Univ. Press, 1993.

———. *Strangers to Ourselves*. Trans. Leon S. Roudiez. New York: Columbia Univ. Press, 1991.

Lejeune, Phillipe. "The Autobiographical Pact." In *On Autobiography*, ed. Paul J. Eakin, 3–30. Minneapolis: Univ. of Minnesota Press, 1989.

León, Juan. "A Connecticut Yankee in Cuban Miami: Reflections on the Meaning of Underdevelopment and Cultural Change." In *Michigan Quarterly Review: Bridges to Cuba* 33, no. 4 (fall 1994): 690–701.

Lima, Rafael. "Tourists Don't Cry." *Miami Herald Tropic Magazine,* 4 Dec. 1994, p. 8.

Luis, William. *Dance between Two Cultures.* Nashville: Vanderbilt Univ. Press, 1997.

———. "Latin American (Hispanic Caribbean) Literature Written in the United States." In *The Cambridge History of Latin American Literature,* vol. 2, ed. Roberto González Echevarría and Enrique Pupo Walker, 526–57. Cambridge: Cambridge Univ. Press, 1996.

Machado, Eduardo. *The Floating Island Plays.* New York: Theater Communication Group, 1991.

Martin, Diane. "Lesbian Identity and Autobiographical Difference[s]." In *Life/Lines,* ed. B. Brodzki and C. Schenck, 77–103. Ithaca: Cornell Univ. Press, 1988.

Martínez, Dionisio. *Bad Alchemy.* New York: Norton, 1995.

———. *History as a Second Language.* Athens: Ohio Univ. Press, 1992.

McNamer, Deirdre. Review of *The Agüero Sisters,* by Cristina García. *New York Times Book Review,* 15 June 1997, 38.

Molloy, Silvia. *At Face Value: Autobiographical Writing in Spanish America.* Cambridge: Cambridge Univ. Press, 1991.

Moraga, Cherríe. *Loving in the War Years.* Boston: Southend Press, 1983.

———, and Gloria Anzaldúa, eds. *This Bridge Called My Back: Writings by Radical Women of Color.* Boston: Persephone Press, 1981.

Novás, Himilce. *Mangos, Bananas and Coconuts: A Cuban Love Story.* Houston: Arte Público, 1996.

Oboler, Suzanne. *Ethnic Labels, Latino Lives: Identity and the Politics of (Re)presentation in the United States.* Minneapolis: Univ. of Minnesota Press, 1995.

Olney, James. "Autobiography and the Cultural Moment." In *Autobiography: Essays Theoretical and Critical,* ed. James Olney, 3–28. Princeton: Princeton Univ. Press, 1980.

———. *Metaphors of the Self: The Meaning of Autobiography.* Princeton: Princeton Univ. Press, 1972.

———. *Tell Me Africa.* Princeton: Princeton Univ. Press, 1973.

Olshen, Barry. "Subject, Persona, and Self in the Theory of Autobiography." *Auto-Biography Studies* 10, no. 1 (spring 1995): 5–16.

Ong, Walter. *Orality and Literacy: The Technology of the Word.* London: Methuen, 1982.

———. "The Writer's Audience Is Always a Fiction." *PMLA* 90 (1975): 9–21.

Padilla, Heberto. *A Fountain, A House of Stone.* New York: Farrar, Straus & Giroux, 1991.

———. *Heroes Are Grazing in My Garden* (translation of *En mi jardín pastan los héroes,* 1982). Trans. Andrew Hurley. New York: Farrar, Straus & Giroux, 1984.

―――. *Poetry and Politics: Selected Poems of Heberto Padilla.* Trans. Frank Calzón et al. Madrid: Playor, 1974.

―――. *Self-Portrait of the Other.* Trans. Alexander Coleman. New York: Farrar, Straus & Giroux, 1990.

Pascal, Roy. *Design and Truth in Autobiography.* Cambridge: Harvard Univ. Press, 1960.

Pau-Llosa, Ricardo. *Bread of the Imagined.* Arizona: Bilingual Review Press, 1992.

―――. *Cuba.* Pittsburgh: Carnegie Mellon Univ. Press, 1993.

―――. *Sorting Metaphors.* Tallahassee: Anhinga Press, 1983.

Peavler, Terry. "Cabrera Infante's Undertow." In *Structures of Power: Essays on Twentieth Century Spanish-American Fiction,* ed. Terry J. Peavler and Peter Standish, 125–45. Albany: State Univ. of New York Press, 1996.

Pérez, Lisandro."Unique but Not Marginal: Cubans in Exile." In *Cuban Studies since the Revolution,* ed. Damian Fernández, 258–71. Gainesville: Univ. Press of Florida, 1992.

―――. "Viewpoint." *Miami Herald,* 28 Aug. 1994, sec. L, pp. 1, 4.

Perera, Hilda. *¡Felices Pascuas!* Barcelona: Planeta, 1981.

―――. *La Jaula del Unicornio.* Barcelona: Noguer, 1990.

―――. *La noche de Ina.* Madrid: Ediciones Libertarias, 1993.

―――. *Plantado.* Barcelona: Planeta, 1981.

―――. *Los Robledal.* Mexico: Diana, 1987.

―――. *El sitio de nadie.* Barcelona: Planeta, 1972.

Pollack, Eileen. Review of *The Agüero Sisters,* by Cristina García. *Boston Sunday Globe,* 25 May 1997, p. N15.

Portes, Alejandro, ed. *The New Second Generation.* New York: Russell Sage Foundation, 1996.

Portes, Alejandro, and Alex Stepick. *City on the Edge.* Berkeley: Univ. of California Press, 1993.

Prida, Dolores. *Beautiful Señoritas and Other Plays.* Houston: Arte Público, 1991.

Prince, Gerald. "Introduction a l'étude du narrataire." *Poétique* 14 (1973): 178–96.

Rebolledo, Tey Diana, and Eliana S. Rivero, eds. *Infinite Divisions: An Anthology of Chicana Literature.* Tucson: Univ. of Arizona Press, 1993.

Renza, Louis. "The Veto of the Imagination: A Theory of Autobiography." *New Literary History* 9 (1977): 1–26.

Rich, Adrienne. "Notes Towards a Politics of Location." In *Blood, Bread, and Poetry,* 210–31. New York: Norton, 1986.

Rieff, David. "Cubans in America: From Exiles to Immigrants." *Miami Herald,* 6 Aug. 1995, sec. L, pp. 1, 5.

————. *The Exile: Cuba in the Heart of Miami.* New York: Simon & Schuster, 1993.

Rimmon-Kenan, Shlomith. *Narrative Fiction.* London: Methuen, 1983.

Risech, Flavio. "Political and Cultural Cross-Dressing." *Michigan Quarterly Review: Bridges to Cuba* 33, no. 3 (summer 1994): 526–41.

Robles, Mireya. *Hagiography of Narcisa the Beautiful.* Los Angeles: Readers International, 1995.

Roses, Lorraine. *Voices of the Storyteller.* Westport CT: Greenwood Press, 1986.

Rumbaut, Rubén G. "The Agony of Exile: A Study of the Migration and Adaptation of Indochinese Refugee Adults and Children." In *Refugee Children: Theory, Research, and Services,* ed. Frederick L. Ahearn Jr. and Jean L. Athey. Baltimore: Johns Hopkins Univ. Press, 1991.

Ruppert, James. "Mediation and Multiple Narrative in Contemporary Native American Fiction." *Texas Studies in Literature and Language* 28 (1986): 209–25.

Said, Edward. "Reflections on Exile." *Granta* 13 (autumn 1984): 157–75.

Sánchez, Marta. *Contemporary Chicana Poetry.* Berkeley: Univ. of California Press, 1994.

Santiago, Fabiola. "A People Ask: Who Are We?" *Miami Herald,* 6 Oct. 1996, sec. A, pp. 1, 2.

Scholes, Robert. *Fabulation and Metafiction.* Urbana: Univ. of Illinois Press, 1979.

Schor, Naomi. "Fiction as Interpretation/Interpretation as Fiction." In *The Reader in the Text,* ed. Susan Suleiman and Inge Crossman, 165–83. Princeton: Princeton Univ. Press, 1980.

Seidel, Michael. *Exile and the Narrative Imagination.* New Haven: Yale Univ. Press, 1986.

Shapiro Rok, Esther. "Finding What Has Been Lost in Plain View." *Michigan Quarterly Review: Bridges to Cuba* 33, no. 3 (summer 1994): 579–90.

Smith, Paul Julian. *Representing the Other.* New York: Oxford Univ. Press, 1992.

————. "Writing the Self in Feminist and Gay Autobiography." In *Laws of Desire: Questions of Homosexuality in Spanish Writing and Film, 1960–1990,* 14–55. New York: Oxford Univ. Press, 1992.

————, ed. *New Hispanisms.* Ottawa: Ottawa Hispanic Studies, 1994.

Smith, Valerie. *Self-Discovery and Authority in Afro-American Narrative.* Cambridge: Harvard Univ. Press, 1987.

Soto, Francisco. *Conversación con Reinaldo Arenas.* Madrid: Betania, 1990.

————. "*El Portero*: Una alucinante fábula moderna." *INTI* (fall 1990): 106–17.

————. *Reinaldo Arenas: The Pentagonía.* Gainesville: Univ. Press of Florida, 1994.

Souza, Raymond D. "Exile in the Cuban Literary Experience." In *Escritores de la Diáspora Cubana,* ed. Julio A. Martínez, 1–5. Metuchen NJ: Scarecrow Press, 1986.

———. *Guillermo Cabrera Infante: Two Islands, Many Worlds.* Austin: Univ. of Texas Press, 1996.

———. *Lino Novás Calvo.* New York: Twayne, 1981.

———. Review of *Before Night Falls,* by Reinaldo Arenas. *American Book Review,* June-July 1995, 1.

Stavans, Ilan. *The Hispanic Condition.* New York: HarperCollins, 1995.

Suchlicki, Jaime. *Cuba: From Columbus to Castro.* McLean VA: Brassey, 1990.

Symmons, Sara. *Goya.* London: Universal Books, 1977.

Torres, María de los Angeles. "Beyond the Rupture." In *Michigan Quarterly Review: Bridges to Cuba* 33, no. 3 (summer 1994): 419–37.

TuSmith, Bonnie. *All My Relatives.* Ann Arbor: Univ. of Michigan Press, 1993.

Ugarte, Michael. *Shifting Ground: Spanish Civil War Exile Literature.* Durham: Duke Univ. Press, 1989.

Valdés, Zoé. *Te dí la vida entera.* México: Planeta, 1996.

———. *Yocandra in the Paradise of Nada* (translation of *La nada cotidiana,* 1995). New York: Arcade, 1997.

Vargas Llosa, Mario. "Is Fiction the Art of Lying?" *New York Times Book Review,* 7 Oct. 1984, 39–41.

———. "Latin America: Fiction and Reality." *World Affairs* 150 (fall 1987): 65–71.

Vásquez, Mary. "Parody, Intertextuality and Cultural Values in *Raining Backwards.*" *Américas Review* 18, no. 2 (summer 1990): 92–102.

Vázquez Díaz, René. *La era imaginaria.* Barcelona: Montesinos, 1987.

———. *La isla del cundeamor.* Madrid, Alfaguara, 1993.

———. *Querido traidor.* Barcelona: Montesinos, 1992.

Veciana Suárez, Ana. *The Chin Kiss King.* New York: Farrar, Straus & Giroux, 1997.

Vera León, Antonio. "Bilingual Writings and Bicultural Subjects: Samuel Beckett in Havana." In *Cuba la isla posible,* ed. J. P. Ballester, M. E. Escalona, and I. de la Nuez, 243–45. Barcelona: Destino, 1995.

Victoria, Carlos. *Puente en la oscuridad.* Miami: Letras de Oro, 1994.

———. *Las sombras en la playa.* Miami: Ediciones Universal, 1992.

———. *La travesía secreta.* Miami: Ediciones Universal, 1991.

Weiss, Timothy. *On the Margins: The Art of Exile in V. S. Naipaul.* Amherst: Univ. of Massachussets Press, 1992.

West, Alan. "Cuban-American Presence." In *American Journey: The Hispanic American Experience.* CD-ROM. Woodbridge CT: Primary Source Media, 1995.

———. *Tropics of History: Cuba Imagined.* Westwood NJ: Greenwood, 1997.

White, Hayden. *Tropics of Discourse: Essays in Cultural Criticism.* Baltimore: Johns Hopkins Univ. Press, 1973.

Wolin, Richard. *The Terms of Cultural Criticism: The Frankfurt School, Existentialism, Poststructuralism.* New York: Columbia Univ. Press, 1992.

Authors' Bibliography

This partial bibliography seeks to give readers information about the creative works available in English by the writers studied in this book. Relevant essays, previous work in Spanish, and selected interviews are also included.

Reinaldo Arenas

ESSAYS

"La literatura cubana en el exilio." In *Puentelibre: Más allá de la isla* 2, nos. 5/6 (summer 1995): 107–12.

NOVELS AND SHORT STORIES

The Assault (translation of *El asalto,* 1991). Trans. Andrew Hurley. New York: Viking Penguin, 1995.

Before Night Falls (translation of *Antes que anochezca,* 1992). Trans. Dolores M. Koch. New York: Viking Penguin, 1993.

El Central: A Cuban Sugar Mill (translation of *El central,* 1981). Trans. Anthony Kerrigan. New York: Avon Books, 1984.

The Color of Summer (translation of *El color del verano,* 1991). Trans. Andrew Hurley. New York: Viking Penguin, 1995.

The Doorman (translation of *El portero,* 1989). Trans. Dolores Koch. New York: Grove Press, 1991.

Farewell to the Sea (translation of *Otra vez el mar,* 1982). Trans. Andrew Hurley. New York: Viking Penguin, 1986.

"Final de un cuento." In *Adiós a Mamá,* 149–75. Miami: Ediciones Universal, 1996.

Graveyard of the Angels (translation of *La loma del Angel,* 1987). Trans. Alfred MacAdam. New York: Avon Books, 1987.

Hallucinations (translation of *El mundo alucinante,* 1969). Trans. Gordon Brotherson. New York: Harper & Row, 1971.

Old Rose: A Novel in Two Stories (translation of *La Vieja Rosa,* 1980; and *Arturo, la estrella más brillante,* 1984). Trans. Andrew Hurley and Ann Tashi Slater. New York: Grove Press, 1989.

The Palace of the White Skunks (translation of *El palacio de las blanquísimas mofetas,* 1982). Trans. Andrew Hurley. New York: Viking Penguin, 1990.

Singing from the Well (translation of *Celestino antes del alba,* 1967). Trans. Andrew Hurley. New York: Viking Penguin, 1987.

SELECTED INTERVIEWS WITH

Interview by Francisco Soto. "Conversación con Reinaldo Arenas," 37–60. In *Conversación con Reinaldo Arenas.* Madrid: Betania, 1990.

Interview by Perla Rozencvaig. "Last Interview." *Review* 44 (1991): 78–82.

Ruth Behar

ANTHOLOGY

Editor, with Juan León. *Michigan Quarterly Review: Bridges to Cuba* 33, nos. 3 and 4 (summer and fall 1994). Ann Arbor: University of Michigan, 1994.

ESSAYS

"The Biography in the Shadow." In *Translated Woman,* 320–42. Boston: Beacon, 1993.

"Cuba y su Diáspora." *Puentelibre: Más allá de la isla* 2, nos. 5/6 (summer 1995): 7–14.

"Juban." *Poetics Today* 16, no. 1 (spring 1995): 151–70.

"Out of Exile." In *Women Writing Culture,* ed. Ruth Behar and Deborah Gordon. Berkeley: Univ. of California Press, 1995.

The Presence of the Past in a Spanish Village. Princeton: Princeton Univ. Press, 1986.

The Vulnerable Observer: Anthropology That Breaks Your Heart. Boston: Beacon, 1996.

Guillermo Cabrera Infante

ESSAYS

"The Invisible Exile." In *Literature in Exile,* ed. John Glad, 34–41. Durham: Duke Univ. Press, 1990.

Mea Cuba. Trans. Kenneth Hall and the author. London: Faber & Faber, 1994.

NOVELS AND SHORT STORIES

Holy Smoke! London: Faber & Faber, 1985.

Infante's Inferno (translation of *La Habana para un infante difunto,* 1979). Trans. Suzanne Jill Levine, with the author. New York: Harper & Row, 1984.

Three Trapped Tigers (translation of *Tres tristes tigres,* 1967). Trans. Donald Gardner and Suzanne Jill Levine, with the author. New York: Harper & Row, 1971.

A Twentieth Century Job (translation of *Un oficio del siglo veinte,* 1973). Trans. Kenneth Hall and the author. London: Faber & Faber, 1991.

View of Dawn in the Tropics (translation of *Vista del amanecer en el trópico,* 1974). Trans. Suzanne Jill Levine, with the author. Berkeley: Creative Arts, 1978. Reprint, London: Faber & Faber, 1990.

Writes of Passage (translation of *Así en la paz como en la guerra,* 1960). Trans. by John Brookesmith, Peggy Boyars, and the author. London: Faber & Faber, 1993.

SELECTED INTERVIEWS WITH

Interview by Isabel Alvarez Borland. "Viaje verbal a la Habana, ¡Ah Vana! Entrevista con Guillermo Cabrera Infante." *Hispamérica* 31 (1982): 51–68.

Interview by Jason Wilson. "Guillermo Cabrera Infante: An Interview in a Summer Manner." In *On Modern Latin American Fiction,* ed. John King, 305–21. New York: Farrar, Straus & Giroux, 1987.

Interview by Marie-Lise Gazarian Gautier. "Guillermo Cabrera Infante." *Interviews with Latin American Writers,* 27–54. Elmwood Park IL: Dalkey Archive Press, 1989.

Margarita Engle

NOVELS

Singing to Cuba. Houston: Arte Público, 1993.
Skywriting. New York: Bantam, 1995.

Roberto Fernández

NOVELS AND SHORT STORIES

Cuentos sin rumbo. Miami: Ediciones Universal, 1975.
Holy Radishes! Houston: Arte Público, 1995.
La montaña rusa. Houston: Arte Público, 1985.
Raining Backwards. Houston: Arte Público, 1988.
La vida es un special/Life Is on Special. Miami: Ediciones Universal, 1982.

SELECTED INTERVIEWS WITH

Interview by Wolfgang Binder. "Interview with Roberto Fernández." In *Americas Review* 22, nos. 1–2 (summer 1994): 106–22.

"Roberto Fernández." In *American Contradictions: Interviews with Nine American Writers,* ed. Wolfgang Binder, 1–18. Hanover NH: Univ. Press of New England, 1995.

J. Joaquín Fraxedas

NOVEL

The Lonely Crossing of Juan Cabrera (translation of *La travesía solitaria de Juan Cabrera,* 1993). Trans. Raoul García Iglesias. New York: St. Martin's Press, 1993.

Cristina García

NOVELS

The Agüero Sisters. New York: Knopf, 1997. Spanish ed.: *Las hermanas Agüero.* Trans. Alan West. New York: Knopf, 1997.
Dreaming in Cuban. New York: Knopf, 1992. Spanish ed.: Soñar en Cubano. Trans. Marisol Palés Castro. Madrid: Espasa Calpe, 1993.

SELECTED INTERVIEWS WITH

Interview by Iraida H. Lopez. "An Interview with Cristina García." *Michigan Quarterly Review: Bridges to Cuba* 33, no. 3 (summer 1994): 605–18.
Interview by Patricia Smith. "An Interview with Cristina García." *Boston Globe,* 18 July 1993, p. 26.

Lourdes Gil

ESSAYS

"Against the Grain: Why I Write in Spanish." In *Inventing America,* ed. Gabriella Ibieta and Miles Orvell, 371–76. New York: St. Martin's Press, 1996.
"Conjugar los espacios: Hacia una liberación por el lenguaje." In *Bipolaridad de la cultura cubana: Primer encuentro de escritores de dentro y fuera de Cuba,* ed. René Vázquez Díaz, 86–96. Stockholm: Olof Palme International Center, 1995. Simultaneously published in Spanish and Swedish.
"La literatura cubana en los E. U." *Brújula/Compass* 19 (spring 1994): 34–37.
"Viaje por las Zonas Templadas." Unpublished collection.

POETRY

Blanca aldaba preludia. Madrid: Betania, 1989.
El cerco de las transfiguraciones. Miami: La Torre de Papel, 1996.
Empieza la ciudad. Miami: La Torre de Papel, 1993.
Manuscrito de la niña ausente. New York: Giralt, 1980.
Neumas. Montclair NJ: Senda Nueva, 1977.
Vencido el fuego de la especie. New Brunswick NJ: SLUSA, 1983.

SELECTED INTERVIEWS WITH

Interview by Carlota Caufield. "Voices of Three Cuban Women Poets in Exile." *El gato tuerto* 12 (1990): 2–3.
Interview by Elena Martínez, "Conversación con Lourdes Gil." *Post-Modern Notes/Apuntes Posmodernos* 4, no. 1 (1993): 33–36.

Carolina Hospital

ANTHOLOGIES

Editor, with Jorge Cantera. *A Century of Cuban Writers in Florida.* Sarasota FL: Pineapple Press, 1996.

Cuban American Writers: Los Atrevidos. Princeton: Linden Lane Press, 1988.

Essays

"Los Atrevidos," *Linden Lane Magazine* 6, no. 4 (1987): 22–23.
"Los hijos del exilio cubano y su literatura." *Explicación de Textos Literarios* 16, no. 2 (1987): 103–14.

Pablo Medina

Essay

"Literature and Democracy." *AWP Chronicle* 30, no. 4 (1998): 23–30.

Memoir

Exiled Memories. Austin: Univ. of Texas Press, 1990.

Novel

The Marks of Birth. New York: Farrar, Straus & Giroux, 1994.

Poetry

Arching into the Afterlife. Tempe AZ: Bilingual Review Press, 1991.
Pork Rind and Cuban Songs. New York: Nuclassics & Science, 1975.

Selected Interviews with

Interview with Belkis Cuza Malè. *El Nuevo Herald,* 21 Oct. 1990, sec. D, pp. 1, 5.
Interview with Margaria Fitchner. *Miami Herald,* 26 July 1994, sec. E, pp. 1, 5.

Elías Miguel Muñoz

Essays

Desde esta orilla. Madrid: Betania, 1988.
"Todos los que son." *Puentelibre: Más allá de la isla* 2, nos. 5/6 (summer 1995): 44–50.

Novels

Crazy Love. Houston: Arte Público, 1989.
The Greatest Performance. Houston: Arte Público, 1991.
Ladrón de la Mente (novella). New York: McGraw-Hill, 1995.
Los viajes de Orlando Cachumbanbé. Miami: Ediciones Universal, 1984.

Poetry

En estas tierras/In this Land. Tempe AZ: Bilingual Review Press, 1989.
No fué posible el sol. Madrid: Betania, 1989.

Lino Novás Calvo

ANTHOLOGIES (IN SPANISH)

Cayo Canas. Buenos Aires: Espasa Calpe, 1946.
Un experimento en el barrio chino. Madrid: Ed. Reunidos, 1936.
La luna nona y otros cuentos. Buenos Aires: Ed. Nuevo Romance, 1942.
Maneras de contar. New York: Las Américas, 1970.
No sé quien soy. Collecciones Lunes, 1945.
El otro cayo. México: Ed. Nuevo Mundo, 1959.
Pedro Blanco el negrero. Madrid: Espasa, 1933.

TRANSLATIONS OF INDIVIDUAL STORIES

"Allies and Germans" (translation of "Aliados y alemanes"). Trans. Harriet de Onis. In *From the Green Antilles: Writings of the Caribbean,* ed. Barbara Howes, 244–56. London: Souvenir Press, 1967.
"As I Am . . . As I Was" (translation of "A ese lugar dónde me llaman"). Trans. Paul Bowles. In *The Eye of the Heart,* ed. Barbara Howes, 159–68. Indianapolis: Bobbs-Merrill, 1973.
"The Cow on the Rooftop" (translation of "La vaca en la azotea"). Trans. Myron Lichtblau. *Latin American Literary Review* 4, no. 7 (fall-winter 1975): 109–16.
"The Dark Night of Ramón Yendía" (translation of "La noche de Ramón Yendía"). Trans. Raymond Sayers. In *Spanish Stories and Tales,* ed. Harriet de Onís, 139–64. New York: Knopf, 1954.
"That Night" (translation of "Aquella noche salieron los muertos"). In *Short Stories of Latin America,* ed. Arturo Torres-Rioseco, 25–54. New York: Las Américas, 1963.

Achy Obejas

NOVEL AND SHORT STORIES

Memory Mambo. Pittsburgh: Cleis Press, 1996.
We Came All the Way from Cuba So You Could Dress like This? Pittsburgh: Cleis Press, 1994.

SELECTED INTERVIEW WITH

"*Memory Mambo* by Achy Obejas: Book Club of the Air." Host: Ray Suarez. Guests: Achy Obejas, Isabel Alvarez Borland, and Jaime Manrique. *Talk of the Nation.* National Public Radio. Washington DC, 24 July 1997.

Gustavo Pérez Firmat

MEMOIR

Next Year in Cuba: A Cubano's Coming of Age in America. New York: Doubleday-Anchor, 1995. Spanish ed.: *El año que viene estamos en Cuba.* Trans. by the author. Houston: Arte Público, 1997.

POETRY

Bilingual Blues. Tempe AZ: Bilingual Review Press, 1995.
Carolina Cuban. Tempe AZ: Bilingual Review Press, 1986.
Equivocaciones. Madrid: Betania, 1989.

SCHOLARLY BOOKS

The Cuban Condition: Translation and Identity in Modern Cuban Literature. Cambridge: Cambridge Univ. Press, 1989.
Idle Fictions: The Hispanic Vanguard Novel, 1926–1934. Durham: Duke Univ. Press, 1982. Expanded paperback edition, 1993.
Life on the Hyphen: The Cuban American Way. Austin: Univ. of Texas Press, 1994.
Literature and Liminality: Festive Readings in the Hispanic Tradition. Durham: Duke Univ. Press, 1986.
"Transcending Exile: Cuban-American Literature Today," In *Dialogue #92,* ed. Richard Tardanico, 1–13. Miami: Latin American and Caribbean Center of Florida International University, 1987.
"The Facts of Life on the Hyphen." *ANQ* 10 (1997): 17–18.

SELECTED INTERVIEWS WITH

Interview with Bridget Booher. "Living on the Hyphen." *Duke Magazine* 82, no. 4 (May-June 1996): 2–6.
Interview with Gigi Anders. "Exile in Carolina: An Interview with Gustavo Pérez Firmat." *News and Observer,* 7 Feb. 1997, sec. D, pp. 1, 3.

Eliana Rivero

ESSAYS

"Cuban American Writing." In *The Oxford Companion to Women's Writing in the United States,* ed. Cathy Davidson and Linda Wagner, 228–30. New York: Oxford Univ. Press, 1995.
"Cubanos y Cubano-Americanos: Perfil y presencia en los Estados Unidos." *Discurso Literario* 7 (1989): 81–101.
"From Immigrants to Ethnics: Cuban Women Writers in the U.S." In *Breaking Boundaries,* ed. Asunción Horno-Delgado, 189–200. Amherst: Univ. of Massachussetts Press, 1989.
"'Fronteraisleña,' Border Islander." *Michigan Quarterly Review: Bridges to Cuba* 33, no. 3 (summer 1994): 669–75.
"Hispanic Literature in the United States: Self-Image and Conflict." *Revista Chicano-Riqueña* 13 (1985): 173–92.
"Of Borders and Self: Constructing Identity on/from the Margins." Keynote address presented at Ohio State University, Nov. 1994, 1–25.
"(Re)Writing Sugar Cane Memories." In *Paradise Lost or Gained? The Litera-*

ture of Hispanic Exile, ed. Fernando Alegría and Jorge Ruffinelli, 164–83. Houston: Arte Público, 1990.

POETRY

De cal y arena. Sevilla: Alderraman, 1975.

Virgil Suárez

ANTHOLOGIES

Editor, with Delia Poey. *Iguana Dreams: New Latino Fiction*. New York: HarperCollins, 1994.

———. *Little Havana Blues: A Cuban-American Literature Anthology*. Houston: Arte Público, 1996.

Coeditor with Victor Hernandez Cruz and Leroy V. Quintana. *Paper Dance: Fifty-five Latino Poets*. New York: Persea Books, 1995.

MEMOIR

Spared Angola: Memories from a Cuban-American Childhood. Houston: Arte Público, 1997.

NOVELS AND SHORT STORIES

The Cutter. New York: Random House, 1991.
Going Under. Houston: Arte Público, 1996.
Havana Thursdays. Houston: Arte Público, 1995.
Latin Jazz. New York: William Morrow, 1990.
Welcome to the Oasis and Other Stories. Houston: Arte Público, 1992.

Omar Torres

NOVELS

Al partir. Houston: Arte Público, 1986.
Apenas un bolero. Miami: Ediciones Universal, 1988.
Fallen Angels Sing. Houston: Arte Público, 1991.

POETRY

Conversación primera. New York: Editorial Niurklen, 1975.
De nunca a siempre. Miami: Ediciones Universal, 1981.
Linea en diluvio. New York: Editorial Niurklen, 1981.
Tiempo robado. Hoboken NJ: Contra Viento y Marea, 1978.

Index

New World Studies

New World Studies publishes interdisciplinary research that seeks to redefine the cultural map of the Americas and to propose particularly stimulating points of departure for an emerging field. Encompassing the Caribbean as well as continental North, Central, and South America, the series books examine cultural processes within the hemisphere, taking into account the economic, demographic, and historical phenomena that shape them. Given the increasing diversity and richness of the linguistic and cultural traditions in the Americas, the need for research that privileges neither the English-speaking United States nor Spanish-speaking Latin America has never been greater. The series is designed to bring the best of this new research into an identifiable forum and to channel its results to the rapidly evolving audience for cultural studies.

NEW WORLD STUDIES

Vera M. Kutzinski
Sugar's Secrets: Race and the Erotics
of Cuban Nationalism

Richard D. E. Burton and Fred Reno, editors
French and West Indian: Martinique, Guadeloupe,
and French Guiana Today

A. James Arnold, editor
Monsters, Tricksters, and Sacred Cows

J. Michael Dash
The Other America: Caribbean Literature
in a New World Context

Isabel Alvarez Borland
Cuban-American Literature of Exile:
From Person to Persona